Work in Progress

by
Reid Vanderburgh

TransGender Publishing

an imprint of
Perceptions Press
Victoria, BC
Canada

2023

Work in Progress

Copyright © Reid Vanderburgh 2023

All rights reserved. No part of this publication may be reprinted, reproduced, stored in a retrieval system, or transmitted in any form or by any means, electronic, mechanical, photocopying, and recording, or otherwise, now known or hereafter invented without the express prior written permission of the author, except for brief passages quoted by a reviewer in a newspaper or magazine. To perform any of the above is an infringement of copyright law.

Published in paperback in 2023 by TransGender Publishing
Cover Design: Margot Wilson

ISBN: 978-1-998924-67-7 (Paperback)
ISBN: 978-1-998924-68-4 (Kindle e-book)
ISBN: 978-1-9900969-69-1 (Smashwords/Draft2Digital e-book)

Published in Canada by
TransGender Publishing
www.transgenderpublishing.ca

an imprint of
Perceptions Press
www.perceptionspress.ca
Victoria BC
Canada

Contents

Volume One
Introduction to Volume I 1
Chapter One
  Childhood 3
    Early childhood 4
    Childhood Memories 5
    Under Pressure 7
    The Sociology of the Day 8
    Family dynamics 9

Chapter Two
  Adolescence 12
    Unrecognized Love 12
    First Love 14

Chapter Three
  Early Lesbian Days 16
    First Attempts 16
    A New Love 18
    Moving On 19

Chapter Four
  20-Something 21
    The First Relationship 21
    Collective Living 23
    First Bicycle Tour 24
    Living Independent 24
    New Self-knowledge 25

Chapter Five
  Something's Not Right! 27
    Looking for Love 27

    Hiding Behind Politics..28
    Yet Another Try for Love..29
    At Loose Ends..30
    Planning the Big Tour..31
    Changing My Life Focus (Who Knew?) 31

Chapter Six
    Big Adventures 34
        A Bicycle Odyssey 34
        The Last Leg..36
        Nesting Again 37

Chapter Seven
    The Relationship 38
        A Fateful Relationship...38
        Idyllic?...39
        Disillusioned 41

Chapter Eight
    Revelations 43
        The Beginning…..43
        Finally Talking..44
        Denial in Action..46
        The Epiphany..49
        Counterproductive Therapy 50

Chapter Nine
    The Crash...52
        The Power of Naming Myself 53
        A Close Call..53

Chapter Ten
    Baby Steps Forward..57
        A New Old Member 57

    A Tourist in My Own Life 59

Chapter Eleven
  The Real-Life Test 61
    A Major Turning Point 61
    Ready for Change 62
    A New Future Emerges 63
    First Crush 65
    New Beginnings 66

Chapter Twelve
  Back to School 67
    My Own Space 68
    An Old Flame 68
    Coming Out 69
    Gender Bending 71
    My Final Moments with the PLC 73
    Family in Transition 74

Chapter Thirteen
  The Countdown Begins 77
    Back to BJ 78
    Last Hurdles 79
    Assessing Priorities 81

Chapter Fourteen
  Transition is a Process 83
    New FTM Experiences 83
    Another Transition Milestone 84
    The Nature of Friendship 86
    Surgery Recovery 87
    Finding My Professional Path 87
    Wrapping Up Portland 89

    My Time Down Under 91

    Hopes for the Future 93

Chapter Fifteen
  My California Sojourn 95

    Balm to My Soul 95

    Peer Education 97

    A Rite of Passage 98

    Final Thoughts—For Now 99

Volume Two
  Introduction to Volume II:
  Reflections on the Wisdom of Time 103

    What was Missing? 104

    A New Family View 106

    How Could I Forget? 107

    Family Reacting to My Transition 108

    What Else Was Missing? 110

    Processing Grief as a Man 113

    Anything Else Left Out? 114

    What Else? 115

Chapter Sixteen
  Transitioning to Therapist 117

    Pacific Center 117

    Grad School Therapy 118

    Navigating the Boundaries 119

    Lessons Learned 121

    A New Companion 122

Chapter Seventeen
  The World Changed 123

    Life Falling into Place 123

    And Then… 124

    A Vivid Memory… 125

    Now What? What Now? 126

    Back North 126

Chapter Eighteen
    On Being Transtherapist.com 128

        Pursuing Licensure 128

        Making a Difference 129

        Families! 130

        A New Chorus Family 133

        Compartmentalizing My Life 134

Chapter Nineteen
    Equilibrium 135

        The "Go-to-guy" 135

        My Own Lack of Therapy 136

        Trans-therapist vs. Cis-therapist 137

        Giving and Receiving Support 138

Chapter Twenty
    The First to Go 140

        The Beginning of the End 140

        The Continuity of Chorus 142

        Really? Again? 143

        A Lonely Season 144

Chapter Twenty-One
    New Directions 145

        Get on it! 145

        Upping the Ante 146

        Arrrrggggghhhhhh! 148

Chapter Twenty-Two

    The First Relationship 150
        Then, There was Nick… 151
        Religion to the Fore 152
        Still on the Path 153
        Conservative Isn't Monolithic 154
        On Hiatus 155

Chapter Twenty-Three
    A New Equilibrium 157
        A New Chorus 157
        Settling into Change 158
        Bolt Out of the Blue 159
        Reinforcement for Leaving 160
        Shifting my Life 160
        And Always, There was Nick… 162
        The Rest of Our Life 164
        Giving Back, Being Honored 165

Chapter Twenty-Four
    Out of Balance 167
        Thank You, Jan 167
        Recalibrating Life 168
        The Clock Ticks 169
        The Kindness of Strangers 170
        Oh Nick… 171

Chapter Twenty-Five
    And Then There was China 174
        And Then There was China 174
        I'm What?! Religious?! 176
        Agnostic to Religious 176

Chapter Twenty-Six

And Then There was China 183
Take Two 183
    PGMC's Finest hour 183
    Complete Uncertainty… 184
    I'm Really in *China* 185
    Communicating in China 186
    Conversations About China 187
    Tourism in China 188
    Me and The Terra Cotta Soldiers 189
    Me and The Terra Cotta Soldiers (Again) 190
    A Musical City 192
    PFLAG China 193
    The Power of Music 194
    About that Music… 196
    China is Changing 197
    Outreach Concerts 199
    See What I Mean? 200

Chapter Twenty-Seven
Change is the Only Constant 202
    Wanting Memories 202
    Finding Home 205
    Time to Go 207
    Now I get it! 208
    Life Goes On Around Me 212

Chapter Twenty-Eight
Summer 'Break' 213
    Shifting Gears 213
    Caregiving at a New Level 215
    In the Midst of Uncertainty 216

    Nurturing through Cooking 219

    Getting to Know My Sister..220

    Work-life-work Balance 221

    Cat Comfort 222

    The End Inexorably Approaches 223

    The Aftermath..225

Chapter Twenty-Nine
  Back and Forth…and Back…and Forth 227

    Back North..227

    Back South..229

    Back North..230

    Back South..231

    Back North..232

Chapter Thirty
  Change is Still the Only Constant... 233

    Back South..233

    A New Opportunity 234

    A New Era for PGMC 235

    Didn't See That One Coming… 235

    Goodbye, Mr. Blue Eyes 239

    It Ain't Over 'Til it's Over… 240

    Not a Birthday—A Lifeday 241

    Living Quarantine 242

    Thank God - I Survived 244

    Life Inevitably Moves On..247

    Wrapping Up Quarantine..248

    Back to the Future…...249

Chapter Thirty-One
  Ends… New Beginnings… Ends... 251

Ends 251

New Beginnings….. 252

… Ends 253

Epilogue **254**
Finale

Volume III **255**

Magical Families **257**

That's it for Now **260**

Appendix
Make Mine a Tailwind: Stories from the Road **262**

The Bear.. 265

The Cemetery.. 266

The Original Remark 267

How Surrealistic 268

God's Bedroom.. 270

It's a Journey... 274

The Vagaries of Wildlife 275

Canadian Camaraderie... 276

Pride 1987 277

Dumb Cows 278

Biking with Others... 279

Pretty Much Flat—Yeah, Right... 280

Journey's End 281

Other Publications by TransGender Publishing **283**

Preface

I wrote Volume I of this memoir in late 2000, stuck at home with a broken leg, in a non-walking cast. I had no clear idea what I would do with it. Volume I resided, unread, on my hard drive for the next 20 years. I wrote Volume II during 2020—the height of the Covid quarantine, this time stuck at home due to a pandemic. All is clear to me now, about the timing of it all, but it sure wasn't when I first wrote Volume I. At that time, my goal was to alleviate boredom. I'd already finished my master's thesis, six months early, and didn't have much else to do all day, other than re-read murder mysteries, hang out with my cat, and watch television long before Netflix or other streaming services. I started my memoir one third of the way through my life and have now written Volume II toward the end of the second third. I've wondered idly where I'll be in twenty years, as the time might come for Volume III. If my life changes as much as it has between Volumes I and II, I can't wait to see what's in store.

Volume One

Introduction to Volume I

In a 1988 interview with Terry Gross on NPR's "Fresh Air," Ray Bradbury stated, "We ensure the future by doing it." I agree with this proactive statement, with the caveat that we also vigilantly remember that the future flows from the present, which flows from the past. History can be viewed at varying levels, from the cosmic to the deeply personal. I write this book from a deeply personal point of view. I leave it to others to write about trans people at a more sociological level.

Trans people need to tell our stories to each other, to provide this continuity that has been sadly lacking in previous times. Isolation and feelings of being negatively unique are common among many trans people, in part because this historical continuity has been lacking.

A friend of mine smiled groggily as she was being wheeled out of her vaginal-creation surgery, whispering to her partner and me, "Another fucking growth experience." My life has been one long growth experience, and though I used to look on the growth experiences (so often the most painful parts of life) with dread, now I look forward to them. Life is for learning, and I'm going for a master's degree in Life.

It's an overwhelming proposition, writing this autobiography. All the layers co-exist from the beginning, and my story can be told from perspectives as superficial as my outward appearance, to the deepest subconscious thoughts and feelings buried in my mind from my earliest childhood. When one questions gender, one is questioning the bedrock of one's existence as a human being and the archaeology involved is formidable. Most people never delve this deeply into their identities, and I alternate between feeling blessed for the opportunity and cursed for the loss of unconscious acceptance of who I am.

My inclination is to begin chronologically, as befits an American, weaving the various layers of my life into a whole that bears some resemblance to my actual experience. We Americans do tend to tell stories from beginning to end, in linear fashion, with little regard to differentiating the layers involved. I hope to transcend this somewhat, as our lives are an ongoing holistic web of social interconnection rather than a straight line, but one must begin somewhere, at some point in the web. So, I begin with what I remember first.

Chapter One

Childhood

First, there is the outward layer, that which everyone else sees. The assumptions people make about others, especially about children, are based almost entirely on observations drawn from this layer. From that first declaration at birth, "It's a boy," or "It's a girl," a child's life is shaped toward a particular adult role. These days, the child's gender is often determined via ultrasound, with a subsequent gender reveal party before the baby sees the light of day.

Gender permeates our culture, as invisible and necessary to our social lives as the air we breathe is to our physical existence. Our autopilot assignment of gender gives us our social boundary with others: how close to stand, how or whether to touch, how or whether to hug or shake hands, what topics of conversation are most appropriate, who we can and can't love. These unconscious decisions are based, in large part, on the gender we have assigned to the person with whom we're in conversation.

Some believe it is possible to transcend gender, that we can create a new culture that is gender-neutral. In such a society, gender would be as important as a birthmark in determining roles and duties. Roles and duties would be assumed based on inclination and talent, not foisted on people by virtue of the assumption of gender. Innate differences in people would be mere observations of tendencies, shortcuts in helping determine a child's aptitude, rather than automatically conferring or denying status to an entire group of people based on perceived gender.

The only way such a culture could evolve is in a society where child rearing is divorced from the concept of personal family, a society where babies are routinely raised in communal settings similar to today's daycare centers. In our current system, gender roles are passed on automatically from generation to generation, effectively preventing the development of any societal transcendence of rigid gender roles.

Loss of rigid roles is unsettling to people. For then, they have to look inward and ask, "Who am I?" Gender roles are the most rigid we've got, and questioning their validity as methods of determination is a scary proposition to many people.

Beyond considerations of how children are raised, such a gender-neutral culture can never exist as long as we are bound by the limitations of the English language. Our gendered pronouns would have to be superseded by a gender-neutral replacement word. As of 2023, "they/them" have become the pronouns of choice among many who identify as non-binary. When I was in grad school in the late 1990s, "hir" or "per" were common gender-neutral pronouns. Language evolves in an attempt to keep up. Who knows what pronoun development will look like twenty years from now? Such morphing of language is an attempt to create cultural space for identities that are beyond the binary.

I have my doubts about the viability of gender neutrality in human interaction. I think it's more likely we are hard-wired as humans to need to differentiate gender, dating back to animal mating instincts. We may very well be able to procreate without sex, but the evolution of instincts will be a long time catching up with technology.

Many people don't agree with the philosophical basis of gender neutrality, adhering to a belief that we are part of nature and not apart from nature. While some animals are dimorphous sexually, we are not among them. Others don't agree with gender neutrality for religious reasons, believing "God created man and woman," end of story.

I believe identities emerge into the light of day in their own time and way. There are so many people, quite different from each other, claiming some form of non-binary identity, I can't help but conclude this is a true identity, finally claiming its place among other available gender identities.

Early childhood

My own upbringing was far from gender neutral. The outward layer everyone saw was a little girl named Nancy, much younger than her three siblings. I was born near Sacramento but had the good sense to move to San Francisco when I was two months old.

My alcoholic father died when I was barely four. He was only 44. I am told I cried bitterly at being denied a place at his funeral. I don't remember this, but I think my tears had more to do with feeling left out than with grief for a death I could not understand. Loneliness and feeling I didn't fit in were constant companions during my childhood.

I only have one lucid memory of my father. He was lying in bed, I believe at home, sick. I went into his room, and he offered me a peppermint lifesaver. This was always a purely innocent memory on my part, until my sister Susan made a remark that illuminates the difference between my small memory of our father and her more vivid, nightmarish memories. When I was in grad school, I told her of this incident, and she unknowingly tainted my sole memory by saying, with some bitterness, "He probably had the lifesavers to disguise the smell of alcohol on his breath."

It never occurred to me to tell Susan how her remark affected me. Another family dynamic played out. I told others in our family, and, eventually, one of them told her. This rather insidious family dynamic may sound like passive-aggressiveness, that I told others knowing it would get back to her. The reality was more complex. It didn't occur to me that anyone else would tell her because it never occurred to me that what I felt or thought mattered enough that another family member would mention the incident to Susan.

For similar reasons, it never occurred to me to talk with Susan directly about how her remark affected me. Many years later, as we watched her wife Rita approach death, Susan herself brought it up to me and apologized. We were both a bit uncomfortable, as this broke all the family rules of engagement, in a good way that resulted in our being able to grow together in our adult-sibling relationship.

We had radically different childhoods, my siblings and me. There is a theory of individual development that all siblings experience different families, based on birth order, age, gender differences, and the like. My sibs and I had more differences between our family experiences than most, such that I grew up feeling like an only child with too many parents, rather than a much younger sibling. Jan was the oldest, 13 years older than me. Susan and my brother, John, were twins, born two years after Jan.

While I never had a sense of being unwanted, I did have the sense of being in the way and of being problematic. I was a late-arriving complicating factor in the already complicated existence of my family. My mother once showed me a letter she had written to her own parents after my birth. She had written, "Warren, of course, is besotted." While I may not remember my father, he adored me.

Childhood Memories

I have only fragmentary memories of childhood. Just about every event I remember with clarity has something to do with gender and is negative. I don't have any purely positive, happy memories of my childhood or adolescence, except those related to some times that I spent alone with my brother John.

He used to take me with him when he went to a local driving range to hit golf balls. He would give me a dime to buy a Coke if I could hit a ball 100 yards. I was so young that there was typically only one golf club small enough to fit me. We also went to the Boardwalk, an amusement park in Santa Cruz, to ride the Big Dipper roller coaster. We would spend all day doing nothing else.

John treated me more like a younger brother than a younger sister, teaching me baseball and using me as a catcher while he practiced his curve ball. We would play catch in the backyard, bare-chested, until I was forced by some unspoken pressure to put on my shirt when I was about 11. Even then, we never stopped doing things together. John was married by this time, but still never treated me as an older brother typically treats a younger sister.

I remember standing in front of a mirror in my bedroom, combing my hair as he combed his, and trying hard to deepen my voice to sound male. I have one embarrassing memory of him overhearing these attempts on my part and teasing me about it.

My denial was a complicated process. It didn't occur to me at the time that I was trying to sound like a boy. I was trying to sound like my brother. It never occurred to me to wonder why I didn't try to emulate either Jan or Susan.

Other, less happy bits and pieces of memory surface...

In second grade, a girl wore pants to school. I have no idea why she did this. In 1962, even in San Francisco, girls were required to wear dresses to public school. This was some years before there was any backlash or overt criticism of such a policy. On the playground, dozens of kids formed a ring around this girl, laughing and mocking her. This incident made a deep and negative impression on me. Her name was Eve. She wasn't in my class, and I didn't know her, yet I remember her name.

Then, there was my ninth birthday party, the only one I remember, which my mother decided should be an all-girl party. I was bitter about this. My best friends were two boys, Jimmy and Danny, from over the back fence, and I was not allowed to invite them.

My mother overheard me complaining vociferously to them about my not being able to invite them to my party. She was furious, and lit into me in front of them, along the lines of, "If that's how you feel, we don't have to have a party at all." In fact, I would have preferred no party at all to what my mother had planned. And I wilted before her anger. The party went on as she had planned it.

I remember this party as nothing but self-conscious embarrassment on my part. Girls from school at my house, myself in a frilly dress, so shy and self-conscious I could say nothing. It was one thing to wear a dress to school—this was the rule in the early 1960s, so it was none of my doing, and I could subconsciously look on the dress as a kind of uniform. But to wear one at home, where one has a choice of clothing, was a matter of complete embarrassment. I never invited girls to play with me at home. I wanted to play with Jimmy and Danny in their sandlot of a backyard. We would build roads in the sand with our hands and run trucks and cars along them.

Since I was born in early September, this all-girl party took place shortly before the end of summer vacation. When I began fourth grade that fall, I was at a new school, a block from home. I sat next to a girl named Gerri, the first tomboy I'd ever met. She and I became best friends, and I never had another close friend who was a boy.

Later, I was to attribute this to being a budding lesbian, though I was not attracted to Gerri. Now, I think it more likely that I'd finally given up and was trying to be a girl. This was bearable with the tomboy role available to me. That birthday party was the last straw. I never wanted to feel that level of embarrassment or self-consciousness again. Driving my true identity completely underground took care of that.

Under Pressure

Prior to this time, I had had behavior problems at school, acting out a lot. From fourth grade on, my behavior seemed to improve tremendously, as did my grades. The "acting out" I'd exhibited prior to fourth grade was, in fact, my behaving exactly as other boys on the playground behaved. But in a girl, in the early 1960s, this was seen as "acting out."

Unfortunately, this "improvement" in my behavior was at the expense of my self-esteem and sense of identity. Instead of acting out, I became very self-conscious and repressed, not wanting to draw attention to myself. To those around me, it appeared that I was maturing. In hindsight, I was stunting myself in an effort to fit into the pigeonhole of "girl."

I am not one of those transmen[1] who knew consciously from an early age that I should have been born a boy rather than a girl. My earlier behavior had been unconscious, me acting in a way that felt natural to me. I gradually came to realize that this was, for some reason, unacceptable. I eventually caved in to the pressure to conform. I knew, somehow, that this meant not being me and believed that there must be something wrong with being me.

Not knowing the exact nature of the problem made it worse, as I assumed that the "something wrong" was an unfixable part of my personality. I was aware, even during childhood, that the "wrongness" I felt was something innate in me, and that it would do no good to tell anyone, as there was nothing anyone could do about it.

In this, I was quite right. In the early 1960s, even in San Francisco, it would have done me no good whatsoever to admit my self-consciousness to anyone. Particularly since I was unaware of the true reason for it, I have no doubt my mother would have been embarrassed by my vague fears and anxiety and would have done her best to discourage me from expressing such feelings.

Unfortunately, like the rest of 1960s society, she had no knowledge that a child's outward gender appearance does not always match their internal identification. That said, it was a no-win situation for me, as it also did me no good (and was harmful to my development) to hide these feelings.

The Sociology of the Day

This was the time period in which John Money was the predominant figure in American sex research, and he was quite vocal in his pronouncement that gender roles were entirely a matter of socialization, that neither genetics nor any other biological factor influenced gender identity at all.

The time period I'm writing about was approximately the same time Money was advising the Reimer's that they could raise their son as a girl after his botched circumcision. The David Reimer story is recounted in John Colapinto's excellent book, *As Nature Made Him: The Boy Who Was*

---

[1] I wrote the first draft of this autobiography in 2000. At that time, I wrote, "I am not one of those transsexuals..." At that time, this was typical self-descriptive language for those of us who had transitioned. I now identify as a transman. This is a perfect example of how terminology morphs over time. I wouldn't be comfortable these days referring to myself as a transsexual.

Raised as a Girl.[2] Of course I knew nothing about John Money when I was in grade school, nevertheless, it was his theories and views that reflected the mainstream view of gender at the time.

Many people now accept as natural the idea that it's not a question of nature *or* nurture, but nature *and* nurture, in combination, that shape a person's identity and personality. However, in the 1960s, biology was not given any credence in shaping identity, and parents thus felt a tremendous pressure to raise their children "right."

At this point in time, most parents would say, "Where did I go wrong?"[3] if their children turned out to be gay, lesbian, or trans, as if it was entirely their fault. Some parents still say this, but most people have come to accept that there is a biological component to a person's identity.

Family dynamics

I was quite a tomboy, a fine athlete, in my pre-adolescent years. I was allowed to play at the schoolyard after school, having first raced home to change into jeans. I was never discouraged from this athleticism, to my mother's credit. Her attempts to feminize me were a dismal failure.

Fortunately, for me, my mother herself was never particularly feminine. She was merely trying to do what she saw as her maternal duty in signing me up for ballet lessons, trying to instill some kind of femininity in me. When this was a patent failure, she quietly stopped trying. She could hardly hold herself up as a feminine role model and had no feelings of personal rejection as she had not adopted a feminine role herself.

My mother was a fair person and hypocrisy was not her way, though she was never one to understand others nor was she able to empathize with others' feelings. She must have seen my obvious unhappiness over that all-female 9th birthday party, as she never tried to force me to do any such thing again. It may be that she had been advised by others to try to "feminize" me, and when my behavior seemed less "boy-like" after that terrible party, she stopped the efforts, thinking she'd been successful enough.

---

[2] I was introduced to this book in a child psychology class in graduate school. The book was on the recommended reading list. The title jumped out at me, and it was the first book I read for that class. I thanked the teacher for including it, and he said he had felt he'd gone out on a limb in doing so, but thought it was a perfect example of how *not* to work with children.

[3] This was precisely my mother's reaction when I came out to her as a lesbian in 1974.

On the other hand, it may be that had she continued to try to force me into a feminine role, my gender dissonance might have come to the surface of my mind much earlier than it did. As it was, I had no reason to rebel against a forced gender role on a daily basis. Hence, the strength of my repugnance for things feminine was not apparent to me.

Unfortunately, my alcoholic family structure was such that I had no self-esteem and never felt safe enough to talk to anyone about my true feelings about anything. At some point, it stopped occurring to me to try.

Given the situation, it's probably just as well I didn't know what was really going on. It would have scared me silly, and I would still have felt that I could not talk to anyone about it. Denial was firmly in place—and with good reason! Defense mechanisms are formed subconsciously to protect the conscious mind from information it can't handle or incorporate. We hide in these fortresses, protected sufficiently to function in our daily lives, until such a time as we are in a position to be able to deal with that which is being denied or repressed. Then, and only then, will the information surface.

My father drank himself to an early grave. My siblings were in their mid-teens when he died. My mother never remarried. I was raised by these three almost-adult children of an alcoholic, and the woman who married him not once, but twice. Hence the age gap between my siblings and me.

One by one, my siblings married and left home when I was a child, each time a personal abandonment of me from my point of view. By the time I was eight, my mother and I were rattling around by ourselves in a three-story Victorian house near Golden Gate Park and UC Hospital in San Francisco.

My siblings did not leave the Bay Area after marrying, and as they began having children of their own, I gradually became reconciled to being an only child in the midst of a growing extended family. I often felt I had no father and was struck fancifully by the cabbage patch story told to young children about where babies came from. It almost felt true to me, as if I'd never had a father at all. No one ever talked about him, except in amusing family anecdotes. He was never three-dimensional to me. I don't even know where he's buried or precisely when he died.

In 2019, I came across a document that listed my father's birthday. With a shock, I realized I'd never known when his birthday was, nor had it occurred to me to wonder. He was never celebrated. I was between generations, three of my nieces and nephews being closer in age to me than my siblings. I had a difficult time defining a clear role for myself in the family structure. This was not aided by my subconscious realization that I had no clear *gender* role to begin with.

Chapter Two

Adolescence

During my pre-adolescent years, gender was not a huge issue for me, aside from those times when my mother attempted to expose me to femininity. But when adolescence hit… When I was 12, I told my mother that I was never going to get married. I was deeply serious and knew what I was saying was Truth. I saw my female friends changing before my very eyes and was dismayed by the sudden emphasis they were putting on boys. I somehow knew I was not going there with them, though I had no idea where I *would* be going in terms of relationships. My feelings of isolation and being different intensified dramatically.

My mother just laughed and said, "You'll change your mind." How sad, to be 12 and have an image of myself as an adult looking exactly as I did at that moment. I resigned myself to living my life alone. I knew I would not be able to have a relationship. Had I known enough to tag on the words, "as a female," I would have been right on target in saying I would never marry.

Children have a clarity of mind and wisdom that is clouded during adolescence. Hormones are not good for clear thinking! I was absolutely right at 12. The relationships I had prior to transition were not intimate emotionally and not successful. Emotional intimacy requires a level of self-knowledge that I didn't have.

I was going through the motions, doing things because they were things adults should do, following patterns of relationship development because that's how such things are supposed to happen. The "shoulds" and "oughts" of adulthood clouded my mind. I knew my mind better at 12 than at any time afterward until I was 39 years old.

One wonderful thing that happened during my early adolescence was the changing of dress codes in the San Francisco Public Schools. Once I entered 8th grade, I no longer had to wear dresses to school. I never looked back, and that one change made adolescence somewhat bearable for me.

Unrecognized Love

In 7th grade, I fell in love with a classmate, a girl named Rosemary. At the time, I did not realize this was what I was feeling. The Stonewall Riots had not yet happened, Gay Pride was in the future, and I don't think I'd ever heard the word homosexual. This may have been San Francisco, but it was also 1967, pre-revolution times for the gay community, and I had no idea my city was a refuge and haven for small-town queers.

My city was the epicenter of Free Love, I knew that much. I could hear the hippy bongo drums in Golden Gate Park from my bedroom window and, through the self-centered lens of adolescence, I knew I lived in a special place. That knowledge of "specialness" didn't extend to understanding my city to be a Mecca for those who were gay or lesbian.

Rosemary intrigued me, partly because she was the first person I'd met who was clearly a genius. Her nickname was "Spock," and she reveled in her logical mind. We spent a great deal of time together, our imaginations soaring far beyond the limited boundaries of Herbert Hoover Junior High School.

When we were 13, Rosemary cut off our friendship. I don't remember the precise circumstances, but clearly remember it had something to do with her feeling that I did not trust her as much as a best friend should. I was stunned not only by her rejection, but that she saw me clearly enough to recognize my lack of trust in anyone.

It floored me, and scared me, to think that anyone actually saw me that deeply. I had not felt I had much of an impact on anyone, a feeling I have fought throughout my life. To learn she was angered by my lack of trust was incomprehensible to me. Why would it matter to anyone what I felt in the depths of my soul? For that matter, why would it make a difference to Rosemary whether or not I trusted her?

Rosemary steadfastly refused to acknowledge my existence for the better part of a year. The first half of 9th grade was a miserable time for me. I stayed home from school for weeks on end, feigning not feeling well. My mother sent me to my pediatrician, a kindly older woman.

In the late 1990s, talking with my mom about the history of my identity, she told me the doctor said I was depressed. My mother was a Depression-Era child, raised on a Missouri farm, and had no time for psychology. Instead of investigating the depression, she latched onto another of the doctor's suggestions, that perhaps I had an undiagnosed allergy. Among the list of likely culprits was down or feathers. So, the end result of my feigning illness was not recognition of my severe depression, but the loss of my favorite feather pillow! Even at the time, I recognized the irony of this and would have laughed had I not been so depressed over Rosemary's rejection.

Only in recent years have I considered that Rosemary's rejection made a fine excuse for my depression, as I really did care deeply for her. I never questioned whether there might not be something deeper going on within me. In any event, I built a wall around my emotions, feelings, and true thoughts that was impenetrable, and, for years, I blamed this on Rosemary. In truth, I walled myself in so no one else would be able to see me as Rosemary had done.

Rosemary eventually repented of her rejection, writing in my junior high school yearbook that she had been stupid, and could I forgive her? We went to different high schools, and, prior to graduation, her family moved to southern California.

Some years later, she called me. She was going to be in San Francisco and wanted to get together with me. We met, and I found my tongue padlocked. I literally could say nothing to her, even at the most superficial levels. I don't think I said two sentences in four hours. I was unable to make myself vulnerable to another human being, and this was the first time I realized it.[4]

First Love

Later that year (1974), I fell in love with a woman in earnest. I was attending City College of San Francisco, as was Mickey. This time, I did recognize the nature of my feelings, and it seemed to me that my entire life fell into place. Though I had a great deal of internalized homophobia, I nevertheless was relieved, thinking, *This is what's been going on all these years! This is what I felt for Rosemary! I must be a lesbian!*

It seemed to explain everything, and I adopted the label "lesbian" and never looked back. I was far from ready to face my gender identity, and adopting lesbian as my identity was a perfect refuge. I never asked questions

---

[4] In 2005, I turned 50 years old. Just prior to my birthday, I felt compelled to try to find Rosemary, who was easily the most important friend from my adolescent years. I did an internet search on her name, not really expecting a quick or easy result. I knew she had married in the early 1980s and didn't know if she'd changed her last name. However, I also remembered her profession and felt I could track her down somehow. Immediately, I'd found someone I thought might be her, but I was understandably suspicious! *It can't be that easy!* I thought. Nevertheless, I sent an exploratory email. The next morning, I had a wonderful long response from Rosemary, who said, among many other things, "You can't imagine how many times I've tried to find "Nancy Vanderburgh" on the internet. But who knew I should be looking for a man named Reid instead?!" We have renewed our friendship, to both our delights.

such as, "Why is my tongue still padlocked?" I was completely unable to talk about my feelings with the woman I loved.

Mickey could see how I felt but could not get me to say it. She was not in love with me, though she was attracted to me. We almost had a sexual relationship, but not quite. This was the mid-1970s, the middle of the sexual revolution, and love and sex were close to being divorced from each other, particularly in Free Love San Francisco. To her credit, Mickey did not take advantage of my feelings by sleeping with me, though the times dictated this as a reasonable course of action. She was 25 to my 19, and our age difference influenced her behavior.

There are few events to which one can point and say with certainty, "My life would be significantly different if I'd made a different choice in this situation." I know with certainty that my life would have been different had I not fallen in love with Mickey. When she was evicted from her apartment so the landlord could give it to his newly married son, Mickey needed a place to live. In my weakness for her, I offered to ask my mother if Mickey could move in with us in our huge three-story house. My mother, thinking this would make me happy, agreed.

It was a miserable time. Mickey had other girlfriends and would bring them home. I sank deeper and deeper into despair, finally deciding I had to leave. In my extreme lack of self-esteem and having no knowledge of acceptable boundaries, it never occurred to me to ask Mickey to move out. Instead, I moved out of my mother's house and left it to Mickey!

I applied to colleges out of town, in order to leave without having to tell my mother the true reason. The closest college I applied to was in Forest Grove, Oregon, about 30 miles west of Portland. I moved in August of 1976, just a few weeks before my 21st birthday. How different would my life have been had I chosen Hofstra University instead? Or Purdue? Both had accepted me. Had I not moved to Oregon, I would never have met Heidi in 1987, and what a difference *that* made, the biggest of all.

Chapter Three

Early Lesbian Days

In Forest Grove, I reveled in living in a small-town atmosphere, with no lesbians around. After my experience with Mickey, I needed a break. I had crushes on several of my classmates at Pacific University, more often than not reciprocated, but the padlock was still firmly closed.

Several straight female classmates pursued me, apparently not realizing what they were doing, though none of these friendships approached turning sexual. This was a post-hippie and still-free-love era, and before the religious right rose to prominence in small-town Oregon. I felt quite comfortable being a fairly open lesbian in this small community.

First Attempts

In June of 1977, I attended my first Gay Pride event[5] in Portland. I met a lesbian couple there, Bev and Jane, who had recently moved to Portland from small-town Virginia. I was just shy of my 22nd birthday. The three of us clicked, and they invited me to come spend weekends with them, to get away from small-town Forest Grove and interact with lesbians.

Bev and Jane were gregarious women and had become quite active in local gay and lesbian organizations. They introduced me to a lot of people when I came for weekends. Through them, I met a woman named Barb. I realized immediately that I was attracted to her and sensed that this feeling was mutual.

One afternoon, we were left alone in Bev and Jane's apartment while they went to the store. This was New Year's Eve, and Barb made her move by asking me, "Don't I get a New Year's kiss?" That's all it took, and it was quite an effort for us to sit up and make ourselves presentable when the others came back from the store.

This was the first time any woman had been attracted to me to the same degree I was attracted to her. My other attractions had not been requited, so I had never been in a situation that would bring my bodily discomfort to the forefront. I now found myself in the confusing position of being intensely

---

[5] These days I would call it the Pride Parade. In 1977, this was no parade, with cheering spectators lining the streets. This was a protest march.

attracted to a woman, and the attraction caused me to not want to be sexual with her! I tried to sort this confusion out. How in the world could it be that being attracted made me *not* want to make love?!

I was not one to openly discuss my feelings with anyone, so I don't remember how the conversation started, but I clearly remember discussing this with Jane and her asking me, at one point, "Are you sure you're really a lesbian?"

I was indignant at the question because I thought the only alternative was to be a straight woman. In hindsight (forty years' worth), I realize Jane hit the nail right on the head without either of us realizing it. I was *not* a lesbian. I didn't want to make love with a woman as a woman. The more attracted to her I was, the more I resisted the attraction. I realize now that it was not that I was repelled by the woman's body. I was repelled by my own and didn't want to be in the position of exposing it to someone I cared about.

This is hindsight speaking, however. At the time, I had no idea where my confusion lay. I found all kinds of negative reasons to lay on myself. Internalized homophobia. Internalized sexism. Some puritanical streak of societal prudism. In exasperation, Barb broke off with me in the spring of 1978, feeling unable to break through to the real me. How could she succeed in that endeavor when I couldn't?

Barb also told me that I had been leaning too heavily on Bev and Jane, that they were tired of my visiting them every weekend. I was an incredibly needy person at that time in my life and had come to look on Bev and Jane as family. They were the first family of choice I ever had, and, in my extreme need, I depended far too heavily on them.

In essence, they had become "mom" to me, and I treated them as I would my actual mother. I visited pretty much every weekend, without checking that this was all right, because they had initially invited me for weekends in Portland. At the time they extended the invitation, I don't think they were envisioning almost every weekend for the next six months. But this is what it had turned into.

Hearing this from Barb, right after hearing that she was not going to see me again because she was, surprisingly, getting involved with a male co-worker—this was a devastating ten-minute conversation for me. Losing Barb was the least of it. Losing my new family of choice was much harder to bear.

It never occurred to me to call Jane and Bev and resolve things with them. I wrote to them, always my communication style at that point in my life, and pretty much blamed them, as I recall, for not making their dissatisfaction known by telling me. I should not have had to hear this from Barb, etc.

A New Love

Cut off from my Portland friends, I developed a much closer friendship with Jacki, a fellow student at Pacific University. She and I came close to having a relationship, and we did talk about it, a little. I wrote her a letter, while I was visiting my family in the Bay Area in the summer of 1978 and acknowledged that our relationship had gone into some gray area that was beyond friendship. She agreed, also by letter. Our friendship had become more intimate than any I'd ever known, though not sexual.

After I got back from the Bay Area, I saw a notice at A Woman's Place Bookstore in Portland, seeking riders to share driving and expenses to go to the Michigan Womyn's Music Festival in August. I asked Jacki to go with me, and she agreed. Her family had moved from Minnesota to Oregon when she was a teenager, and she still had many friends back there who she wanted to visit.

An unspoken reason I'd invited her, and she'd agreed, was that this would move our friendship to a new realm. Jacki could experience how it felt to be with me in the context of the lesbian community, rather than a small-town college community. She had never been involved with a woman before but was open-minded and not at all averse to self-exploration.

As we neared Michigan, she called two friends of hers to say hello. She learned that her favorite teacher, a mentor, had died unexpectedly the week before. She lost her focus on me and the festival and went off with her friends, to attend his funeral and grieve her loss.

In hindsight, this was completely understandable. In the moment, I saw this as yet another abandonment of me, that Jacki was running away from the lesbian context because she couldn't handle it. The former was a very self-centered reaction. The latter did Jacki an injustice she did not deserve.

Ultimately, Jacki did not attend any of the 1978 Michigan Womyn's Music Festival. Her two friends drove her onto the land the last evening of the festival, looking for me. When she found me and said her friends were there to give us a ride, I was furious. One of her friends was a man. She had told him to just drive and not speak, and he'd be taken for a masculine woman. He was Mayan and had no beard, so this did work.

But I had just spent four days on my own in women-only space and, for the first time in my life, had made some tenuous connection to the lesbian community that was not mediated through Jane or Bev or anyone else. I had begun to feel a part of a larger community in my own right. Now, Jacki had brought a man into what I viewed as sacred space, and I was so filled with rage I couldn't speak to her.

I don't remember how we reached St. Paul. My memory is hazy, but I do remember being with Jacki and another friend of hers, Paul, thinking as I did that she always seemed to attract nice guys. I was still so furious with her that I couldn't even speak to her. I walked away from the two of them in downtown St. Paul where Jacki had just booked an airline ticket back to Oregon. I had no money, no idea where I was, and no idea where I was going to sleep that night.

Moving On

After consulting a phone book, I found my way to Amazon Books in Minneapolis, after a very long walk, and threw myself on the mercy of the woman behind the counter. She called two friends of hers, Jackie and Dawn, who were quite willing to take me in until I could find a ride back to Oregon.

I ended up staying with Jackie and Dawn for three weeks, a healing time for me. They had an inflatable kayak and were happy to let me take it down to one of the many lakes in Minneapolis, just a few blocks from their house, and paddle all over. I fell in love with Minneapolis, and almost moved there until I found out their first frost is in mid-September. Too much for this California kid!

I did not go back to school that fall. When I finally got back to Oregon, I stayed in Forest Grove just long enough to pack up my things. Jacki wouldn't speak to me. Bev and Jane re-entered my life out of the blue, calling me as if nothing had ever happened. Though things were never as innocently happy between us as they had been, we spent some enjoyable time together late that summer. Jane agreed to help me move and was going to arrange a moving van. She showed up at my apartment and asked me where the van was. I reminded her she'd said she would take care of it, and she angrily denied this.

The unresolved and undiscussed issues Barb had brought up earlier that year still lay between us. The moving van issue gave Jane and I a forum in which to be angry with each other, without discussing the real underlying issue of my needing them too much and them feeling alternately burdened and guilty for not being able to meet all my neediness.

Jane agreed grudgingly to pack her station wagon as full as possible, make one trip, then I was on my own. I was moving in with a friend of theirs, Diane, who had a large apartment in Portland near S.E. Hawthorne. I didn't have much stuff at that time in my life, so most of my possessions fit in this station wagon. I ended up leaving quite a few odds and ends behind, however, as I didn't have the wherewithal to carry them and didn't like to ask people for favors like a ride to Forest Grove to bring things back to Portland.

This trivial issue over the moving van ended my friendship with Jane and Bev once and for all[6]. Fortunately, though Diane was a casual friend of theirs, there were so many other friends in her life, it was not a big deal that I wasn't on speaking terms with Jane and Bev. In a small town, such meltdowns in lesbian friendships just can't persist. There is not a large enough community to absorb complete ruptures. Such is not the case in Portland, and I simply developed other friendships and turned my back on my life in Forest Grove, completely and permanently.

---

[6] During Covid-19 quarantine, I sought connection any and everywhere. On a whim, I searched Facebook for Bev and Jane. I learned that Jane had died some years before. But I did find Bev. I sent an exploratory message, verifying this was indeed the woman I'd known forty years ago, and received the response: "Oh, my heavens, I've been thinking about you recently and wondered how you are!" We now have a delightful Facebook-based friendship.

Chapter Four

20-Something

The first few months I lived in Portland were wonderful. I made new friends, realizing I'd depended so much on Jane and Bev to provide companionship, I had never developed friendships in my own right. Diane and I discovered a mutual passion for Yahtzee and Monopoly. We spent many evenings playing marathon games. She had recently broken up with her girlfriend, hence the need for a roommate to help pay the rent. We were both single and hung out together happily. It was a balm to my soul to form a close friendship with someone to whom I wasn't, in fact, attracted.

My mother had sent me a tuition check for the fall term of 1978, and I didn't go back to school. She told me to keep the money to get myself established in Portland, though she was not happy at my dropping out of college. Since I had this money in the bank, I was in no hurry to get a job.[7] I wasn't really qualified to do anything anyway. I had no particular job skills, though I had taught myself how to type.

I was aimless, in my early 20s, and reveling in discovering the lesbian community. I was still smarting from my break-up with Jacki, if it could be called that, and wanted a clean break from my small-town life in Forest Grove. Though Portland is only 30 miles east of Forest Grove, the difference was such that I might as well have been in another state.

The First Relationship

On New Year's Eve of 1978, I met a woman at a party. She was visiting from the Oregon coast, and we were immediately attracted to each other. Perhaps, it would be more appropriate to say that in my extreme need for others' approval and acceptance (upon which my own was predicated), I was attracted to Elena's[8] attraction for me. We became lovers in early January, my first true relationship. I moved to the coast to be with her, living in a coastal cabin for nearly a year.

---

[7] To put this in perspective: tuition at my private liberal arts college was about $2,000 a semester at that time. My share of the rent was $100/month.

[8] I have not used pseudonyms for many people in this memoir. Elena, however, isn't the real name of my first lover.

Had I been ready to have my denial tampered with, this relationship could have given me major pointers in the right direction: "Hey, look over here at your relationship to yourself as a woman!" At that time in my life, I beat myself up with the question, "What kind of lesbian _____???" Fill in the blank in various ways: "hates going into women's bathrooms," "isn't comfortable being sexual with women," and "hates referring to herself as a lesbian or as a woman."

Those questions were never answered in my mind, in part because it never occurred to me to take them seriously. Yes: "What kind of lesbian *is* it that hates going in women's bathrooms?" Not being ready to face the answer, I couldn't afford to take the question seriously. So, I moved through the world with those questions hovering in a vague cloud of anxiety.

Elena had caught my enthusiasm for bicycle touring, captured by the romance of it. Though I had yet to do a tour and it had never before occurred to her, both of us had the idea that it would be a wonderful way to see the country. In the summer of 1979, we decided to ride to the Michigan Womyn's Music Festival.

This was a disastrous trip because Elena had a bad back. Had we done sufficient training in riding prior to attempting this trip, she would have realized sooner than eastern Oregon that she was not going to be able to ride 2,500 miles. As it was, I felt frustrated at our 30-mile-a-day pace, while she was in pain much of the time.

Near the border of eastern Oregon, she gave up and hitch-hiked on. We agreed to meet in Missoula, Montana, without the least idea how long it would take me to get there or how we would connect once I arrived. Looking back on it, I find our decision-making processes ludicrous! Nevertheless, the next three or four days were blissful for me. I rode about 60 miles each day, at my own pace and with the peacefulness of my own companionship.

I arrived in Missoula and found a hikers/bikers' hostel in a church. Shortly after I checked in, I was informed that there was a phone call for me. I picked up the phone in astonishment, and Elena was just as astonished that she had found me. She had connected with a lesbian household, and we stayed with them for about a week before proceeding on eastward.

Because of Elena's back problems, we knew we would not have time to ride the rest of the way to Michigan, so we decided to hitchhike. I was intent on spending another three weeks with Jackie and Dawn in Minneapolis. The previous summer had been so idyllic. To have the full three weeks, we needed to hitchhike the rest of the way. We arrived in Minneapolis, and I called Jackie and Dawn. I'd already asked them via letter if we could stay with them on our way to the festival.

Again, looking back on it, I do not understand my own thought processes. Why I thought they would welcome houseguests for three full weeks is beyond me. The previous summer, I had been stranded and had connected with them in a family kind of way.

This time, I was with a lover they had never met and pretty much foisted the two of us on them. Jackie was surprised to hear from me so long before the Festival, as they had assumed I had meant we would stay with them for the weekend prior to the festival, not attempt to recreate the previous summer's stay.

Not long after our return from that bicycle trip, Elena and I broke up. I don't remember now what caused the final breach. It doesn't matter. I was so out of touch with my identity that I couldn't have formed a lasting relationship with anyone at that time, including the woman who is my wife today.

Collective Living

When Elena and I broke up, I moved into a lesbian household, a big mistake for me. I did not have good boundaries or communication skills. I was not assertive, and I found myself in a household with a strong personality running the show, though it was called a collective household. The best thing about that experience is that I met Neuma and Kim, a lesbian couple who moved from Boston and took two available rooms in our household.

This was the late 1970s, a time when monogamy was a dirty word in the lesbian community. The household was suspicious about accepting Neuma and Kim as roommates because they were a couple (oh, horrors!) and only wanted one of the rooms as a bedroom. Kim was a musician and wanted the second room as a practice room. The suspicion was that monogamous relationships were unstable and inherently unhealthy, that Neuma and Kim might fight, break up, and leave the household in a lurch when it came time to pay the rent.

Years later, I told Neuma about this, and she roared with laughter. She told me that she and Kim had never had a monogamous relationship, though neither had had an outside affair at that point. Our collective household had assumed monogamy where it did not exist!

Neuma and Kim bought a house and moved out a few months after moving to Portland. Our entire household relocated sometime after that. Shortly after our move, my relationship with the most powerful member of the household (Kate) deteriorated sharply. I was used to not picking up after myself and have never been an innately tidy person. Kate tried bluntly to inform me that my habits did not mesh with collective living, and I just got defensive about it and began avoiding being home when she was awake. I would be away from home until past midnight, sneaking in and going to my room. I'd wait until Kate was gone in the morning to come out again.

First Bicycle Tour

In the summer of 1981, I decided to ride my bicycle to the West Coast Women's Music Festival in Yosemite, partly to get away from the tension in my household and partly to recapture the idyllic experience I'd had riding on my own a few years before.

I told my mother I would not have time to visit the Bay Area for the annual September Birthday Party (four of my family members, including my mom and I, have a Virgo birthdate). This was not true, however. Conniving with my sisters, I made plans to ride to San Francisco prior to the Yosemite Festival. The family planned to take my mother out to dinner, and I would be the big surprise.

My mother was more than surprised when I showed up at that family dinner. She didn't immediately recognize me. I had cut my hair very short for this trip, and my mother had thought I was a male friend of her youngest grandson's that he had brought along to dinner. This was just one of many incidents involving mistaken gender during my life. I ignored this one, also.

The effect it had on my mother was interesting. She never forgot that incident, and from this point on, she would comment that she wished I wore my hair longer. She had never let me wear my hair short when I was a kid, largely because she wasn't allowed to have long hair as a kid growing up on the farm. I cut my hair short when I moved to Forest Grove and wore it lesbian-style from then on. My mother never commented on this, until that dinner where she mistook me for a guy. For the first time, she felt the deep gender dissonance in me, and it jarred her.

Living Independent

That touring experience changed my life. I had felt competent, secure in my aloneness, and independent. I was about to break out in Portland as well. I moved out of the collective household in the fall of 1981, less than a month after returning from that bike trip. For the first time since I moved to Portland, I rented an apartment on my own.

I was adopted by a neighbor cat, Bear Cub, who was to be my constant companion for the next 16+ years of my life. Except for one brief period of crisis, I never again lived with anyone who was not my lover and doubt I ever will. I had too little self-knowledge at that point in my life to realize that I'm too private a person to live easily in a collective situation.

Shortly after I moved, I took stock of where I was geographically in relation to various friends. I was living in NE Portland. At that time, most of the lesbian community still lived in the Hawthorne area of SE Portland. In checking addresses of friends, I realized that I had inadvertently moved within six blocks of Neuma and Kim!

I walked over to their house shortly after my move. They were home, and delighted to hear I was now a neighbor. I became much closer to them over the course of the next year or so that I lived in that neighborhood.

New Self-knowledge

That winter of 1981, I became involved as an almost-founding member of the Portland Women's Theater Company. As with most things in my life during my twenties, I got involved with groups largely because people would ask me and I didn't know how to say "no." In the case of the theater company, however, I would not have wanted to say "no." This was pure luck on my part, as I said "yes" to a job for which I was perfect without having the faintest idea what it entailed.

The friend who asked me to be stage manager knew it would be right up my alley. The theater company needed and valued the organizational abilities I'd never known I had, and, over time, my tongue became less padlocked. I was able to voice my opinions in meetings.

I was even able to audition for a part in the third play the theater company produced. Just a few years before, it would have been unthinkable for me to be on stage, speaking lines in front of an audience. Certainly, I felt stage fright along with everyone else, but it did not affect my ability to remember my lines.

I was exhilarated to realize that I was the only one in the cast who did not mind individual scenes with one of our best actors. The other actors dreaded being onstage alone with her. She did not reliably remember her lines. A scene with her often turned into a form of improvisational theater—with a paying audience. I rather enjoyed this.

In my first play, this actor played a realtor. I played a naïve young woman in search of a suitable space to rent. With some friends, I was going to start a restaurant (vegetarian, of course—this was a 1970s lesbian play!). The realtor and I were supposed to have a conversation that would reveal information that would become relevant later in the play.

Toward the end of the scene, she was supposed to ask me how big a space I had in mind. The answer was supposed to be in terms of numbers of tables for which we wanted to have room because we were opening a restaurant. We sat down at the beginning of the scene, looked at each other, and my realtor said right off the bat, "So, about how many square feet do you think you'll need for your restaurant?"

At this point in the scene, she was not supposed to know we were opening a restaurant! And square footage was never even mentioned in the script! Without missing a beat, I replied, "Oh, about 1600 square feet." And we salvaged the scene from there. At intermission, she approached me and said, "That wasn't quite right, was it?"

This experience, as well as my ability to deal with onstage emergencies in my capacity as stage manager for the previous two plays, showed me some abilities I'd never known I possessed. My self-concept was slowly being altered by this experience, and I developed some degree of self-confidence.

I also learned how to play a part, and this allowed me to play the part of "lesbian" more convincingly (to myself—no one else had reason to question it!) than I had to date.

Chapter Five

Something's Not Right!

By my late twenties, sex had become an obsession with me, because I knew with misplaced certainty that the root of my problems in relationships lay in my warped view of sex. However, I did not yet understand that there was a difference between sex and gender. My real obsession was with *gender,* and it played out through my sexuality. I was existentially confused at that time in my life. I knew I wasn't attracted to men sexually. I knew the only people I ever fell in love with were women, and I knew something was wrong.

I kept a daily journal at that time in my life. Those journals are full of angst about attractions, feelings of self-worthlessness, wondering why I was so unlovable. The bottom line always was, "What's wrong with me?" As long as I continued to wail that question from a sexuality context, rather than a gender context, the answer remained elusive.

Looking for Love

At about the same time I began my involvement with the theater company, I had also started working on a women's newspaper in Portland. I had an ulterior motive. Alicia was helping produce this newspaper, and I wanted to get closer to her.

The chemistry between us was dynamic and volatile. We exchanged lengthy passionate kisses on several occasions. One evening, I could tell she was nervous, that she was working up to telling me something big, so when she finally blurted out, "I'm bisexual," I'd been prepared to hear she'd fallen in love with someone else.

To put her announcement in context, this was the early 1980s in the lesbian community, a time when being bisexual was generally suspect. Most of my friends viewed bisexual women as either confused about whether they preferred men or women, or as women who preferred sex with women, but were too cowardly to give up the safety of heterosexual relationships.

In neither case were bisexual women regarded with trust or much respect. Bisexuality was not viewed as a sexual orientation in its own right. Hence Alicia's nervousness in making this confession to me. She was very relieved when I just said, "So?"

This was not the first time a woman had made such a confession to me, but it was the first time that the thought crossed my mind to wonder what it meant that nearly all the women I'd loved were either bisexual or had ended up in relationships with men. Over the ensuing years, this was to become an ongoing pattern. To my knowledge, only one of the women I've loved over the years had never been with a man.

When I said, "So?" to Alicia, my reaction was not based on any well-considered politic of supporting bisexual women. My reaction was based on my attraction to Alicia, and I was not going to let any revelation drive her away from me.

In fact, I *was* uncomfortable with her statement, because I had no idea what it really meant to be bisexual, and because this was bringing men into the conversation, however obliquely, and I didn't want to go there at all! That was a little too close to a personal truth that I was avoiding like the plague. I just knew her confession left me feeling anxious and a bit scared.

Hiding Behind Politics

My politics were a hodge-podge of whatever was currently most popular in the lesbian community. I was cynical about lesbian politics in general and tended to make fun of some of the press releases that came my way while I worked on the women's newspaper. When a story was prolonged and press release updates would come every month, I would say, "That story still!" with no empathy for the people involved.

One story, in particular, used to get me every month as updates came in. It went on for over a year, and I got increasingly callous about it. I cringe now when I remember my sarcastic comments about the story of Sharon Kowalski and her lover Karen Thompson. If ever a story cried for empathy, theirs did.

They were closeted lovers in small-town Minnesota and led a conservative life. Sharon was in a car accident that left her in need of physical therapy. Karen ended up coming out to Sharon's parents, in an effort to get Sharon home with her. Karen was a physical therapist and could have helped Sharon regain much of her functioning.

Upon hearing about their relationship, Sharon's parents refused to believe Karen, saying their daughter was not a lesbian and that she had been seduced by Karen. They succeeded in getting a restraining order to prevent Karen from ever seeing Sharon. They then put Sharon in a nursing home where she received very little physical therapy at a crucial stage in her recovery.

I was callous and sarcastic when updates on their situation would come in each month, very effective defenses against feeling emotion. On the one hand, I was eaten up with envy that Sharon had a lover who cared for her so much. On the other hand, I knew, deep down, that I could never be in that kind of relationship myself.

I realize now that I was quite right about that. What I didn't understand is that I could never be in such a close relationship with someone else because I wasn't in a right relationship with myself. At the time, however, my belief was that I was too unlovable to be in that kind of relationship, that no one would ever come out in small-town America in order to win the right to take care of me.

Yet Another Try for Love

By the mid-1980s, Alicia had long since moved on and was no longer working on the women's newspaper. She had given up on the lesbian community, finding too little support for a bisexual woman. I had fallen in love with another woman working on the paper, Sharon. My love for her about drove me crazy, nearly to suicide.

There were several times during the 1980s when I came close to suicide. The pattern was always the same. I would fall in love with a woman, always a woman who was not in love with me. I could not voice my feelings and felt my very life depended on her not finding out how I felt. She would always know, however, by my actions. I would find my work deteriorating, my self-esteem (never very high) disappearing, and my journals filling with angst about being unlovable.

Eventually, the woman in question would get tired of her role in my trauma-drama. But things would get sticky, as we were usually very good friends. I would deliberately form friendships with women to whom I was intensely attracted. I assumed, from the time I met a woman to whom I was very attracted, that I should form a friendship with her because I was so unlovable, no other kind of relationship would be possible.

I never allowed for the possibility that she might be attracted to me yet not fall in love with me, which happened with Alicia and Sharon both. For me, it was all or nothing.

At Loose Ends

In mid-1985, my work with the women's newspaper abruptly came to an end due to a conflict with the woman who owned the typesetting equipment we used. She was a very abrasive and opinionated woman. I saw her as a loose cannon, whose benefaction was not doing the newspaper any good in the long run.

I proposed that we take advantage of my new computer and the then-new capacity of printing out documents on a laser printer at a local copy shop.[9] When the typesetter owner learned of my proposal, she abruptly denied me further access to her equipment. Scared of her overwhelming personality and uncertain about the efficacy of this new laser printer technology, the newspaper collective chose not to rock the boat, which forced me to leave the collective.

I also left the theater company in the mid-1980s. Tensions often ran high in lesbian organizations, and several of us techie-types felt the tension wasn't worth it in the theater company. The actors had the audience applause coming their way to help balance the tension. Those of us mostly-behind-the-scenes folks didn't.

With my relationship with the newspaper and the theater company severed, I felt at loose ends. I was working on a half-time basis for a law firm in Portland, transcribing deposition tapes. I was in my late twenties at this point. I still had the thought, "I wonder what I'm going to be when I grow up?"

I had no direction in my work life, had never had a job that paid benefits. I didn't have career plans, just drifted from job to job as opportunities arose. My half-time $8.00 an hour job paid all my bills easily, so I thought no more of it.

My mother inherited a great deal of money in the mid-1980s and felt it was unfair that she was the sole heir. She shared the wealth with various family members and bought me a small house.[10]

---

[9] No one I knew had a laser printer at home at this time. They cost many thousands of dollars.

[10] To put this gift in perspective—a small house in Portland at that time cost about $25,000.

Planning the Big Tour

Now, without having to worry about money and having no organizations demanding any of my time, I was becoming too comfortable. If I were not constantly busy, I would have too much time to think. And to feel. And possibly to realize a few core truths about myself. Can't have that! I decided it was time for another bicycle tour and began planning another ride to the Michigan Womyn's Music Festival.

One of my closest friends had recently moved to Boston, and I missed her a great deal. In looking at a U.S. map, I realized how close Michigan was to Boston (relative to its proximity to Oregon!), so the thought occurred to me to ride to Boston on this trip to visit Sylvan.

Then, I considered logistics. The festival is in August. If I rode on to Boston from Michigan, would summer weather hold until I got there? Then I thought, *Maybe I should ride to Boston first, then to Michigan from there.* It was a short step from this idea to thinking, *Jeez, I should just ride both ways!*

I wrote letters to various Contact Dykes in *Lesbian Connection,* an international publication consisting entirely of lesbians writing letters in response to letters in response to various topics raised in previous issues or raising new issues or questions. The Contact Dyke list consisted of women who were willing to be contacted by other lesbians for information about their town or part of the world. I'd been a Contact Dyke myself since the late 1970s.

I published my intent in *Lesbian Connection,* looking for contacts along the way. By the fall of 1986, I had amassed quite a few replies, offers of places to stay, which largely determined my route. I was planning to do the trip during the summer of 1987.

Changing My Life Focus (Who Knew?)

In October of 1986, the Lesbian Community Project produced the first lesbian conference Portland had ever known. Over 400 women attended workshops on a variety of topics. I went, though I had no intention of joining any political group. Politics (and particularly processing) bored me. However, something happened at that conference that changed my life once again.

A few women had been trying for a month or so to form a women's chorus in Portland but had had little success. Only four women had shown up at the first few meetings. Their advertising had been a little too minimalist. One member offered to announce the formation of this group at the Lesbian Community Project conference.

With two friends, I heard the announcement, and all three of us decided to go to the next rehearsal to check it out. We did, and I stayed. For the next eleven years, the soon-to-be-named Portland Lesbian Choir was my spiritual center and the only place I ever felt truly at home in the lesbian community.

I had always loved to sing, but my innate fear of exposure to others prevented me from being able to sing when not alone. There had been times when I had sung along with records or the radio knowing I would be overheard, as I knew I had a good voice and that this was likely to impress the person who heard me. I only had problems when others were watching me sing. In joining this newly-forming chorus, I knew I was coming home to a key aspect of myself.

I don't want this to become a history of the Portland Lesbian Choir, though I know more about the early history of that organization than all but a handful of people. The bond I feel with that handful is profound. My first rehearsal brought Amy and Karen into my life, and we quickly became the three musketeers.

Between the three of us, we steered a course of professionalism and performance for the new chorus. I was one of the first production coordinators and also held positions as publicity coordinator and fundraising coordinator. There was never a time when I was not in a leadership position within that organization, following the trend I'd always done in the lesbian community since my theater company days.

I understand now that I was buying my place as a lesbian in good standing. If I did enough work for an organization, I could stay. I would have felt very uncomfortable simply joining a lesbian group for the sake of sociability or because I believed in its mission and wanted to be associated with it.

One could make the argument that I am a workaholic of sorts, or that my perfectionist nature is such that I can't stand watching someone else do a job I know I could do better. The former is certainly not true. The latter has an element of truth to it but does not tell the whole story.

If I joined a chorus now, I might offer my graphics skills for publicity purposes but would probably not take on the leadership role of making sure publicity was done as needed. I no longer have that feeling of needing to buy my membership in any group I care to join, beyond any required membership dues.

What I was buying in the case of the Choir was the right to sing in a *lesbian* chorus. In the back of my mind was the thought, *If I do enough work, no one can contest my right to be here.* Of course, the thought never entered anyone's head to contest any such thing until years later, when the thought finally entered *my* head.

Throughout my twenties, I visited my biological family in the Bay Area as often as I could. I was not yet to the point where I was able to talk about deep feelings with other people. For this reason, it did not bother me that feelings are not talked about or dealt with in my family.

In my thirties, as I came to have some self-esteem and an understanding of the level of intimacy possible in a family, I developed a family of choice in Portland whose company I preferred. Every member of my family of choice was a member of the Choir. The Choir as a whole was like my extended family, and a small circle of five or six was my family of choice.

Only with that small circle of friends did I ever feel truly at home, as if I never needed to do a thing to "buy" my place or justify myself. And it was to this group that I turned later, when my life turned upside down and I needed support as I'd never needed it before.

Chapter Six

Big Adventures

I had just turned 31 when the Choir formed in October of 1986. And, I had already decided to ride my bike once again to the Michigan Womyn's Music Festival in 1987. I was planning to be gone for about five months, and now felt conflicted about this, as the Choir had quickly become central to my life. Nevertheless, my plans had been set, and I was also looking forward to my prolonged adventure.

The Choir had its first performance for the Portland lesbian community on International Women's Day 1987. When we were announced, the audience of perhaps 400 gave us a standing ovation for setting foot on the stage of the Northwest Service Center. This was the last time any standing ovation was so easy. It was difficult for me to imagine spending months away from these women, who had already become the most important family I ever had.

A Bicycle Odyssey

On May 2, I departed on my odyssey. As I rode east toward Mt. Hood, the only thing that kept me from turning around in sheer terror was the knowledge that I'd sublet my house until late September.

I had financed this tour by banking the $2,000 I had received the previous summer for my work on Artquake, a regional arts festival. Back in 1984, a friend (a lesbian, of course) had asked me to be a volunteer at this festival, which I'd never even attended (too straight!). I ended up coordinating all the signage for the festival, producing much of it myself. I was intrigued by sign-painting.

The fact that this was a non-paying gig didn't faze me. All my work for the theater company and the women's newspaper had been volunteer. In 1985, I was invited to be one of the festival coordinators and was paid to do so. I held this position for nine years, only taking off the summer of 1987 for this bike tour.

What got me through the first weeks of this tour was the following quote I'd copied out of Reader's Digest:

I did not see the whole. I only saw this rock ahead of me; I only saw this poisonous snake, which I had to kill in order to take the next step. I only saw the problem directly in front of me. If I had seen the whole thing, I would have been too overwhelmed to have attempted this."
~Sir Henry Morton Stanley, jungle explorer

I affixed this post-it note quote to a large U.S. map I'd put on my living room wall, with my route drawn in felt-tip pen. Later, this quote would also become the paradigm for my transition.

After the first two weeks or so, I had adjusted to living on the road and no longer had any doubt that I would succeed, that I could go anywhere. I rode through 22 states and two Canadian provinces that summer. I've always been a baseball fan (thank you, brother John). I had become a Chicago Cubs fan because, at that time, they broadcast all their games on WGN television. That summer, I saw two games at Wrigley Field, the last season before lights were installed.

I rode my 80-pound all-terrain bicycle over Trail Ridge Road, 12,183 feet, the highest paved road in the continental U.S.[11] I dipped my wheels in the Pacific and Atlantic Oceans (a tradition among those who bicycle cross-country). I visited my friend Sylvan in Boston, enjoying bombing around that town, which has too many potholes and too little traffic control. I went to Provincetown. And I went to the Michigan Womyn's Music Festival, the only time-delineated goal I had all summer.

There is nothing like bicycle touring to spark conversations with strangers, often leading to offers of meals or places to stay for the night. I rode on county and state highways, through towns that were off the beaten path, and met dozens of wonderful people that summer. As promised, I sent them all postcards when I arrived home safely.

I felt strong and powerful, feelings I seldom had when not on my bike. Only once during that summer was this feeling shattered, once again in a way that could have been a pointer to me had I been willing to see. I was riding on U.S. Highway 1, north from Boston up the Atlantic coast. It was

---

[11] At the end of this memoir, I've included some stories from the road, tales from various bicycle trips, including this trek into the heights of the earth over Trail Ridge Road.

very hot and muggy in Boston, and it was Saturday. It seemed the entire city was leaving town heading toward Maine.

In a small town, I was fending off traffic and feeling very hot and bothered by it all. I was wearing a tank top and shorts, my usual biking garb in such hot weather, and a man on the sidewalk whistled at me and said in a very turned-on voice, "Oh, babe."

I immediately felt a rush of hot fury that had me shaking for hours. I turned my fury on him and said, "Fuck off!" in my most drop-dead voice. I reached into my pannier and fished out a Hawaiian shirt, putting it on over my tank top. I was absolutely furious with him for reacting to me as if I were a woman, though, of course, I did not put it that way to myself consciously.

I used to react the same way when someone would call me "sir," or if a woman saw me in a public bathroom and questioned why I was there, both of which were common experiences. I am six feet tall, with short hair, and seeing me as a man was a natural "mistake." I really had no reason to react to such incidents with intense anger. No reason, except that "sir" was more appropriate for me and I wasn't ready to admit it.

For the most part, however, I felt happier and more centered that summer than at any prior time in my life. I was producing endorphins by the truckload, and my body was in such wonderful condition, I couldn't help but have a happier outlook on life. Yet still, it has never been a body image issue for me. No matter what kind of shape I was in, it was still a female shape, and that would never please me.

After the music festival, I felt flat and aimless. I slowly rode to Minneapolis. Once there, I realized I just could not stand the thought of riding the Midwest twice in one summer. I flew to Seattle on my 32nd birthday, September 1. I called my sublet and made an arrangement with her that I would return on September 19.

I spent the next 18 days riding around the Olympic Peninsula, my first trip to that part of Washington. I was in such splendid physical condition by this time, spending 18 days riding 400 miles was much too easy and fairly torturous. I bought the thickest paperback book I could find and did my damnedest to make it last nearly 3 weeks.

The Last Leg

I spent my last night on the road in the public park that was part of the Trojan Nuclear Power Plant, 44 miles north of Portland. The next day, I fairly *flew* to Portland, I was so excited to be coming home. I was in town by noon.

I'd asked Neuma, who was overseeing things in my absence, to invite my friends (Choir and otherwise) to a welcome-home party for me at 5:00 that Sunday afternoon. Obviously, I was early. I spent the afternoon in a SE Portland park, finishing the book I'd bought. As I rode up Hawthorne on my way to Neuma's house, two good friends passed me in their car, on their way to my welcome-home party, and I thought, *I'm home!*

Few Choir members were at my welcome home party, as the group had just spent most of the afternoon in a tense processing meeting that culminated in the then-director leaving. This was to become a familiar type of scenario as the years went by, but, at the time, I was merely disappointed so few of my Choir buddies were there to welcome me back from my odyssey. But Amy and Karen were there, the people I most wanted to see.

After the party, Amy and Karen insisted on loading my bike and gear into their truck and giving me a ride home. It was nearly dark by then, and I had no light on my bike. Somehow, it just wasn't right that I didn't pedal that last three miles on my own, arriving home under my own power as I'd left it 5,285 miles and 4½ months before, but I did not insist.

As we pulled up, I saw a cat lying on the sidewalk outside my house. She was thinner than I'd remembered, and it was fairly dark by then, so I said, "Are you my cat?" She ran to me, meowing and rubbing against my legs, so indeed, she was my Bear Cub, welcoming me home at last.

Nesting Again

I spent the next few months doing all kinds of projects around the house. I had so much energy, I just didn't know what to do with myself. Despite my very minimal riding the last three weeks of my trip, I had never been in better physical condition. Upon my return, my resting pulse rate was that of a marathon runner—38 beats per minute. Hills that had seemed somewhat daunting prior to my departure didn't even quicken my breath or require a gear change.

Little did I know that within months of my return from this wonderful odyssey, I would meet a woman who would rock my world and change me to the core of my being.

Chapter Seven

The Relationship

That fall, I reconnected with the Choir. Amy, Karen, and I became the best of friends. I had never discussed relationships with anyone before, but I began to talk about my feelings more with Amy and Karen. I confessed to them that on entering into a relationship, I always had the thought in the back of my head, *I wonder how this one is going to end?* I remarked that I just did not understand why anyone would ever want to get involved. It just leads to heartache in the end. It was not long before I learned, for the first time, why people get involved.

A Fateful Relationship

On New Year's Eve of 1987, two friends from my Artquake days invited me to a beach house on the Oregon coast. The gathering was a hodge-podge of their biological families, friends from Portland, and friends of theirs from Eugene. I didn't know anyone except the two women who had invited me.

It was during this weekend that I met Heidi, who lived in Eugene. We recognized an immediate affinity for each other and spent the weekend acknowledging this to ourselves, though not immediately to each other.

Upon my return, I got her address from our mutual friends and wrote her a card in which I told her I was attracted to her and wanted to see her again. Two days after mailing this card, I received a card from her which merely said, "I'm glad I met you." No acknowledgement of my card at all. I thought I'd misunderstood, that she was saying, "It was nice to meet you. See you around someday."

I talked to Neuma extensively about this, dissecting the possible meanings of this short message, until finally Neuma said the obvious, "Do you think maybe Heidi sent this card before she got yours?"

Feeling like a fool because this possibility had not even occurred to me, I admitted this might be the case. Sure enough, when I got home that day, there was another card waiting for me. Heidi had gone home after mailing her initial card to me, read my card, and sent me another to say she felt the same way.

Soon thereafter, Neuma called me excitedly and told me a print shop in downtown Portland was going out of business and auctioning off their equipment, among which was a typesetting machine. Neuma owned a print shop of her own and kept track of such possibilities. State of the art for the 1980s, this typesetter actually had a disk drive for storing jobs. Unheard of at the time, this meant not having to re-type previous jobs in order to make revisions.

I went to the auction and bought the machine for $800, intending to set myself up as a typesetter and work out of my home. It looked as if the volunteer typesetting I'd done for the women's newspaper some years before was going to pay off. With my future employment solidly envisioned, I was free to worry about having met Heidi.

I first visited her in Eugene the same day I took delivery of the typesetter. More than once, I have found momentous events occurring either on the same day or in close relative proximity to one another, as if the cosmos had several plans for me that all converged at once.

Heidi was in the process of writing a book and was now in the final editing phase. Realizing she would not be able to concentrate on this most-hated phase of writing if I were there, she limited our first visits to one day of a weekend. So, I went down via Greyhound on Friday evening and came back Saturday evening. (I had still not acquired a driver's license). We were similarly shy with each other, which bonded me with her quite effectively. After a month or so, we acknowledged to ourselves and each other that we'd fallen in love. She moved to Portland in June of 1988 to be with me.

Idyllic?

The following March, we bought a large house together, and I sold my little house. The typesetter never worked right after the move, and in exasperation, for it had always been temperamental, I bought my first laser printer. Once this was hooked up to my computer, I was off and running and never used traditional typesetting equipment again. I named my business "Your Type Typesetting," later changing that to "Your Type Design Services."

Heidi had a music degree, and, at first, worked an office job until she had developed sufficient contacts in the local music community to be able to offer her services as a private music teacher. She then quit the office job and taught students in several locations. Between the two of us, we barely made sufficient money to pay the mortgage each month[12]. We never had quite enough, and saving for household emergencies or retirement was simply not an option. But we had a beautiful older home in a wonderful neighborhood and were quite happy, for a while.

I had always had the attitude, "The right relationship is what I need to feel happy and complete." On some level, I knew this wasn't quite the answer, but still I had kept searching. Now, on paper, my life looked complete, as if I'd achieved all my dreams. I had a work-at-home business, doing work I loved. I owned a beautiful house. I had cats. I had *the* relationship. So why was I more anxious and unhappy than ever? I had thought the relationship was all I'd needed to fix my life, and it hadn't worked.

Amy and Karen fully accepted Heidi into the equation, and we became the four musketeers, rather than the three musketeers we'd been before. They considered our home their home away from home, and would often drop by unexpectedly, bringing beer and food for a "barbecure." We would complain about the Choir, barbecue on the back patio, and generally have a wonderful time together.

We had some good times during our relationship, Heidi and me. I had the most enjoyable times when we were away from home. I love adventuring and traveling. Heidi was always much more anxious while traveling, but my enjoyment of such situations bolstered her, and she came to enjoy our trips also. She did not sing with the Choir. Professional musicians tend to be easily bored with amateur groups.

Our relationship was far from idyllic, however. My own discomfort with living female had been steadily growing, and now that I was in my thirties, I was living with a low-grade anxiety that was increasing as the years went by. I could no longer ignore the fact that I was not living as an adult, contributing member of society.

During my early twenties, it did not bother me much that I didn't know what I wanted to do with my life. I had an unconscious sense of marking time until I grew up. But as this feeling stayed with me into my thirties, I had a growing unease that something was seriously wrong with me. My friends all had careers, were beyond the stage of having mere jobs, and I felt this difference keenly. I was still marking time, waiting to grow up.

---

[12] To put this in perspective—our mortgage was $625 a month.

My business was never successful financially, which meant Heidi was contributing the lion's share of our income. At first, this was not inappropriate. The bulk of the down payment for our house had come from the proceeds of selling my smaller house. But, as time went by, Heidi grew more resentful of my inability to generate income.

My lack of self-esteem infected every area of my life, including my work. Though I produced high-quality work for my clients, I always felt uncomfortable being paid for the work I did. I also had a difficult time marketing myself, relying primarily on my skills in developing print advertising and not being able to sell myself in person at business events.

During those years from 1989 to 1995, I was unconsciously using my home-based business as a way to hide myself away from the "real world." My gender dissonance had grown to such an extreme that I was very uncomfortable interacting with anyone outside my family of choice. Yet still, I did not recognize the reason for my extreme anxiety.

Disillusioned

By 1995, I was very unhappy in my relationship with Heidi and knew it consciously. I was also very unhappy with myself, and while I knew it consciously, I was still unaware of the reasons for it. Being with a partner I loved and who loved me brought to the forefront my gender dissonance, as I didn't want to be sexual, yet knew I *should* want it.

In addition to my own discomfort with myself, I knew, even then, that there was something in Heidi that I just wasn't reaching. I would eagerly wait for her to come home from teaching, having prepared dinner. I would hold Bear Cub and we would stand by the back window, waiting for the sound of the garage door opening that meant Heidi was home.

Yet, when she walked through the door, I was always conscious of a feeling of being let down, as though the person I was waiting for wasn't the person who came into the house. I constantly berated myself for these feelings, which confused and distressed me. And, of course, it never occurred to me to talk to anyone about it.

At this point, I fell in love with another member of the Choir. I never told her about my feelings, though I hinted sufficiently that had she reciprocated, I would have left Heidi for her. Fortunately, she did not feel as I did and, eventually, my feelings shifted into a close friendship. However, this was the first time I seriously entertained the notion of leaving Heidi. I never quite recovered from that experience, and from that time on,

I knew it was just a matter of time before we broke up. I could never have foreseen, however, the circumstances under which our relationship finally ended.

Chapter Eight

Revelations

During the Choir season of 1994-95, we were working on a four-chorus, three-city concert tour, with groups from Seattle and Vancouver, B.C. The *Under One Sky* concert was the most ambitious project the Choir had undertaken to date. Karen was the overall coordinator of the event. I was coordinating the housing for the other choruses when they visited Portland, as well as being publicity coordinator for the Choir that season.

It was a productive, busy time. Yet I was increasingly unhappy because I was so unhappy in my relationship with Heidi. I talked with Amy about a lot of things (she is the only person I ever told about my unrequited love for a fellow Choir member), but I never articulated even to Amy the extent of my growing restlessness in my relationship with Heidi.

The Beginning...

By April of 1995, I didn't have much to say to Heidi and was very disillusioned with her. I didn't know why I felt as I did. I just felt she wasn't *there* most of the time. Even so, I was completely unprepared for what happened one night that month. Heidi bolstered her courage and said to me, "I've always felt like a gay man inside, and, if I had the money, I'd have an operation tomorrow."

We were lying in bed at the time. It was very late at night. I lay absolutely rigid with terror and anxiety. I could not speak and felt paralyzed. My emotions shut down, and I went numb. I had absolutely no idea what to say. I don't remember how or if I responded, but Heidi, at one point, asked if I'd like a cup of tea. I managed to say, "No," and she went downstairs and made herself a cup. By the time she came back, I was feigning sleep. She got back into bed quietly and, shortly after, was asleep herself.

But I was not asleep. I spent that night quietly crying my soul out. I lay in bed next to her, sobbing silently. Before dawn, I rose and dressed. I went downstairs and wrote a note. I don't remember precisely what I said but do remember one line. "I can't be in a relationship feeling like I'm a poor substitute for a gay man." And I left.

I was in a state of shock, not thinking clearly at all. I wandered all around our neighborhood, passing houses of friends and seeing their cars parked out front. I wanted desperately to connect with sanity again, yet what I was going through was so momentous I could not bring myself to knock on anyone's door. What could I say? "Sorry to wake you up at 6:00 on a Saturday morning, but I'm having a breakdown because my girlfriend just told me she feels like a man inside. Can I come in and cry in your arms?"

Eventually, I went out for breakfast. Not that I was hungry, but I felt I needed some kind of nourishment, since I wasn't getting any nurturing. I picked up a paper and turned to the classifieds to look for apartment listings. The enormity of the implications of breaking up began to sink in, and I cried again, silently. I tried to pull my thoughts together, but they would not remain coherent for long.

I realized I would have to go back to our house to pack up a few things, though I had no idea where I would go then. I waited until I thought Heidi would be gone to teach—Saturday was always her busiest lesson day—then walked slowly back. Approaching our house, I saw Amy and Karen's truck parked out front.

I thought Heidi had called them to come over and wait for me to come back while she went off to teach. It never occurred to me that on reading my note, Heidi would have gone off the deep end herself. Of course, she had. She had canceled all her students for the day, and then called our dearest family, our musketeer allies, who had immediately canceled their day and come right over.

I felt so alone and isolated, I didn't want to see anyone in the extremity of my shock and grief. I snuck onto our back patio, intending to wait there until Amy and Karen left. I still did not realize Heidi was inside with them.

Then, I saw her at the kitchen window, looking outside. She saw me out on the patio and came rushing out to me. We hugged, and Amy and Karen joined us. At that point, they asked if we were going to talk. We both said "yes," and, wonderful family that they are, they left us to it, making sure we both knew they were right there for us.

Finally Talking

Heidi had called them immediately after reading my note and had told them exactly what had happened. Thus, Amy and Karen were the first to find out about the gender issues that were later to rock all our lives and change us all so profoundly.

As we talked, it emerged that she had had a life-long fantasy figure in her mind named Alan Jones.[13] All the times I'd thought she was not fully present, it was *true*. She was engaging in some fantasy scene with Alan. She had never talked about her fantasies of being male and only brought it up because she had just discovered that transition in this direction was possible. She had seen a magazine article about Loren Cameron, an FTM photographer. This crystallized her fantasies, and she knew this was the direction she had to go in life.

During all this turmoil, the Choir's *Under One Sky* tour was happening. At the early April concert in Seattle, I had no idea about Alan, or Heidi's feelings of being male. By the concert in Portland, in late April, I knew what was going on and was freaked out. By the early May concert in Vancouver, the dust had settled a bit. We cared a lot about each other, and this was becoming more apparent as the weeks went by. Yet, the nature of transition is so deep and the changes so profound that I became increasingly terrified as Heidi began acting on this life-long feeling.

She found a support group for trans people. She began going to therapy. She started redefining her identity with frightening speed. Our relationship was in chaos. Heidi's gender identity had moved into limbo-land, a phase that I now understand is the beginning of transition. At the time, all I knew was that all *my* identities were suddenly insecure. In the moment, the one that rocked me most was our relationship.

I found it impossible to concentrate on work. I had to give up my typesetting business. I lost my companion, as Heidi moved out. A Choir member had just bought a house in NE Portland and was looking for a roommate to help her with the mortgage. Heidi moved in with Allison, ostensibly only for a while, to gain some perspective and have the space to create this new identity of "Alan."

I also "lost" the Choir, as the ending of the *Under One Sky* tour was the end of the Choir's season and the beginning of summer break. Choir would not be meeting again until mid-September. I had never needed my family more, or the structure that rehearsals provided for me, and suddenly both were missing.

---

[13] Though 'Heidi' is not a pseudonym, "Alan Jones" is. In present time, "Alan" is a transman off living his life privately, not involved in the trans community at all. Were he more "out there," I would use his real name now, with his permission.

For historical accuracy, I have used female pronouns for Heidi/Alan to this point in my narrative, but I am now about to switch. When Heidi became Alan, the pronouns switched also. Easy to type—incredibly painful in the moment. In accepting Alan as male, I had to let go of Heidi.

Essentially, when I think of Heidi, it's as if my partner of seven years had died. I don't believe it's true of someone who transitions that they remain "the same person only in a different body, with a new name and a different pronoun," as I've heard some describe it. Transition involves such profound changes, the person on the other side is not at all who they were previously.

Denial in Action

Though I'd kept a journal religiously during my twenties and on into my thirties, I had given it up after becoming involved with Heidi. Now, I tried journaling again, but stopped after only a week or so. The events of that time were so painful for me, writing was no salvation. Rather, it was the equivalent of salt in a deep wound. The following is the only writing I did during that time period. I re-read this journal occasionally, homage to the incredible journey I've taken.

> I try not to laugh at the bitter irony of the name of this journal. "A Woman's Journal" indeed. I wonder if this means Heidi couldn't use it. Actually, Heidi could. It's Alan who would hesitate.
>
> I can't quite shake the feeling this whole thing is merely sick, and that I'm going to lose big time out of it.
>
> I used to think life was hard. The pain of unrequited love. The constant wondering about attraction—is she, isn't she? I handled it in stride when Alicia told me she was bisexual. I will never fall in love with a man, but I can see the attraction (at least, with some men!). But all previous pain and especially doubts pale compared to the concept of Heidi as transgendered.
>
> I have a strong aversion to calling her Alan because I know that, to her, it's an affirmation of maleness in herself. And I

want no part of being involved with someone who isn't glad to be a woman. That's it, in a nutshell. How can I be in a happy life-partnership with someone who'd rather be a man? I'm a ***dyke!!!***

I should know by now that my first reactions are usually true and right. My first reaction was, "Let me out of here!" I calmed down from that, but the more time passes and the more I learn, the more that reaction returns. I'm rather glad for the down time, the alone space, for centering.

Leaving Heidi would be incredibly painful. But she's becoming Alan, and that person, I can leave easily. Particularly since I think the next step will be changing pronouns to "he." I know Heidi. She'll never be satisfied until she's gone as far as all her resources (financial and emotional) will permit. Which means just shy of surgery. I don't want to be involved with a man!

She says, "This is who I've always been. I'm the same person." But all that means to me is that there was a side of her she kept ***really*** well-hidden.

I don't know how far I can go toward overcoming my socialization. Men are men, women are women. Period. I feel uneasy around transsexuals. I don't understand them. I am very well aware that this is the exact reaction homophobes have to gays and lesbians. I know that, in time, I will come to accept Lily, or Kendal, and say, "That's just their way."

The question is, do I want to be in a life-partnership with someone I can't understand on such a fundamental level? I can see that I could come to an acceptance of transgenderism. But understanding deep enough to sustain a lover relationship requires an empathy, a sharing of feeling, that I will never have.

I wish to God Heidi had had the courage to face these fantasies at their initial appearance. None of this would be happening if she had. She's going to lose me. And her friends. Is it really worth it? I guess it is—to her—because she's doing it.

I wish I believed this was all going to be taken care of by her name change. But I truly see that as the first step, not the end of anything. When I think of our past life together, it brings tears to think how much we've shared, knowing that even if, miraculously, our relationship continues, it will never be the same. I don't trust that I will ever know my lover again, and that makes me insecure. And this process is so deep, so overdue acknowledgment, that I don't trust it will ever end. That even if we stay together, she'll wake up one morning and announce she's ready to take hormones. Pass as a man.

Certain things about Heidi do fall into place for me. Like why she had so few women lovers before me. I thought she was shy, happy alone, waiting rather than looking. Philosophical about it, an "if it happens, fine" kind of attitude. Now, I see there was more to it. How did I manage to get past all those fantasies long enough to have an impact?

Whatever the hell kharmic debt brought all this on me, rather than someone else, I hope I'm handling it well enough to never have to face this hell again.

As is clear from this writing, I had not yet realized the implications of Alan's revelation for my own identity. I was still trying to fit my round self into a square hole. Yet, deep down, I knew that the intensity of my reaction was not normal for me. No break-up had ever affected me like this.

I sought therapy, for the first time in my life, because I somehow knew I was not going to survive this without professional help. I called Phoenix Rising, a local gay and lesbian mental health agency, and made an appointment with the first therapist who had an opening. I didn't ask any questions about expertise with forms of identity. I wouldn't have known what to ask. I knew nothing about therapy. Or about trans identity.

The Epiphany

My memories of this time period are quite hazy, but there are a few moments that stand out with crystal clarity. One took place on a hot summer afternoon in July while I was walking around downtown Portland. I'd had a few sessions with a therapist who had embraced cognitive behavioral techniques. Margo was concerned about my depression, which was severe, and gave me cognitive therapy tools to challenge negative thoughts as they arose.

That day, I applied these techniques in a new way. A stranger on the street had just called me, "sir," and I had startled myself with an entirely different reaction than I expected. Time was, I would have been furious. This time, *I liked it*. What the hell?!

Stepping back from Alan's transition to ask from the perspective of an outsider, or one approaching the idea as an intellectual curiosity, I queried, "What *would* it be like to wander around the world male instead of female?" I had Alan in mind as I asked this question.

However, my reaction had little to do with Alan. I had a sudden feeling of personal excitement, almost euphoria, that led me, finally, after 39 years of being female, to go that monumental further step and ask the right question: "What would it be like for *me* to wander around the world male instead of female?"

This simple question changed everything. It was not a change in my thoughts or beliefs. It was a change in the processes underpinning my thoughts and beliefs. In asking that question seriously, I shed the negative self-esteem that had colored my self-concept all my life.

New revelations came fast. Perhaps I hated going into women's bathrooms simply because I didn't feel I belonged there, not because I had high levels of internalized sexism. Perhaps I was too self-conscious to enjoy sex because I couldn't share that intimately while being seen as a woman, not because I had high levels of internalized homophobia.

I experienced a wonderful high feeling of rightness—for about two minutes. Then, the implications of my revelation hit me hard, and I went into a tailspin. The logical outcome was that I would be much happier with life living as a guy than as a lesbian. And from there, it wasn't long before the thought surfaced, "My God, this means leaving the Choir." The tailspin was the result of knowing that this final stripping away of my denial was going to lead me away from the Choir forever, a thought so painful I didn't know if I could survive it.

The enormity of change sank in. Amy and Karen. All the friends I'd accumulated through nearly twenty years in Portland. My family of choice. Would these lesbians remain my family? Would I retain my place as family to them?

My voice. I would lose my fine alto singing voice. I would lose my place in the Choir. I would lose my place as an alto in Bridges Vocal Ensemble, a mixed chorus I'd helped create in 1990. I wailed in despair, "Why does it have to be my *voice?* Why couldn't I have been a tuba player???"

All I could focus on was what I would lose. I could not envision what I would gain. Unlike Alan, I'd never had conscious fantasies about being male. I had no pre-created identity to step into. Now, I not only had no business, no job, no chorus for the summer, no companion, no Heidi, I had no "Nancy" either. All my identities had been stripped from me, and I sank. The bedrock of my life had turned to quicksand.

Counterproductive Therapy

Naturally, I took this revelation to my next therapy appointment. Because I knew nothing about therapy, I did not realize that I didn't have the right therapist. I had thought from her age (mid-40s) that Margo was experienced. I didn't know then that therapy is often a second career for folks, and that many therapists don't embark on this career until mid-life.

I also did not know that working at an agency is often a stepping-stone for a therapist, accruing their hours toward licensure. Margo was an intern, not an experienced therapist, which I'm sure I was told when I embarked on therapy. However, the information had no meaning for me at that time in my life.

When I told Margo about my revelation, she immediately tried to convince me that since I had not had these fantasies consciously all my life, I did not fit the official criteria for gender identity disorder and, therefore, that couldn't be it. She concluded, snap judgment, that I was trying to convince myself that I was male in the hope that if I transitioned also, Alan and I would remain partners, since he was identifying as a gay man.

Now, I was very unsure of anything anymore, but even in the midst of this major breakdown, I knew Margo was wrong about this. I wasn't sure what or who I was anymore, but Margo's interpretation didn't feel right at all. The thought of remaining with Alan had not even occurred to me when I had my revelation or experienced the resulting tailspin. I tried to tell her this, and she recommended I read a book called *Goddesses in Every Woman.*

Clearly, she thought I was a maladjusted lesbian. She gave no credence to the power of my epiphany, or to the fact that the only positive thoughts I'd had recently were when I visualized myself moving through the world as male.

I also thought it quite significant that thoughts of Alan had not even entered into my vision of myself as male. This vision had to do with me, alone in the world, centered in an identity for the first time in my life, and nothing to do with myself in relation to anyone else. I hadn't gotten that far yet!

Despite my reservations, I bought the book *Goddesses in Every Woman,* and read about two paragraphs before putting it aside with the thought, "*This is not it.*" Though I had no idea who I was, I had come to a clear realization of who I *wasn't*. I gave the book to a lesbian friend who had recently broken up with a lover and was having self-doubts.

It was a shock to me that my therapist discounted my revelation so thoroughly, and I began to believe therapy was not going to help me. I grew increasingly desperate for peace, sanity, and some semblance of identity.

When Alan moved out, I had taken in boarders to pay the mortgage. Living with strangers in the house that had once been our home was too much for me, and, after about a month of this existence, I asked Alan if we could trade places. He agreed, and I moved out the same day he moved back in.

I saw more clearly than Alan did that our relationship was over, and when I told him how sad I was because I knew I'd never live in our home again, he was very taken aback by the observation. But I knew I had to move out. I was not sleeping and knew I stood no chance at all of moving forward in any direction as long as I remained in that house. So, in the late summer of 1995, I moved in with Allison, a fellow tenor[14] in the Portland Lesbian Choir, and Alan moved back into "our house."

---

[14] The Portland Lesbian Choir has never used traditional SSAA nomenclature in naming its sections. The PLC sections are soprano, alto, tenor, and bass.

Chapter Nine

The Crash

Allison experienced some of Alan's story while he was living there but had not had an opportunity to hear my story. Amy and Karen helped me move a bedroom's worth of stuff over to Allison's. When they left, she made tea, and we sat down at the kitchen table and looked at each other.

Allison said, "So, tell me what's been going on."

Thus, Allison was the first Choir member (aside from Amy and Karen, who were far more than just Choir members to me) to hear my story. She was immediately supportive, and my room became a haven for me.

Allison lived much further north in Portland than I'd ever lived before. You can see the remnants of a segregation history in Portland even today.[15] This particular neighborhood had been primarily black since shortly after WWII. Allison is white and was among the first white lesbians to recognize this area as one of the last affordable neighborhoods in the city.[16]

It took some getting used to, not living walking distance to downtown or to major grocery stores. I took to walking to the nearest mall, a couple of miles away down a steep hill. I would buy some little thing or other and then walk back. I had nothing else to do all day.

During this summer, I visited the Bay Area three times. Prior to this crisis, I had never visited more than once in a year. During my 1995 visits, I stayed with Susan and Rita. Rita had reacted very negatively to Alan's revelation, holding the view (not uncommon among older lesbians) that anyone transitioning from female to male was doing so, at least in part, to gain male privilege, and she resented this.

Now that I was questioning my own gender identity, I didn't share this with anyone in my biological family. I didn't want to experience their reactions to my own process. I was having enough negative reactions of my

---

[15] Oregon is the only state to have had laws on the books preventing anyone not white from owning land. The last such law was repealed in 1926. This created a "'whiteness'" to the state that is very slowly dissipating over generations.

[16] This neighborhood gentrified considerably beginning in the mid-2000s and is now called the "Alberta Arts District."

own and did not feel strong enough to handle anyone else's negativity or misunderstanding.

Beyond that, it was typical of my family to question unpopular decisions, to disallow and disrespect family members' personal processes. I had no answers to give and felt I would be derided by some family members for asking questions with no answers in place. And I didn't believe the others would speak up in my defense. I kept silence, using my visits as a refuge from my sterile existence in Portland, not as an opportunity to process what I was going through.

The Power of Naming Myself

Another moment from that summer that I remember with crystal clarity is when I found my new name. I was on my way back to Susan's house from the store. I was casting about in my mind for a name for myself, and the name "Reed" flashed into my mind.

Immediately I felt at home with this name. I have had the rather entertaining experience over the years of having store clerks compliment me on my name, without their having the least idea that I chose it for myself! I loved the images it brought to my mind. Reeds bend with the strongest wind, rooted in earth and water simultaneously (homage to my Virgo sun and Pisces moon), able to withstand the stormiest weather because of their flexibility, when rigidity would cause another plant to break. I spelled it Reid just to be different.

Still fearful of family reaction, I casually said to Susan that I was thinking of changing my name (without telling her I'd already found "Reid," and certainly without telling her of my huge identity shift) because I didn't think "Nancy" fit me. I wanted to gauge her reaction to this fairly innocuous step.

Susan, bless her, said, "Your name hasn't fit you since you were five."

I initiated the legal name change process shortly after I returned to Portland from that visit. This was one of the few positive incidents of that summer.

A Close Call

One of the three visits I made to the Bay Area that summer was a horrendous mistake. I was still clinging to Alan, knowing our relationship was over, yet not allowing myself to begin the process of relating to him in a new way. I use male pronouns now in referring to Alan, but, in the moment, I was unable to do so without bitterness and anger. This, despite having finally recognized my own identity.

Because of this clinging, I could not say "No" when he asked me to go to the first FTM conference in San Francisco, held in August of 1995. Though I'm sure he did not want to go this route, he agreed to stay at my mother's house with me. I knew he'd developed some online friendships and that he intended to meet some of these folks at the conference. I was quite jealous and wanted him to stay with me so I would know he wasn't having an affair with someone else.

I don't remember much about the content of that conference. At the initial gathering on Friday night, I could not take in the import of the occasion, the first time any official gathering of FTMs had ever happened, anywhere. There were about 400 people there, FTMs with friends, wives, lovers, and family members, all grinning ear to ear at seeing so many of their own kind when they'd been isolated for so long. I just wanted to kill them all for shattering my old life so effectively and permanently.

I attended a few workshops on Saturday, I have no idea on what topic or who else was there. Saturday night was disastrous. My therapist had referred me to a psychiatric nurse who worked at the same agency, and he had prescribed a mild antidepressant for me. The theory was that if I took this medication prior to going to bed, I should sleep through the night. If I could just establish a normal sleep pattern again, much of my depression would lift. In theory.

I was supposed to take half a pill the first night, as the dosage was uncertain. I tried that, prior to leaving for the Bay Area, and still woke crying in the middle of the night. On Saturday night of the FTM conference, at my mother's house with Alan there, I took a whole pill, reasoning that half a pill had been insufficient. Within twenty minutes, I had a major depressive episode, worse than any I'd had to date, crying uncontrollably and feeling suicidal. Had Alan not been there, I don't know what I would have done. I had not been feeling this way prior to taking the pill.

Four hours later, the length of time the pill was intended to work, the depressive episode ended. I felt it in my brain, as if someone had turned a switch off. The impulse to cry and feel suicidal was just gone. I looked at the bottle of pills in absolute horror, and never again dared to try another psychotropic medication.

Next morning, I bottomed out emotionally, feeling flat and frozen. I went to the conference with Alan, but at the door, I said to him calmly, feeling like an automaton, "I'm starving. I'm going to go find some breakfast. I'll see you later." I thought he knew what I was going to do, but felt I had to fight this demon on my own, that either I would survive or not. He couldn't help me.

I knew intellectually he was right. He couldn't help me any more than a spouse can help an alcoholic stop drinking. The impetus has to come from within, and all the outside agency in the world is not going to make a damn bit of difference if the alcoholic doesn't want to stop drinking. Alan could not give me the will to live.

Still an automaton, I went back to my mother's house to get my credit card, which I had neglected to bring with me that morning. I snuck into the house, intending to tell my mother that we'd forgotten the card and that I'd come back for it. But she was working in the backyard and never even heard me come in and leave again.

I went to three different stores, purchasing small bottles of sleeping pills in each, and threw in a few additional random items so no one would think my purchase was odd. I bought a bottle of water. I went into a liquor store and bought a pint of 151 rum, thinking it had the highest alcohol content of any booze around and would be the most effective. The water was to wash down the alcohol so I would not throw up, since I was not a heavy drinker and was unused to the taste of hard liquor.

I planned all this in the moment, with total detachment and the numbness of one whose emotions have shut down due to overload. I didn't have the energy to feel anything anymore. I went to a remote corner of the Arboretum in Golden Gate Park and began methodically removing the sleeping pills from their individual foil pouches, lining them up on a handkerchief next to me. I had the rum ready to go, the bottle of water open next to it.

I sat there for four hours, unmoving, occasionally putting a sleeping capsule in my mouth, tasting the gelatin of the capsule. I had a paper napkin with me, and on it I wrote down all the reasons I could think of why I shouldn't do this. I don't remember any of them now, except the deciding factor: the thought of the look on my mother's face when she had to identify my body. Despite my own pain, I knew hers would be greater yet in that moment, and I couldn't do that to her. I wrapped the sleeping pills in the handkerchief, capped the rum, and drank the water.

Still an automaton, I got on a bus and went back to the conference. The look of relief on Alan's face when he saw me simultaneously angered and gratified me. *How could he have let me go like that if he knew I was going to kill myself?* warred with *He must still care about me to look that relieved to see me.*

I told him what had happened. He was very shaken and said he wanted to spend some time with me. Alan has told me since then that he did not realize what I was going to do when I left the conference, and only started worrying about me when I didn't come back. He wanted me to get something out of this conference, which had obviously been meaningful for him, and said he wanted to go to a workshop with me, any workshop I wanted to attend. I picked one but have no idea now what the topic was.

Though I had begun to face my true identity, clearly I was not ready to have its reality reflected back to me. Nor was I ready to have Alan's true identity shown to me so baldly. I looked at the roomful of 400 FTMs with a strange mixture of envy, jealousy, hatred, and nostalgia for my unconscious identity as a lesbian.

I got nothing positive out of that first conference at all and do not remember that time period fondly. When writing this book, I was already writing about the fall of 1995 before realizing I'd skipped writing about this conference experience altogether.

Chapter Ten

Baby Steps Forward

In late summer, I stopped seeing my therapist, Margo. I was frustrated by her lack of understanding and was in search of a new therapist. Alan had found the only trans support group in town. He got there first, preventing me from participating. I tried not to resent this, but I needed support also and was feeling very isolated. I could not help but resent that he had a support group, and I did not.

It only seemed fair that I found a private-practice therapist who understood gender identity issues much better than Margo had. BJ Seymour was the only private-practice therapist in Portland at that time who had worked extensively with trans clients. What made this time period bearable for me was the two hours that I spent with her in September of 1995, just before the Choir reconvened for its ninth season.

I told BJ that I thought I was transgender and didn't know whether or not transition was the route I would go, and that I was trying to avoid it if possible because of the Choir. I told her that I had no idea who I was anymore and was completely confused. She gave me an exercise to get to know all my sub-personalities and how they each felt about gender and transition.

I went off and did the homework she'd assigned, came back, and told her what I'd found. The tools she gave me in the two hours I spent with her were enough to keep me on my path for the next year and a half, on the path toward transition. It was not long after my last appointment with BJ that I finally admitted to myself that I was going to end up transitioning, that I could no longer live female. I did not see BJ (or any other therapist) again for nearly two years, but she had given me the tools I needed to get through the next part of my life unaided by therapy for gender issues.

A New Old Member

By September of 1995, Choir was back in session. I felt like a new member and very unsure of myself. I had a new name, a new address, no partner, no business or job, and a new relationship to myself. Everything in my life was different from what it had been when the Choir broke for summer.

Yet despite the magnitude of the visible changes in my life, the deepest change of all was invisible to my fellow Choir members. I had changed to such an extent that they looked like strangers to me, as if I was meeting them for the first time. And, in fact, I was. The scenario was surrealistic: I was "Reid, the guy who is going to transition," no longer "Nancy, a founding member of nine years standing." And feeling very bizarre about the whole thing because not a soul in the room could see this about me.

The Choir always had some kind of icebreaker at the beginning of the first rehearsal, to help new members feel a sense of belonging. This term, the icebreaker outed my new name quite thoroughly. The instruction was to form a circle, alphabetized by first name. I kept being shooed away from the Rs by folks who thought I belonged with the Ns.

By first rehearsal, I had written a coming out letter, telling people what my process had been and that I was heading toward transition. In my letter, I included a list of my own answers to frequently asked questions. I wanted to disseminate the information, and some of it was personal enough that I felt more comfortable writing than saying it. Further, I knew these were the questions most likely to come up. If I didn't do this, I'd get very tired of repeating the same information over and over again. I also said that if anyone had any questions not listed, I'd be happy to answer them.

I first sent this letter to the leaders of the Choir, both administrative and musical. I had been on the Music Committee for several years and knew the Choir was planning to produce its first CD to coincide with its 10th anniversary season, and that the recording was still more than a year and a half away. I was determined to hold off my physical transition until that recording was finished.

As I put it in my coming out letter, I knew that in five years, the pain of living between genders would have faded while the CD would be on my shelf forever, a source of pride in an organization I'd helped create. I was wrong about this, by the way. Though the pride remains, the pain faded much more quickly than five years.

I knew that if I did not have the support of the movers and shakers in that organization, I couldn't stay during that year and a half. For I also knew that my transition was going to be the biggest gossip ever to hit that organization and that there might be some serious opposition to my staying in the group since I was planning to transition. I knew that Rita's reaction was not an uncommon one among lesbians, and that her negative views might well be shared by some Choir members. However, I received nothing but unqualified support from Choir leaders about remaining to sing on the CD, and this comforted me.

A Tourist in My Own Life

The Choir's first concert of that season was particularly difficult for me to rehearse and perform. Titled *Simply Love,* it had to do with love relationships of all kinds. Singing the love songs was difficult for me, but nowhere nearly as difficult as singing *Suite in Four Movements,* written by a woman whose long-term relationship had ended painfully.

I had often made rehearsal tapes for my section, and made several for this concert, but our artistic director didn't even consider asking me to make the rehearsal tape for this particular piece. She did that herself. Rehearsal tapes are made during the summer prior to Choir reconvening, and there was no way I could have sung the following lyrics during that summer of 1995.

>I'm wand'ring around you
>Nowhere to rest my head
>Nowhere to lie down and wait for morning
>Nowhere to find an answer
>Nowhere to find a reason
>No one home in my heart.
>I took your name off the checkbook
>I took your name off my heart
>I am a tourist in my own life.
>But I still see your face.
>I wait for the healing they say time will bring,
>but time only passes and it can't do a thing
>To ease all the hurting that you left behind
>To comfort my heart or settle my mind.
>Your face in the morning, your arms in the night
>My darling, my dear one, my sweetness and light
>My grief is a hollow that nothing can fill.
>~Diane Benjamin
>from "Suite in Four Movements"[17]

---

[17] Permission to quote received from Diane Benjamin, email January 4, 2023.

All that fall of 1995, we rehearsed these songs of love, longing, and grief. The performance was January 20, 1996, and I was already in countdown mode, thinking, *Two more concerts are all I have left with this group that has meant everything to me*. The line from "Suite in Four Movements" that stuck with me most during this time period was, "I am a tourist in my own life." I have seldom come across a better description of that early-transition time.

During this time, I did not share much of my internal process with friends. I'd never been very good at asking for help from people or allowing myself to be vulnerable with people who really mattered to me. This legacy of an alcoholic family kept my lips sealed at a time when I badly needed connection.

Listening to the recording of that concert evokes the feelings of extreme isolation and despair I felt at that time as nothing else can. Music has always had that effect on me, which is the very reason the Choir had such a hold on my soul. It was not just the group itself, but the power of sharing music that created the deep bonds between me and my family of choice.

In October of 1995, I read that a local gay and lesbian foundation was looking for a half-time administrative assistant. I thought, *That's a job I can do*. I needed some stability in my life, and a half-time job seemed ideal.

For the first time, my oldest nephew, John, came to visit me from the Bay Area, having received my coming out letter and wanting to show his support. He, Alan, and I went clothes shopping for my job interview, and I bought my first men's dress shirt, tie, and wool suit jacket. Wearing these splendid new clothes, my first overt and deliberate step toward wearing men's clothes, I went for a job interview. I was hired and, on October 16, 1995, I began a new phase of work life.

Chapter Eleven

The Real-Life Test

I set my own work hours and chose 11:00 a.m. to 3:00 p.m. I joined Gold's Gym and worked out every day after work, then hopped a bus back to Allison's. My female body was giving me no joy. Now that I was conscious about how I felt about it, I didn't set foot in a locker room, but the endorphins released by these daily workouts kept the worst of my depression at bay. Though I was still depressed and had little sense of centeredness about my identity, having a job provided sufficient stability and focus for my life, as well as having weekly Choir rehearsals, that I was no longer in danger of committing suicide. Most of the time.

A Major Turning Point
I still had periodic bad moments, however, particularly on Friday nights. Sundays had structure because of evening Choir rehearsals. But Saturdays had no structure to them, and a structured schedule was much of what held me together that fall and winter. I dreaded Friday nights, always followed by a day with no structure. Whenever I had bad nights, I would wake from a crushingly depressing dream, always, it seemed, at 3:00 a.m. I came to dread 3:00 a.m., a time when I felt no one else existed in the world.

One such night, I woke and was so depressed and in such despair that I just said through my tears, to no one in particular, "Help me. I can't do this anymore." And suddenly, I felt...lighter. I would not describe it as the presence of God, or any other deity known (or unknown) to humanity. I just felt a release from the sense of isolation I'd lived with for so long. I no longer felt alone and knew I had come through a darkness that would never be quite so overwhelming again as it had been in recent months. I later learned to call this "the dark night of the soul" and to realize that I had survived a spiritual emergency. All I knew at the time was that I was through the worst.

Through Alan, I found several online mailing lists for FTMs and developed some close online correspondents. I found this particular method of support most comforting. I was becoming increasingly self-conscious about my body as I became more comfortable with the degree of masculinity in my personality.

I relished being able to sit alone in my room, out of sight, sharing my turmoil and feelings with others in much the same situation. In hindsight, this was a much more useful source of support to me than a face-to-face group would have been. I highly recommend online support for those in the very earliest stages of figuring out who they are.

One perceptive Choir member, herself a survivor of clinical depression, asked how I was doing, and I confided to her that I'd been feeling isolated and was enjoying online support. She suggested I sign up on the GALA Choruses'[18] online mailing list. I did so and enjoyed chorus correspondence as well as FTM mailing lists.

The internet became an important aspect of my life and a godsend. I had no one else to talk to in Portland about trans issues, or how I was feeling, and don't know that I would have made it through as well as I did without the online support I received during the winter of 1995-96.

I also read a few autobiographies of trans people and received some inspiration from the stories of those who transitioned at a time when there was no peer support and very little medical support available. Alan had lent me some books in the fall of 1995, but I was too scared to touch them. I read the back cover of Kate Bornstein's *Gender Outlaw* at that time and was so terrified and vaguely repulsed that I put the book back on the shelf. Every time I saw it among my other books, I felt anxiety, fear, and anger rush through me.

Ready for Change

Internal, unconscious processes act on their own timeline, and milestones sneak up on us undetected. One evening in the spring of 1996, the thought crossed my mind to take *Gender Outlaw* off the shelf and read the back cover again. This time, I felt intrigued and exhilarated by her words.

I read *Gender Outlaw* that evening and immediately felt, as many other FTMs have, that Kate Bornstein was my ally. The attitudes I'd heard expressed envisioned transition as a switch from one gender to another, without looking back, without loss or grief for what went before, and without retaining any part of one's previous existence. It all seemed very

---

[18] GALA is the Gay and Lesbian Association of Choruses, an international organization of nearly 200 men's, women's, and mixed choruses from all over the world. Both the Choir and Bridges were member choruses, as was the Portland Gay Men's Chorus.

black and white, cut and dried, and not reflective of my experience. And it depressed me, for it seemed inevitable that I would be totally cut off from the Choir—my family of choice—forever. I emailed Kate, and we had a correspondence that supported me well during this time of uncertainty, in the face of certain transition. Kate showed me another way, giving me a vision of gender as a social construction, malleable to suit my life.

Alan and I were still seeing each other socially on occasion. One afternoon, I saw a newsletter in his car, produced by the partner of an FTM and aimed at families and friends of FTMs. Alan had picked it up for me on a recent trip to Seattle. I looked at the masthead and my heart leaped. The name of the editor was Rachel Borlin,[19] and her partner's name was Stephen. Alan had met them in Seattle, and I excitedly asked him what Stephen had looked like.

Alan was a bit mystified but thought back to their meeting and described Stephen sufficiently that my hunch was confirmed! Though I had never officially been introduced to them, Rachel Borlin and her lover Stephanie Norman had been actively involved in the Portland lesbian community at the time I'd moved there in the late 1970s. I had not heard either of their names for years. It appeared that the reason for this is because Stephanie had transitioned and was now Stephen!

As soon as I got home, I emailed Rachel and said, "We never officially met, but I know your name, and I think you will know my former name. I was Nancy Vanderburgh. I'm now Reid Vanderburgh and am in the process of transitioning FTM."

Rachel replied that she did, indeed, recognize my name. A week or so later, the three of us met at a local restaurant for dinner. I recognized Rachel when she walked in the door, but I would never have recognized Stephen as the former Stephanie. We had a good time, and I knew that I had met a couple who were going to be family to me. And, this time, I would have the added bonus of having an FTM as part of my family, to mentor me. Things were looking up!

A New Future Emerges

A few months after we met, Rachel told me that she and Stephen had been discussing my future and that they thought I should go back to school

---

[19] "Rachel" and "Stephanie/Stephen" are also pseudonyms. Like Alan, Stephen is quite private about having transitioned thirty years ago.

and get a Ph.D. in clinical psychology. Both are academics. Rachel was close to finishing her Ph.D. in sociology and Stephen was partway through a Ph.D. in anthropology. I was astonished at this proclamation on their part, and the thought crossed my mind that I didn't think I could do it.

I was also amazed at this coincidence, because I had been toying with the idea of getting an MA in psychology and becoming a therapist, though I had not articulated this to anyone as yet. Though their ambitions for me were higher than my own, they were along the same lines. I had found myself in the position of peer counseling others online and realized that I had a knack for reframing problems, helping people come to terms with hard choices in their lives.

I derived such satisfaction from helping others through my online correspondence, it occurred to me that I'd probably be very good at it in person as well. Through my own experience and from hearing others' stories, I had come to realize how few therapists understood anything about gender identity at all, and I decided peer education would also be on my list of "things to do when I grow up."

Rachel and Stephen had had their own discussion and come to similar conclusions about my future, but with far higher degrees in mind than I had! A Ph.D.! I remember walking home from their house that afternoon thinking, "I can't get a Ph.D.!" I thought I could probably handle an M.A. But first, I had to finish my B.A.!

In late spring of 1996, I attended Rachel's graduation ceremony, the granting of her doctorate from Portland State University. During the ceremony, my resolve hardened that I would go back to school myself, perhaps finishing my M.A. in the year 2000. (I was not off by much. I finished in 2001.)

By the summer of 1996, Alan and I had not seen each other for some months, as I'd been unable to really let go while he was wanting to move on. One evening, we had an argument on the phone, and he said something to the effect that it wasn't easy for him to let go either. I was incredulous.

I asked, "You're having a hard time letting go?"

With some impatience, he replied, as if I should have known this obvious fact, "Of course I am! It's really hard!"

I wish it weren't the case, but knowing it was also hard for him made it much easier for me to let go. I learned a hard truth about myself in the process. I was clinging because of my own fear of not being needed or loved. After that conversation, I was never seriously depressed about our breakup again, and my own life started coming together in a way it had not before. I was finally ready to face the world again as my own person.

During that summer of 1996, I traveled with the Choir and Bridges to Tampa, Florida to sing at GALA V, my third GALA festival of queer choruses. It was a bittersweet experience, as I knew it would be my last GALA with my beloved PLC. Bridges was one of the hits of the festival, but that group had never meant as much to me as the Choir. I was acutely aware of my countdown as a Choir member. The next PLC concert would be the tenth anniversary, and that would be my last. Then would come the CD recording.

First Crush

There was great energy and back-and-forth correspondence on the GALA Choruses listserv after the festival. I was struck, in particular, by a singer in a women's chorus from the Midwest, Katie. She and I took our email correspondence private and exchanged long emails every day. Coming home to her emails became one of the most important aspects of my day. Several times, we talked on the phone for long periods, quite expensive in those days of long distance.

At one point, Katie got into it with a rude man on the GALA listserv. I was incensed on her behalf and emailed her privately. Our exchange that evening became quite passionate, and it was clear we'd fallen in love. This "in love," however, had the adolescent quality of first crush about it. I was growing up anew, despite not having started hormones yet. Katie was dissatisfied with her current relationship, and I was a convenient outlet, a way of putting a foot out the door without me as a real destination.

We met in person that summer at a conference, and it was clear to both of us that the chemistry needed for a relationship just wasn't there. And— seeing me in person for the first time, Katie could not get past misgendering me. The visual of my still-female presence shifted her perception of me. By the end of that trip, I knew it was a no-go, as did Katie.

Our email correspondence faded away after our return to our respective homes. At the time, I was crushed, as an adolescent would be. Nevertheless, I'd had my first interaction with a woman who treated me like a man (until we met in person), and it left me with a heady feeling. More confirmation that I was, indeed, on the right path.

As summer continued without Katie, I was surprised how quickly I moved on. At the time, I was surprised. In hindsight, I wasn't in love with her at all. I was in crush. In the self-centered way of early transition, I had fallen for her falling for me as Reid, not Nancy. She was one of the first people I met who had never known me as "Nancy," and that was a powerful draw.

New Beginnings

I felt the pressure of leaving the Choir mounting. I worked out with a vengeance, producing those wonderfully anti-depressant endorphins and, as a by-product, becoming very physically fit. I enjoyed life very much during that summer and looked forward to attending the second FTM conference, scheduled for August in Seattle.

What a difference a year made. That second FTM conference was so meaningful to me, meeting friends I still consider my litter mates. Kai. Lukas. Aaron. And Kate Bornstein, throwing her arms around me and calling me "brilliant." I returned to Portland feeling a newfound sense of community, allowing me to feel somewhat better about leaving lesbian community behind.

And then, a new chapter beginning, I registered for fall term classes at PSU.

> I will not die an unlived life.
> I will not live in fear of falling or catching fire.
> I choose to inhabit my days,
> to allow my living to open me,
> to make me less afraid, more accessible,
> to loosen my heart
> until it becomes a wing, a torch, a promise.
> I choose to risk my significance,
> to live so that which came to me as seed
> goes to the next as blossom
> and that which came to me as blossom,
> goes on as fruit.
> ~Dawna Markova[20]

---

[20] From the poem "Wide Open," used with permission from Dawna Markova, email January 4, 2023.

Chapter Twelve

Back to School

I took three psychology classes during my first quarter back at PSU. The first night of class, I noticed an older woman sitting not far from me in our very full classroom. She asked good questions. As was typical in lower division psychology classes, there were about 100 people in the class. When my next class met for the first time, there she was again. Wanting to make a friend during this lonely time, I struck up a conversation with Ann, and we became study mates.

Near the end of that first quarter, I moved out of Allison's house. I was doing my "real-life test" at this point (though without hormones, still waiting on the Choir CD) and feeling more private than I'd ever felt in my life. Never had I needed to live on my own as much as I did then!

I was wearing tweed jackets, ties, slacks, and dress shirts to work and school. I never used the women's bathrooms at PSU, though I felt completely at home in the men's bathroom and used it regularly. I was working out at Gold's Gym every day, sneaking into a tanning booth to change my clothes in order to avoid using a locker room. I was pre-hormones and pre-surgery and wanted no part of either locker room at that point. I had always felt much too dissonant with my female body to feel comfortable walking into a women's locker room. Now that I understood why I'd always felt the dissonance, the feelings were all the stronger for living on the surface.

Nor was I willing to experience the scene I knew would result if I tried to use the men's locker room. I've never been an "in your face" kind of activist and did not have the kind of brazen courage required to use the men's locker room, even though I knew it's where I would eventually feel most comfortable.

With all the challenge of presenting male and being seen as a lesbian every time I opened my mouth, what I needed most at day's end was to come home to a place of my own. Because Allison already had a cat, I'd had to leave my beloved Bear Cub with Alan, still living in "our house." I wanted a place to call my own, to come home to Bear Cub each evening and shed the real-life test until the next day.

My Own Space

I began looking at apartments. Our house was on the market by that time, and I knew we were going to make a significant profit on the sale. I told one prospective landlord that I expected to come into some money within a few months, and he suggested I check out some apartments down the street that were being converted to condos. He thought some were going to be as cheap as $79,000. I took his advice and ended up purchasing a condo not for $79,000 but for $74,000. I put a lot of work into making it beautiful, and Bear Cub and I were quite happy there.

For the first time, I was living in NW Portland, about six blocks from where I worked, and a half-hour walk to Portland State University. I had moved from a completely residential area, with no stores within comfortable walking distance, to an area where absolutely anything I needed was a five-minute walk! I moved toward the end of 1996, just in time for Christmas, to a neighborhood that looks like something out of Norman Rockwell at that time of year. It snowed that year, and the trees lining the major streets were all hung with little white lights. I was ecstatic!

An Old Flame

Shortly after my move, an old girlfriend called me out of the blue. Annie had heard about my transition from her sister Chris,[21] a friend of mine from my theater company days. Back in the early 1980s, Annie had come from the Bay Area to visit Chris, and had come to a play with her. Annie and I had taken one look at each other and realized an immediate attraction.

Getting together with Annie mirrored me back to myself. I found it difficult to measure my own changes during transition, particularly during this pre-hormones phase. When you live it, the changes are so incremental, it's difficult to chart progress. I found that I had become less judgmental of other people's life choices, that I was less abrasive in manner, and more masculine in both my reactions to her and my mannerisms in general. Walking around with Annie, I felt like a man walking with a woman. It was a heady feeling!

Annie had some interesting observations about me, dating from our 1983 affair. She had perceived the discomfort I felt about sex but had interpreted it to mean I was not as attracted to her as she was to me, which

---

[21] "Chris" is also a pseudonym, as is "Annie."

was certainly not the case. As she lived in the Bay Area and was already in a primary (though non-monogamous) relationship, she didn't push it.

We never actually broke up. Annie's primary partner left her for another woman. Annie was so heartbroken that she lost all interest in me. Our reconnection that winter evening in 1996 was healing for both of us, though we've seldom been in contact since. In the winter of 2001, I ran into Annie in a coffeeshop in Oakland, quite by accident. I was fully transitioned by that time, and she did not recognize me. When I went up to her and jogged her memory, she simply said, "Oh, my God!" Then, we had breakfast together.

Coming Out

December was finals time, and Ann and I were studying furiously. This was the first quarter back at school for both of us after many years away from academia, and we wanted to do well. I had found, to my pleased surprise, that just about every one of my textbooks contained a brief description of gender identity as separate from sexual orientation.

At some point during our studying for finals, Ann said to me, "You know, I just don't understand this gender identity thing. I'm comfortable being a woman. You're comfortable being a woman..." At which point, I interrupted her and said, "Well... no, I'm not. I'm transitioning from female to male."

Ann was very taken aback and left my apartment shortly thereafter. I wondered whether she'd been thrown for too much of a loop. I'd nearly backed away from pursuing a friendship with this woman when I found out that she is a conservative Republican and devout Christian.

Nevertheless, her openness to new ideas and the innate integrity I sensed in her had pierced my defenses, and I maintained the friendship. At first, I was on eggshells, not quite trusting that a person who claimed those particular labels would befriend me once she knew who I really was. I had lived through the anti-gay ballot measure era of the 1990s, ballot measures spearheaded by fundamentalist Christians, and this experience had distorted my view of Christians in general.

After our finals were over, it became clear to me that Ann was intrigued by me and wanted to know more. I told her what she wanted to know, being careful not to reveal more than I felt she was ready to hear at any given time. We had wonderful conversations about life, our goals, school, and any other subject under the sun.

We took classes together whenever we could, though it wasn't long before this was no longer possible. I had taken two quarters of statistics right off the bat, knowing this was required for all senior level psychology classes. Ann was intimidated by statistics and eventually switched her major to avoid taking statistics at all. After my first year at PSU, we never had another class together. I felt bereft, as did Ann. We still met on campus to study whenever we could, but it wasn't the same, as we weren't studying for the same exams.

I rarely came out in classes, though I often came out in papers written for classes. I wanted to educate my professors, to give them a different perspective for the next time they taught the same material. However, my classes were large and full of people I didn't know. So, I wasn't comfortable coming out. I didn't want to be that much the focus.

Along with 150 or so of my peers, I took a sociology course titled Marriage and Family. At the first class meeting, the teacher (Pete) announced that the next time the class met, we would hear from a panel of transgender people. He wanted us to read certain parts of our text in advance and think up good questions for the panel. As Pete put it, "This is going to be new to most of you, and I want you to put some thought into it before you hear from the panel."

I read the parts of the text that Pete had mentioned. It was the same basic explanation I'd seen in several other of my textbooks. I also realized, however, that this explanation was anything but basic for most of my classmates! Keep in mind: this was 1996. The following week, a panel of four spoke to our class about their experiences. The panel consisted of two MTFs and two cross-dressers. In other words, people who had been assigned male at birth. The class asked intelligent, respectful questions and received intelligent, respectful answers.

I was impressed that Pete had put this together, but the community representation was incomplete. I went up to him afterward and asked why there had been no FTM representation. Pete told me that a friend of his wife's was a member of a group called the Northwest Gender Alliance (NWGA). As Pete had not been in Portland long, he had not had an opportunity to meet anyone who might be able to direct him to any FTMs. Knowing that NWGA is a group for male-to-female transgender people, I understood Pete's position.

I told him I was an FTM, and that if he planned on doing this panel in the future, I would be glad to participate. He thanked me profusely and said he would keep this in mind. A year later, I spoke before nearly 200 students in Pete's Marriage and Family class, as a member of his gender identity panel. What a difference that year made. By that time, I'd been on hormones for six months and had had chest surgery less than a month before. A new man, indeed!

Gender Bending

I continued to rehearse with the Choir that fall of 1996 and spring of 1997, though it felt more surrealistic with every passing week. As long as I didn't speak, I was beginning to be seen as a man more and more often, which felt very right and natural to me. Yet here I was rehearsing Portland Lesbian Choir music in preparation for the tenth anniversary concert and CD recording! The disparity was beginning to chafe, and though I was sad about leaving the Choir behind, I was also increasingly irritated at delaying my process.

I also realized that I was being given a priceless gift, living this year and a half between genders. Though at times uncomfortable, it also gave me the experience of transcending gender labels, as much as one can. I could be either or neither or both at any given time, and it really sank in what a joke it is to define marriage as being between a man and a woman. First, you have to define "man" and "woman"!

Upon being told of his transition, one of our mutual lesbian friends said to Alan, "What a gift, to be able to live as both sexes in one lifetime!" Alan told me this during my breakdown period, and that reframe shifted my own perspective significantly. I was given a further gift of being able to live as both sexes, alternately, during the same year.

Doing this by choice, having deliberately postponed my own process, gave me a sense of personal power that has been with me ever since. I felt I had complete control over my own gender, an identity so fundamental that this sense of power spilled over to every other aspect of my life as well. I felt there was nothing I did not control, and it is this feeling that has stuck with me throughout the years. I am my own man, and I know it much more fully than I ever felt I was my own woman.

In the spring of 1997, a few months prior to beginning hormones, I had a disconcerting experience in one of my classes. I asked a minor favor of the woman sitting next to me, and she was agreeable. Yet, there was something in this woman's attitude toward me that was disconcerting and a little uncomfortable for me. The feeling was familiar, as if I'd seen it before, yet I knew it was not an attitude I'd experienced coming my way. It was rather like being mothered by a peer, and I didn't like it.

At our next class meeting, she referred to me as "he," and I realized that, for the first time, I'd experienced a woman interacting with me as a man. Her attitude had been that unconscious deference some women show toward men.

On the one hand, I was exhilarated that I was passing as a man to this woman, that she had never revised her opinion of me from "male" to "lesbian," though we had had a fairly lengthy conversation about the course material. On the other hand, this deference made me really uncomfortable, socialized as I'd been in the lesbian community to be outraged at women showing deference to men simply because of their gender.

At this point in my transition, I assumed that everyone who heard my speaking voice would no longer see me as male, so I was not particularly trying to pass. I was going about my life, just being myself. This made it especially gratifying to be seen as a man when I was not putting forth any effort to that end.

In this particular class, I had my first experience of being a "gender bender." Most of the people in the class saw me as a lesbian and referred to me using female pronouns. A few used male pronouns for me and looked puzzled when others referred to me as "she."

This was a sociology class titled "Minorities." The teacher thoroughly enjoyed being on a soapbox, espousing her socialist views of our society and its despicable history where non-white, non-male, non-Protestant, non-heterosexual people are concerned. Though I agreed with her assertions, I found her smugly self-righteous manner a little hard to take at times.

I came out in a class paper early on, and the teacher indicated support of me in her written comments. I asked a question at one point late in the quarter, and the teacher said into her microphone, "Did you all hear what she asked?" I wanted to sink into the floor, and one of my classmates who'd seen me as male turned to me and said, "She???" I looked at her and shrugged my shoulders, as if I didn't have a clue why the teacher had said that.

I went up to the teacher afterward and told her I preferred male pronouns. She looked very puzzled and said she didn't remember using pronouns for me at all in that situation! She had been so very righteously indignant about the treatment of minorities in this culture, it was a bit satisfying for me to give her an object lesson. No one is immune from making mistakes in dealing with others. We have all been socialized and can react automatically based on the influence of that socialization, no matter how evolved we believe ourselves to be.

I did not come out to my classmates in that class. Being seen as a guy was such a new and exciting experience for me, I wanted the opportunity to revel in it.

My Final Moments with the PLC

The Choir CD was recorded at about this time. Jenni had sung next to me for years. At one point during the recording process, she said to me, "Do you *have* to become a man?" I laughed and said, "Yes, Jenni, I've come too far to turn back now." And then, she said, "Can't you stay anyway? I mean, we'd all know, but we wouldn't have to *tell* anyone."

Jenni was deliberately missing the boat. Singing in a group creates such powerful bonds, and she didn't want to lose me in that capacity. It was a wrench for me to leave, but it was also a wrench to many Choir members to witness my leaving, and under such circumstances that it was clearly a final parting.

On the date of the Choir's tenth anniversary concert, I held a drop-in time at my apartment. I sent a flyer to every Choir member, inviting them to come over sometime in the afternoon, prior to the concert, bringing with them some memento that reminded them of me. Quite a few showed up and brought me interesting gifts and cards full of loving support.

Later, I put the cards in a photo album and created an altar with the gifts. A mustache cup. A geode, split open to reveal shiny mica inside plain rock—as fantastic a metaphor for living trans as I've ever seen. This gift was from my Musketeer allies, Amy and Karen. A new copy of the score for Handel's *Messiah,* as my old one had the alto part highlighted. That afternoon stands out as a highlight of my transition process[22].

---

[22] In 2016, a young non-binary member of PLC said to me, "I think the PLC owes you an apology!!!" Astounded, I said, "What for???" Taken aback by my demeanor, the backpedaling was immediate. "Well, for forcing you to leave." Shocked, I said, "What? WHAT???" It emerged that this person had heard, or assumed, that, as a transman, I had been told to leave the Choir when they learned of my impending transition. I was incensed and wrote a piece that I posted to PLC's Facebook page and sent to the current director, publicly thanking the PLC for the support I've described herein.

Family in Transition

My nephew, John, saw his first Portland Lesbian Choir concert that night, having traveled from the Bay Area to support me for that last performance.

I saw John as representing my biological family, which had largely been silent on the subject of my transition. As is the case in alcoholic families, mine is terrible at showing genuine emotion or expressing honest feelings.[23] Only four family members had responded to the coming out letter I'd sent all of them in the fall of 1995. John had come to visit me several times, and, though we never talked much about my transition itself, his presence spoke volumes.

When I first came out as a lesbian, I followed the family pattern of not telling anyone formally, except my sister Susan (as usual, via a letter), shortly after I'd moved 700 miles away to Oregon. I let the rest of my family come to a gradual realization that I was having relationships with women. No one ever said anything about it to my face, though I'm sure they talked amongst themselves.

In this case, I was honest with them all and knew it was going to be interesting at family gatherings. When they realized I was a lesbian, they did not have to say or do anything to acknowledge the fact. Now, however, they would actually have to do something to acknowledge my transition—use a new name and new pronouns for me.

Several family members had come to Portland for my 40th birthday party in September of 1995. Jan and Susan were both there, and my mother. John would have been there had travel from his home in Guam not been prohibitively expensive. I had never had so many family visit at one time since I'd moved to Oregon nearly 20 years before. While they didn't talk about my coming out letter, they showed their support by visiting *en masse*.

At times, I would look at Heidi's family with extreme envy for their closeness. When Heidi graduated from the University of Oregon, every member of her immediate family made the trek from various parts of the country to participate. Every Christmas and Thanksgiving, the entire immediate family gathers in one part of the country or another, taking turns

---

[23] I wouldn't put it this way now. At the time I wrote Volume I, however, I was early in transition and only viewing how transition was affecting me, not how it might be affecting my family to have to let go of 'Nancy.'

hosting the family gathering. This means quite a few small children are traveling, but that's the way their family operates.

I cannot begin to imagine that kind of closeness in my own family. When I first met Heidi, I envied this family closeness while at the same time feeling stifled when I was at her family dinners. It was this experience that showed me that no family dynamic is perfect.

Over time, my own family reconciled itself (for the most part) to my transition. John, Susan, and Jan were so much older than I am that it was hard for them to change their view of me. After all, they babysat me when I was in diapers.

And as for my mother, she slipped on pronouns occasionally for the first couple of years, especially when I wasn't present. She was very much the type to live in the past and had never allowed me to grow up in her own mind. She did not slip on my name, or on pronouns, when I was present.

I knew my mother had completed her transition of me when she told, for the umpteenth time, some story from my early childhood and called me "Reid" in the story. She was completely unconscious of having done so. I thought to myself, *"Good for you, Mom, you made it!"* and never said a word to her about it.

John's reaction had been a mystery to me as he lived in Guam and had little contact with any of his family. I had sent him a coming out letter also, but never heard a word from him. John rarely visited the Bay Area after his move to Guam, and our visits had never coincided.

When I moved back to the Bay Area in the fall of 1998, my mother told me John was going to be visiting soon. The date of his visit kept getting postponed, but as my mother had been keeping me posted for years about family doings, I assumed she would let me know when he was finally going to be there.

Some months later, she let slip that he'd been in town for ten days, stayed with one of his daughters (who lived about five miles from my Oakland apartment), and was gone again. I was very hurt by his silence. John had visited everyone in our family, except me. I never even knew he was in town.

I expressed my hurt feelings and anger to my mother, who did not know what to do with them. She was never one to express her own feelings, particularly if they were feelings of pain or vulnerability. She then told me that when I sent my coming out letter four years before, John had shown it to a doctor friend of his, who was "very impressed by it," as my mother put it.

It would be the family way for me to nurse a grudge against my brother for not contacting me and use this to maintain a posture of righteous anger, to be dissected and rehearsed with my mother and Susan for years to come, to never speak to my brother of it at all and treat him icily when I finally saw him again.

More foreign to me is what I actually did about the situation. I wrote to him in early 2000, said I was very hurt by his actions (or non-actions) toward me, and that I'd like to see him the next time he visited. I included a number of pieces I'd written since 1996, primarily layperson explanations of various aspects of "transness," and one paper I wrote in graduate school for a Human Sexuality class.

About a week after mailing this packet to him, I came home from school to hear a very surprising voice mail from John. His message of support was one of the most genuine statements I've ever heard from anyone in my family.

Among other things, he told me he'd wished very much for a little brother and reluctantly reconciled himself to having a baby sister when I was born. I don't know that he would have said all he did if he hadn't had a few drinks, but people do tend to say exactly what they feel when under the influence, without the usual social inhibitions in place, so I was most gratified by this message.

Chapter Thirteen

The Countdown Begins

In the spring of 1997, I began to feel the change of pace of my transition. I'd felt "on hold" for a year and a half and, suddenly, I was faced with the realization that this time spent between genders was approaching an end. At that time, the Standards of Care included a requirement of ongoing therapy for those seeking referral letters for hormones or surgery. The Standards said at least three months of therapy; I couldn't afford to see BJ Seymour for that long. She was in private practice, so sessions with her cost considerably more than those at an agency. I tried Phoenix Rising once again. Not Margo this time!

My new therapist Lois was not as experienced as she wanted to believe in dealing with trans people. She was suspicious of my attempts to explain the richness and depth of experience I was having during this time leading up to transition. She told me at one point that if she seemed to be "bursting my bubble," it was because she saw her role as devil's advocate, in keeping with the DSM model of diagnosis.

At the time, this merely irritated me, and I resented her implications. I realized that she represented the unfortunate paradigm of most therapists of that era, that of seeing my condition as a disorder rather than as a core identity. Any problems I had related to gender identity were acquired during my female socialization and were not innate to my trans identity. It's hard for me to imagine growing up with gender dissonance in this society and not acquiring a few psychological problems along the way. However, given that many of these problems are caused by the dissonance, it follows that if the dissonance is alleviated, the problems that are due to the dissonance will mostly sort themselves out.

In my case, I also had the legacy of an alcoholic family with which to deal, and it's impossible for me to tease apart the effect of gender dissonance and my family's addiction issues. Lois, however, insisted on seeing the gender identity issues as a presenting pathology, rather than as an existential issue of reinventing, or rediscovering, who I was. And we never talked about my alcoholic family structure.

The tools of self-knowledge BJ Seymour had given me proved invaluable during this time. When Lois tried playing devil's advocate, I would check in with my personality aspects and confirm that, yes, I was on the right path. I stayed in therapy with Lois because I assumed that, eventually, someone in a gatekeeper role was going to ask if I'd been in therapy for a prolonged period of time. I wanted to be able to answer, "Yes." Seeing Lois through an agency cost me about a third what an appointment with BJ would have cost.

Back to BJ

Once the CD recording was finished, I called BJ for the first time in over a year and a half. Though I still knew little about therapy at that point, I had a good sense that Lois and I just were not on the same page, and that she did not understand me at all. Though it would be more expensive, I wanted my final evaluation and referral for a hormone prescription to come from a therapist whose judgment I trusted.

Lois had tried to get me to talk about the difficulty I would have relating to women as a man without a penis. I grew angry with her and said, "I can't have a penis, and I'm not even sure I want one. Therefore, any woman I get involved with is just going to have to deal with the fact that I'm a man without a penis, or we won't be able to have a relationship."

She got angry in turn, reacting in a way I now realize is inappropriate for a therapist, and said there were women for whom the presence of a penis is very important. Her anger told me that she was talking about herself. She was out of her depth and just could not chart a helpful course into this territory.

I went back to BJ in May of 1997. When I talked with her on the phone, she sounded startled by the depth of change in me, and I could almost read her mind through the phone, "Has he been taking under-the-table hormones?" My voice was somewhat deeper, my manner definitely masculine and forthright. I made an appointment to see her, jubilant at taking the first step toward the acquisition of hormones.

I expected that BJ would insist on following the Standards of Care and would want to see me for at least three months. Possibly, I thought, she might lessen that amount of time because I'd seen her before and had seen other therapists in the meantime.

When we met, she asked me how my year and a half had been. I told her all the steps I'd taken toward changing my identity legally, that I was very peaceful and centered in myself, that I'd come out to all and sundry in my life, that I'd participated in recording the CD, and that I'd officially left the Choir. At the end of our hour, I fully expected her to ask if this was a good time to meet regularly.

Instead, she said, "When would you like your hormone referral letter?"

I was astonished and stammered something about the Standards of Care.

She replied, in a matter-of-fact tone, "The Standards of Care are just guidelines. You've already done your real-life test, without benefit of hormones or surgery, and I don't see any reason to hold you back."

She further astonished me by saying that when she'd last seen me leave her office, trying to avoid transition, to avoid leaving the Choir, she'd thought then that I would eventually find my way toward transition. But, of course, she did not tell me that. No matter how clearly a therapist thinks they see a client's path, it's the client who has to find it and live it.

She prepared a letter and sent a copy to me, and one to Barry Maletsky, a psychiatrist she had worked with for years around gender identity. They had never disagreed on a diagnosis. One reason I'd gone back to BJ was because I knew she and Dr. Maletsky worked so closely together. I reasoned, *"If she thinks I'm ready, Maletsky is sure to agree, and I'll be over that hurdle."*

At that time, there were no physicians in Portland that BJ could have referred me to for a hormone prescription. She had developed a close working relationship with Dr. Maletsky, covering several bases at once. As a psychiatrist, he was a physician and could write hormone prescriptions. As a mental health professional with a doctoral-level degree, he was also eligible (according to the Standards of Care) to write the second referral letter required for lower surgery.[24]

Last Hurdles

Little wonder so many trans people viewed the mental health profession as a gatekeeper system. It remains so to this day, though informed consent models are more prevalent than in the 1990s. I always saw that gatekeeper system as a series of hurdles to overcome. One of my goals as a therapist was to try to change that attitude on the part of my trans clients,

---

[24] As of 2023, two letters are still required for lower surgery, according to the Standards of Care. However, it's no longer required that one have a doctoral-level degree; both can be master's-level therapists. The requirement now is that they both be well-versed in trans issues.

so they would view me as an ally rather than as a gatekeeper with the power to keep them from transition.

Even with BJ, the thought was in the back of my mind, *She's not trans. She can't know what it really feels like*. I felt that even more strongly with Dr. Maletsky, as a member of the very profession that wrote the DSM. The more I studied that book and the medical model paradigm it represented, the more strongly I felt that gender dissonance has no place in the DSM at all.

In May of 1997, however, I was not thinking in these kinds of "larger picture" terms. As with my bicycle trip in 1987, the quote from Sir Henry Morton Stanley was operative at this time:

> I did not see the whole. I only saw this rock ahead of me; I only saw this poisonous snake, which I had to kill in order to take the next step. I only saw the problem directly in front of me. If I had seen the whole thing, I would have been too overwhelmed to have attempted this.

Transition is a series of little baby steps, and each step must be taken with care and attention. I did not have my eye on the larger picture at all and did not think about transition beyond the next step.

My personal experience with the gatekeeper system was easy, and I never felt held back by the service providers who facilitated my transition. Nevertheless, I saw all of them (BJ Seymour, Barry Maletsky, and Toby Meltzer) as having an inappropriate amount of power over my life decisions. Furthermore, some of the horror stories I'd heard from other trans people (particularly FTMs) caused me to re-evaluate my decision to become a therapist. Did I want to align myself with the very professions that are seen in such a negative light by other trans people?

On the other hand, if trans people turn their backs on these professions because the current paradigm does not serve us well, nothing will ever change for future generations. I knew the therapy profession had undergone a major shift in the 1970s, when gay men and lesbians entered the field to serve their own, changing from a model of attempting to "cure" homosexuality to one of helping clients adjust to their sexual orientation. With this example in mind, I decided to stick it out. Later developments, which showed me a non-pathologizing perspective on psychology and therapy, strengthened my resolve.

My first appointment with Dr. Maletsky was in mid-May 1997. He asked me questions that I recognize now were a humanized version of the information required for diagnosis according to the criteria in the DSM. At the end of our hour, he astonished me, as BJ had, by saying hesitantly that he was almost ready to make a diagnosis on the spot and give me a prescription for hormones.

However, being an older man and set in his procedures, he vacillated and, ultimately, decided that he should not break his own tradition of sitting with a diagnosis for thirty days before making a decision. I understand his process, given the medical model paradigm within which he was working. The introduction of testosterone has far-reaching consequences for an FTM, and it would be his signature on that prescription. He wanted to be very sure of himself.

He also said he wanted to allow me the time to think about it (as if I'd been thinking of anything else for nearly two years!), to make sure it was what I wanted. Given my history, I thought this a rather silly argument, but I did not challenge him. I was too happy that neither BJ or Barry Maletsky were going to hold me back by adhering rigidly to the Standards of Care.

Assessing Priorities

At the time of my next appointment with Dr. Maletsky, I had two houseguests from Australia visiting me, members of a chorus that was planning to perform with Bridges the following year. We had become close friends via email, and I invited them to come along with me to get my prescription and have my first injection. I wanted to share this momentous occasion!

We took the bus to Dr. Maletsky's office, and he wrote the prescription. But then, he informed me that the pharmacy most FTMs go to for their hormones was in downtown Portland. It was late in the day, and I didn't think I'd be able to get there and back by bus before his office closed.

Dr. Maletsky suggested I come back the following afternoon, and he'd inject me and show me how to inject myself. I'd been planning on doing a daytrip with my Australian friends, and, at first, told them I would not be able to go along with them to the Oregon coast, as I wanted to get my first shot. The more I thought about it, the better able I was to put this into a more appropriate perspective. The opportunity to spend time with my Aussie friends, only visiting for a week, was more important than postponing my shot for an extra day.

I have never lost this perspective. There have been times when other things have come up that have made it impossible for me to inject myself on a specific date, but I don't worry about it when that happens. I even experimented with going off hormones altogether for a time, during a hormone shortage. I never had a hysterectomy, and, thus, going off hormones allowed my body to revert to its estrogen base. I found that invaluable during the process of writing this book. I no longer have access to the same emotional angst I experienced while living in an estrogen-based body. Unlike some FTMs, I still cry easily at emotional movies and the like, but my own life does not cause me angst.

While I was in grad school, writing Volume One of this memoir, I ran out of hormones. The company that produced the most common version had gone out of business, and there was a hormone shortage for some months. I took the opportunity to write the most painful portions of this book—my experiences during my 1995 breakdown. Those emotions were readily accessible and on the surface as estrogen was once again the dominant hormone in my body.

Postponing my first shot by a day was the right decision, though it also meant I did not have any company to the doctor's office that day. My friends were busy elsewhere. I found it very anticlimactic, that first shot. There was no indication from the doctor that he had any notion how important this injection was to me. He jabbed me in the upper arm and that was that. I was disappointed at the lack of ceremony. But I was also jubilant! At last!

June 20, 1997 became my second birthdate, as important to me as my actual birthdate of September 1. I sent a notice to *Just Out,* the local gay and lesbian paper, to be published in a section of the paper appropriately titled "Transitions." This section primarily announced AIDS deaths and gay weddings, but my announcement was a little different: "Reid Vanderburgh (formerly Nancy Vanderburgh) would like to announce a new birthday, June 20, 1997, and a new pronoun, male." I hoped this would take care of informing those who had not heard the gossip.

Chapter Fourteen

Transition is a Process

That summer was a time of self-discovery. The hormones made me unbearably cocky and arrogant, as a teenage boy often is. I was not taking classes during the summer, though I was still working. In my newfound arrogance, I tried unilaterally to bring organization to my mixed chorus, Bridges, which had never had much formal structure in its seven years of existence.

Though many members said they supported this move on my part, the director did not; ultimately, she prevailed simply by refusing to leave or change. It was impossible to oppose this tactic on her part. The very lack of structure of the group meant there was no way to oust a director who did not want to leave. My voice began changing about two months after beginning hormones, and I used that as an excuse to go on leave from the tension in my chorus.

New FTM Experiences

Late in the summer of 1997, I attended the third FTM conference, in Boston. By this time, I was seen as male most of the time. I enjoyed the Boston conference and made a new friend, Jon.[25] He'd been on hormones for nine years, isolated in a small town in the Midwest the whole time.

Jon had gotten his original prescription from a doctor who had no idea what he was doing. He was trying to be supportive and didn't know how to find out the right dose. This doctor had Jon inject himself with a normal dose (1 cc.) every three days, rather than the usual every other week.

It was three years before Jon discovered this was a massive dose of hormones and not the typical dosage for an FTM. Fortunately, Jon seemed to have suffered no ill effects from this overdose. He did tell me he'd wondered why his periods had never stopped until he lowered his dosage to

---

[25] 'Jon' is a pseudonym. I've lost touch with him, and don't want to use his real name without permission. So many whom I consider my litter mates are now off quite happily living their lives privately, only telling intimate partners and close friends they were assigned female at birth. That's not the closet—every use of the right name and pronoun affirms their identity.

the right amount. He now understood that the excess testosterone had been converted to estrogen in his system.

Jon's story reinforced for me, yet again, the importance of having trans people become service providers for each other, every step of the way. Jon and I had long discussions about therapy for trans folks, as I was becoming a therapist and Jon was a social worker.

I also met a PFLAG member and conference volunteer, Mark, who was a student at Lesley College at the time. He tried hard to talk me into coming to Lesley, which was a pioneer in the field of expressive arts therapy. At the time, I had no idea what this form of therapy entailed, and I did not like Boston as a city, so I did not seriously consider Lesley.

Now, having studied expressive arts as a graduate student, I understand its efficacy. It's a natural fit for working with trans clients, and, in some ways, I do wish I'd investigated Lesley College more thoroughly. However, we make choices for a reason, whether we see that reason immediately or not, and it just didn't feel right to apply to Lesley College.

I went back to PSU for my senior year sounding like a man. The hormones had also caused my breast tissue to kind of collapse downward even more than it already had due to age. I stopped wearing the custom binder I'd bought back in 1996, which was giving me shoulder problems and wore tight-fitting t-shirts under baggy button-down shirts that I would leave untucked. Sloppy, yes, but this allowed me to be seen as male easily that fall, pre-surgery.

Another Transition Milestone

The moment I had my referral letters from B.J. and Dr. Maletsky, I made an appointment with Dr. Toby Meltzer, surgeon extraordinaire and all-around nice guy. How different would my life have been had I chosen Hofstra University instead of Pacific University, back in 1976? I would not have been living in Portland, Oregon, a city with an experienced gender identity therapist, a sympathetic psychiatrist, and one of five or six surgeons in North America whose practice includes extensive experience doing trans surgeries. Toby's office was a five-minute walk from PSU, in downtown Portland.[26]

---

[26] Toby Meltzer has since relocated to Scottsdale, Arizona, unable to find a hospital in Portland that fit his requirements and would extend him operating room privileges. Once his home base Eastmoreland Hospital was purchased by a conservative consortium of

If it had fit my schedule, Toby could have fit me in during early September, shortly after my 42nd birthday, but I had to go back to school. The next available date that fit my schedule was December 9.

As is the case with BJ and Dr. Maletsky, Toby Meltzer considered the Standards of Care to be guidelines, not laws. He was not going to make me wait six months to a year on hormones prior to considering surgery. I'd done my real-life test, he trusted my therapist's assessment, and he trusted my own desire to have chest surgery as soon as possible. He would have done it within a month or two of my beginning hormones had it fit my schedule. My chest was very large, and he quite understood the urgency I felt in dealing with it.

Once my voice changed and I realized I passed well enough with loose-fitting shirts on, I lost much of that sense of urgency about having surgery immediately and was quite willing to wait until it fit my class schedule.

However, I no longer felt comfortable working out at Gold's Gym. Without my voice giving me away, I just could not wear workout clothes, knowing people would revise their assessment from "male" to "female." My gender dissonance had increased in direct proportion to my ability to be seen as male.

When I planned my class schedule for the fall of 1997, I realized I would have to take two of my final exams early in order to make my December 9 surgery date. I waited until after I'd taken several exams and gotten As on them to let my teachers know about my surgery date, as it would mean I would be taking the exams unmonitored.

Following my pattern of only dealing with what was on my plate for the immediate future, I studied for my finals and took three final exams on December 8, 1997, which quite effectively distracted me from the idea of having surgery the next morning!

I got up at 5:00 a.m. on December 9, 1997, went into Eastmoreland Hospital, and had chest surgery at 7:00 a.m. I'd seen Toby a couple of days before, and he had closely examined my chest and made markings to outline the cuts he would make. As he worked, he said in a supportive man-to-man tone, "Bet you'll be glad to see the last of these." I couldn't agree more and felt quite well-supported.

---

doctors, Dr. Meltzer's days in Portland were numbered. These days, Dr. Meltzer would have no problem finding a home base in a Portland hospital, but not in the early 2000s.

He chastised me for never having had a mammogram. He immediately called the mammography department and had them see me then and there. Even before I was aware of my gender dissonance, I'd always been too self-conscious to ever have any such "female exams" before. This one was bearable because Toby would not perform my top surgery without it and because I knew it would be the last time I would ever experience having my breasts looked at or handled (at least, while I was conscious).

I had no idea how I might react to the anesthesia, so I asked Amy and Karen to call me before coming to visit me in the hospital. They called the afternoon after my morning surgery, and I said I felt great. Which was quite true. I was not putting a bold face on it. I felt great as long as I didn't try to move.

Amy and Karen came to visit me in the hospital, a couple of other people dropped in, I ate two hospital dinners, and we watched some movie on TV. I felt lighter by much more than the 6-7 pounds that had been removed from my chest. Between the hormones and top surgery, I'd done everything I wanted, and all I had to do now was...live. Scary thought that. I no longer had any external circumstance to blame if I was unhappy with life.

The Nature of Friendship

I came home the next day and discovered one of my close friends, Lisa, had come over while I was gone and had set up and decorated a Christmas tree for me. I'd arranged for Choir friends to come over at various times and do things for me. I had two weeks off work (my bosses were very supportive of my transition), and three weeks off school.

I sat in my recliner all day, Bear Cub on my lap, and watched a lot of television, or read from the stack of murder mysteries I'd acquired with this time period in mind.

I sat and thought a lot about the nature of family and friendship. Lisa was a fairly recent addition to the alto section in Bridges, and I'd met her since my 1995 epiphany. She had never known me as Nancy. When Lisa found out through the grapevine what I was doing with my life, she came to me and proactively offered her friendship and support. She had become as close a friend to me as Amy or Karen.

I have often found that to be the case, that my friendships have shifted somewhat because of my transition. While no one I'm close to actively rejected me, some of my friends were more flexible than others and were better able to transition with me. Of course, I found myself seeking out the company of those who were more comfortable with me. If I made a list ranking my friends by how close I feel to them, the names would be much the same, but the order of ranking would be somewhat different than prior to my transition.

Surgery Recovery

During those first few weeks, post-surgery, I was extremely limited in my range of upper body motion, though I had no complications from the surgery. My grafted nipples stuck on fine, and there was never any sign of infection.

I wasn't in pain, as long as I didn't try to move much, and I never used any of the painkillers prescribed for me. However, the stitches were more binding than I'd imagined anything could be. I felt as if there were staples in my chest. Stretching my arms more than a few inches in any direction was out of the question.

After a month or so, I attempted to go back to the gym. Though I was using the lightest weights possible, I still felt something pull in my pectoral region, and I gave it up. I had not been able to stretch at all but thought using low level weights would perform the same function. Wrong! Gradually, I noticed a pain developing in my right shoulder area. I had some massage, but the pain did not go away.

By the end of each day, my right shoulder was in a great deal of pain from the weight of my arm hanging down. Each morning, it was pain-free upon waking, from the alleviation of gravity. But, by the end of the day, I'd be in pain no matter how I held my right arm. I bought a sling, but this did not help much.

This pain lasted for nearly a year and only went away when I went back to a gym and hired a personal trainer. I told him I'd had some chest surgery, though not what for, and the nature of my problem. He gave me some exercises to do that began the healing process. Within a week or so, the pain was gone. I highly recommend that anyone who has a large chest reconstructed, seek out some physical therapy, or a good trainer at a gym, after recovering for a few months.

Finding My Professional Path

Once I'd had those few weeks off to recover from surgery, it was back to school and work. I was nearing the end of my undergraduate education and taking senior level classes that were somewhat more interesting than lower-level coursework tends to be.

Just about every class I'd taken to this point had treated psychology as a science, and some had followed the medical model to an extreme. Psychopathology was one of the most depressing and dehumanizing courses I took at PSU. The more I studied within this paradigm, the more convinced I became that this was no way to work with people. I came to see the fundamental flaws in the scientific method as applied to human beings, and I despaired of being able to help clients at all.

I saw quite clearly why it was that so many people joked about therapy and saw psychology as a pseudoscience. They are right. Clinical psychology is not a science. However, I came to see that those who assumed therapy to be non-effective because its results are not scientifically measurable were illogically assuming that everything worthwhile and effective can be assessed via science.

I came to a different conclusion, that people cannot be reduced to variables that can be scientifically manipulated as one can manipulate drug dosages to determine their efficacy. If people can't be reduced to variables in laboratory settings, then it follows that they cannot be studied using the scientific method, as manipulation of variables under controlled conditions is the very basis of that methodology.

Taking this line of reasoning further, it occurred to me that assigning people to DSM categories is also a flawed methodology, as there is no objective testing method that can back up the categorical assignment. Assessment itself is subjective, one human being assessing another. I became disillusioned as it became clear to me that therapy and assessment is an art, rather than a science.

This might have made me question my future in the field of clinical psychology, since it was still being taught using the scientific medical model that I now believed to be the wrong approach. Fortunately, I took one class during my senior year that provided me with a different avenue. The class was called *Loss and Grief*. In discussing how various psychological perspectives view the grieving process, I heard of transpersonal psychology for the first (and only) time in my undergraduate career.

This perspective holds that people are a psychospiritual whole, and that spirituality is a basic human need. Further, transpersonal psychology is holistic, believing one can't separate mind from body. In this, it combines western psychology with the eastern philosophy of healing. I had begun to wonder if I was ever going to find a perspective that would speak to me, and now I finally had!

I had come to see that my transition could be viewed as spiritual, psychological, emotional, *and* physical, depending on which level I cared to examine. The view that fit the transition process worst was the one that is most commonly used, the medical model and definition as outlined in the DSM. Finding out that there was a form of therapy that was non-pathologizing and that combined the spiritual, psychological, and emotional, felt very much like coming home.

I decided this was going to be my path as a therapist, helping others deal with the ramifications of their own transitions. Transition affects all aspects of one's life; nothing is untouched, nothing is unchanged. A holistic approach to therapy seemed essential to me in helping people going through any major life transition, whether due to gender dissonance, dealing with loss of a spouse or child, sudden career changes, etc. I knew I'd finally found my path.

Ironically, the *Loss and Grief* class was an elective course, not offered very often, and only eight people signed up as it was taught as a weekend intensive. With this kind of exposure at the undergraduate level, it's no wonder transpersonal psychology is still largely unknown.

I did an internet search on "transpersonal psychology" and the name John F. Kennedy University kept turning up. I sent an email asking for more information, though from what I'd read on the website, I knew I'd found my graduate school. I did not apply to any other schools. I sent in my application in early summer, to begin that fall.

The only qualm I felt is that JFKU is located in the Bay Area. I would have to leave Portland and move back to the Bay Area. I had not lived close to my biological family since I was 20, and I had serious reservations about how enjoyable that might be.

Wrapping Up Portland

That spring, my beloved Bear Cub died. She was nearly 17 and had been my companion since 1981. She saw me through transition, and then began a slow decline. I called Alan during the last week of Bear's life, as he had lived with her for seven years and loved her also. The two of us buried her on March 6, 1998, and I felt a chapter in my life close. One of the few things that had been constant in my life since my mid-twenties had been this wonderful tabby girl, and now she was gone.

I have noticed about my life that momentous events are often paired with each other. My Australian friends visited the same week I began hormones in June of 1997. A year later, in June of 1998, the entire Australian chorus visited Portland for a week and performed with all three Portland queer choruses on the evening of June 13. I quit my job at Equity Foundation a week before the concert. I knew I would be doing this eventually, to move away for graduate school, but timed my leaving the job to allow me to devote the entire week to the Australian visitors. I was the overall concert coordinator and partially responsible for finding housing for the 50+ visitors.

On concert morning, I graduated from Portland State University. Commencement seating was limited for the first time in PSU's history because President Bill Clinton delivered the keynote address. I was not happy with the coincidence of the concert with graduation, as it meant I could not devote my full emotional energy to either.

My mother and Susan made the journey from California for my graduation and to attend the concert. I knew Alan was going to be there, 3½ years after beginning hormones, and I wanted very much for at least a few members of my family to have this object lesson. Alan had been quite feminine as Heidi and had changed so much, I did not think they would recognize him. They had not seen him since my 40th birthday party, in September of 1995, when he was still some months away from beginning hormones.

When he arrived at the concert, I brought him over to where my mother and Susan were sitting and watched the stunned amazement on their faces as they finally realized who he was and who he had been. They would not have known him had I not brought him over to where they were sitting.

In July, I received a postcard from my former therapist, Lois. She was starting her own private practice and was advertising to former clients. My gut instinct that she'd never believed in my transition was validated by the fact that she hand-addressed the card to "Ms. Reid Vanderburgh."

I spent some time carefully writing a response to this card, calling her on the fact that I'd done my real-life test right under her nose for some months and yet here she was, addressing a card to me as "Ms." I suggested to Lois that she obtain some further education about trans clients before attempting to work with others.[27] I never heard from her again.

That summer of 1998, I worked full time at an HMO, a temp agency job I despised, though they were impressed enough with my work to offer me a permanent position. This job provided me with a wonderful reminder of how the corporate half lives and how much I wanted to avoid working in that sector ever again. My resolve to attend graduate school was strengthened every 5:30 a.m. when my alarm clock went off.

My Time Down Under

What made the job bearable was the reason I was earning this money. My Australian friends were so grateful for the work I put into hosting them in Portland that two of them had offered to pay my airfare if I would visit Australia. I worked like a demon that summer to have sufficient spending money to be able to enjoy myself Down Under.

Though I was excited to go abroad for the first time (Canada and Mexico have never quite seemed "abroad" to me), I had a few misgivings about traveling with testosterone. I brought along my prescription in case I needed to justify having a controlled substance in my possession. My luggage was not searched, going either direction, so the question never came up. I was only gone long enough to need one injection and was able to purchase a syringe at a pharmacy in Melbourne without having to prove I needed it for a prescription medication.

Because I still did not have a driver's license, I had never bothered to change my official Oregon ID card from "F" to "M," though BJ Seymour had given me a letter for just this purpose. At that time, in Oregon, a therapist's letter was required for changing a driver's license, and the therapist had to be on the DMV's list of "approved" therapists. I never used the ID card, so did not see the point of spending $15 to change the pronoun.

However, because I had no official ID that identified me as male, I had an adventure getting a passport that said "M" instead of "F." I filled out all the forms, had my picture taken, and followed the appropriate procedure, which included sending the federal government my original birth certificate.

---

[27] Now, in 2023, I regret putting it this way back in 1998. Some years later, I became the source of education for local therapists about issues related to trans identity. Calling Lois out rather than calling her in effectively prevented her from ever taking one of my CE classes on working with trans clients.

I checked "Male" on the application form and sent the whole packet off Express Mail. I did include a copy of my legal name change through the state of Oregon, so my passport would not say Nancy Vanderburgh.

As I left the post office, however, it occurred to me that the passport officials were going to assign gender based on my birth certificate, regardless of how I filled out the application form. I went back into the post office, explained the situation to the clerk at the passport window, and asked her advice. She said they would most certainly go by what my birth certificate said, regardless of what box I checked on the application form.

I had a copy of my letter from Toby Meltzer with me, a notarized document saying I'd had sufficient surgery to be considered male, and after reading it, the clerk said I should enclose that with the other documentation. She also said that she had no idea what would happen, or what my passport would say. She had never had this situation come up before.

I apologized for her having to hunt through the outgoing Express Mail packages, and she laughed supportively and said, "That's okay. It's not like you've ever done this before!" She found and opened the Express Mail envelope I'd prepared and gave me a new one, free. A few weeks later, I received a passport that said "M." No comment, no fuss, no bother.

In early August of 1998, I took off for Australia via the Bay Area. I had a free layover option and spent four days in the Bay Area. On the second day, I rented an apartment. On the third day, I went to John F. Kennedy University for my admissions interview to the Graduate School for Holistic Studies. They accepted me. On the fourth day, I flew fourteen hours nonstop to Sydney (a three-movie flight).

I fell in love with Australia and felt as if I'd come home. I'd never realized before how depressing it is to live in a culture where "conservative" and "religious" seem inextricably linked. It was during this trip that the word "impeachment" was first mentioned in connection with Bill Clinton's affair with Monica Lewinsky. I was having breakfast in a café in Sydney one morning and saw a newspaper on the next table. The *very* large headline read "Impeach the President?"

My first thought was idle curiosity about Aussie politics, *I wonder what Australians consider an impeachable offense?* followed in a heartbeat by the thought, *They don't have presidents in Australia.* With a sinking feeling of foreboding, I walked over to look at the article and was mortified to see a picture of Bill Clinton on the front page.

I thought, in a panic, *I've only been gone two weeks! What the hell is happening over there?!* I hoped there had been some major political controversy on par with Watergate. When I read further and realized the impeachment talk was related to Monica Lewinsky, I wanted to slink back to my room at the YMCA and not come out again, not be seen abroad as an American.

I'd already realized that Australians regard the U.S. with an odd mixture of tolerant, amused contempt and admiration for our audacious expansion, our constant pushing the envelope, and our talent for innovation. Regarding the Clinton-Lewinsky affair, the general opinion Down Under seemed to be the laughing response, "Thank God, we got the convicts, and you got the Puritans." Yup. Damn.

There is a streak of moralism in everything about which an American is passionate. Whether a person is far to the left or to the right, the tenor of the rhetoric retains the self-righteous moralism of the religious zealot. It was more than refreshing to be in a culture in which politics and religion are divorced, in which churches are progressive institutions that actually help people in need, rather than having political agendas of their own.

Hopes for the Future

I enjoyed my time in Australia to such an extent, it still brings tears to my eyes to hear an Australian accent. While it did occur to me that I'd love living in Australian culture, I also know myself well enough to realize that I can't live anywhere but in the U.S. I don't want to leave the U.S. I want to live to see it change. This may be a fool's hope, nevertheless, I cling to it rather than despair that this country will always be as it currently is.

Having lived between genders, with all my identities up in the air for months on end, gives me hope that the country can change too. I survived my own upheaval and believe that it takes a lot to completely destroy a person—or a community. To all who say, "You can't change the government unless you have a clear idea what to change it to," I say, "I think anarchy, shaking up the current system, is not such a bad idea." That, after all, is exactly what the American Revolution accomplished. We would still be a British colony if we'd had to wait until we had a clear idea about what future system might suit us.

Most people live on autopilot, a luxury no longer an option for me, and I'd love to turn off that autopilot for a time, to force people to really talk to each other about what they want their country to be.

I loved being in a country where even the most conservative politician would never dream of challenging the existence of their national health care system, the most popular government program in Australia. There was a sense of national pride and security that I've never felt in the U.S., and I think it is attributable, in large part, to their health care system. They have a safety net, and they know it. Conservative is a fiscal position, not a moral one.

In fact, due to their convict heritage, Aussies tend to regard with suspicion people who are extremely wealthy. Anyone who tried to use their wealth as a basis for obtaining political power or social status would quickly find this cuts no ice with Australians. While Aussies might admire a person who became wealthy through their own hard work, if that person tried to adopt an attitude of superiority as a result, they would quickly find their neighbors putting them in their place.

Upon my return from Australia, I had a little over a week to pack up and move. My close friend, Lisa, was going to drive a rental truck to California with me (I still had no driver's license at this point), and I bought her a plane ticket for the return journey.

I was excited and scared at the same time, much as I had been prior to my cross-country bicycle trips. I was going to be gone for three years, which seemed an eternity at the time. Though I knew I would return to Portland, I also knew that after that length of time, nothing would be the same by the time I moved back. So, what else is new?

Chapter Fifteen

My California Sojourn

Synchronicity has played a large factor in my life. My mother's health had been slowly deteriorating as the years went by, and it was during the early summer of 1998 that she finally realized she just could not maintain the big old Victorian on her own any longer. She had come close to dying that spring, being stubbornly unwilling to call her nearby children for help. Susan found her at death's door, and she spent several days in the hospital.

At this point, my mother gave up her independence, and Susan and Jan spent weeks preparing the old house for sale. None of them were savvy about the San Francisco real estate market, which was enjoying a price surge the likes of which had never been seen before.

Balm to My Soul

My mother's house sold for a ridiculous amount of money that summer, enabling me to move to the Bay Area and live for the first year of graduate school without having to work. My siblings and I had legally owned an eighth of that house each, and my mother owned half. I felt rich!

And I felt leisurely, for the first time in a long while. I was accountable to no groups. No non-profits had any claim on my time. The only people I knew in the Bay Area were my family. I'd left my family of choice behind and moved back to the bosom of my biological family, at a time in transition when I needed my family of choice more than ever. Nevertheless, my education was of primary importance to me, and the program for me was in the Bay Area.

My first few quarters at JFKU were a balm to my soul. My B.A. in Psychology was nearly meaningless. I might have done better to have gotten a B.A. in Cultural Anthropology, had I known it at the time. I found that I had indeed chosen the right school, as the paradigm of psychology I was now learning was the antithesis of the medical model I'd been taught at PSU. How refreshing!

For the first time, I was presented with a non-pathological view of various psychological conditions. Though we studied the DSM, we viewed it as a language with which to converse with colleagues, not as a Bible that held all the answers. My fellow students and I needed to know this language in order to pass our licensure exams and converse with each other about a client's behavior. We were very clear that this was the extent of its importance to us.

The smallest required course I took at PSU had about 60 people in it. At JFKU, the largest class I took had about 75 students, because it was required of all students in the Graduate School for Holistic Studies. Most of my classes had about 15 students. All were held in a seminar format, and I never again saw a multiple-choice test.

Group Process was the most difficult class for me. Every time I felt tempted to chastise myself for the difficulty I felt talking about my feelings, I would step back from the situation and remind myself how absolutely impossible this kind of class would have been for me at earlier times in my life. I would remember the times in my late teens when I could not speak in group settings at all, my tongue padlocked, and I would nearly cry experiencing the deep peace and inner joy that has never left me since I began my psychological transition back in 1995.

I also took *Effective Communication,* beginning to learn the tools of the therapy trade. During our second quarter together, the teacher had us each draw a defense mechanism from a hat. Synchronicity struck again, and I drew "denial." Our instructions were to do a class presentation about our defense mechanism, making it so personal and powerful that our classmates would remember it vividly five years later.

We were doing these presentations in pairs, and my classmate Felicia had also drawn "denial." When we got together to plan our presentation, Felicia said she was going to tell a story that she was sure people would remember. (Note from the year 2023: I certainly do!)

Felicia is a recovering alcoholic. She is a highly intelligent woman, fairly skeptical and concrete in her observations. When she was an undergrad, before she faced her drinking problem, she took a psychology course in which the teacher had the class take the AA test "Are You an Alcoholic?" This simple questionnaire has been used for years as a time-tested method of helping a person determine whether or not they have a drinking problem. After scoring her test, Felicia went to the teacher and said, "I think this test is flawed. I answered yes to just about every question, but I'm not an alcoholic."

For my part of this presentation, I created a single page titled "Denial in Action." At the top of the page was my high school graduation photo, stunningly feminine. At the bottom of the page was a photo my Australian friends had taken a few months before the class presentation.

I put my name beside each photo—Nancy beside the high school photo, Reid beside the other—and in between the photos I wrote, "There's a whole lot of denial in between." I printed these out in color and handed one to each of my classmates. The *Effective Communication* teacher still uses our presentation as an example to her students of something people will remember after five years.

Peer Education

Opportunities for this type of peer education cropped up in more than one of my graduate classes. For a *Human Sexuality* class, I asked a number of trans friends of mine and their partners to answer a questionnaire about their sexuality and relationships, pre-and post-transition. I sent a copy of the questionnaire to each of my classmates, about a month prior to my presentation, and asked them to consider how they thought a transsexual might answer the questions.

Three of my trans friends and their partners came through with flying colors, writing thoughtful and honest answers. I wrote a lengthy introduction to their answers and made copies of this 17-page document for each of my classmates. This was the paper that I sent to my brother John early in 2000. I then stood in front of them all and said, "You can read the answers on your own time. For now, I will tell you a bit about what it means to be transsexual, how that differs from sexual orientation, and will then be open to questions."

I then launched into a presentation of what I consider to be "Trans 101," beginning with the common distinction made between gender identity and sexual orientation. I went through this fairly quickly, as I was merely using this information to preface my talk on relationships and sexuality.

However, I had no way to gauge what was basic information to me and what would be new information to my classmates. Several stopped me at times, wanting clarification about why it was important to differentiate between sexual orientation and gender identity.

I then realized that though these were intelligent, empathetic folks with good intentions, they were still products of American socialization and had never been presented with this information before. Further, many of these folks were my age or older and had never even heard the distinction made before, that gender identity and sexual orientation are not synonymous. Keep firmly in mind: this was 1999.

The teacher, himself a brilliant psychotherapist, wrote on my paper that he thought I ought to publish it, which both gratified and floored me, making me realize, for the first time, that I was approaching a time in my life when I could reasonably expect to publish articles and make waves in the therapy community.

At this point, I began thinking and writing in concrete terms about how therapists can facilitate the self-insight and depth of self-knowledge necessary for a smooth transition. I started making notes about what had worked for me in therapy and what had not. I began asking trans friends the same question. I jotted things down as they occurred to me, in no particular order, formulating the beginnings of my master's thesis, a new vision of working with trans clients from the perspective of identity emergence, rather than a medical model of pathology and diagnosis.

A Rite of Passage

After about a year of living on the money from the sale of my mother's house, I knew I would have to find work. A friend who worked on campus informed me that university jobs come with the tremendous perk of a partial tuition waiver, to the tune of six free units per quarter.

I looked at the job postings on campus. There was an opening for Outreach Coordinator for the Graduate School for Holistic Studies. In reading the job description, I realized there was no aspect of the job that was new to me. All those years of volunteer work were about to pay off, as I had learned most of the tasks required for this job in the context of the theater company or the Choir. I was hired and began work in late May of 1999.

The one requirement of the job that I did not have was a valid driver's license. For years, I had steadfastly refused to learn to drive. I always had good and valid reasons, mostly to do with wanting to avoid inflicting damage on the environment. However, I'd had an underlying reason deeply hidden from consciousness—not feeling able to grow up. I was growing up with a vengeance now, finally feeling I was reaching the maturity of adulthood, and I viewed getting a driver's license as a rite of passage into adulthood. I'd been stunted in early adolescence long enough!

I contacted a driving school that specialized in teaching adults and took my driving test after six hours of lessons. All those years of riding a bicycle had given me a very good sense of how to behave in traffic. In July of 1999, a few months before my 44th birthday, I received my first driver's license. I was finally beginning to feel like an adult, two years after starting hormones.

In September of that year, I bought my first car, a Subaru Impreza Outback. Shortly after I purchased this car, one of my lesbian friends informed me, with some amusement, that Subaru Outbacks had become the car of choice among Portland lesbians. Figures!

I drove to Portland for Christmas in 1999, yet another rite of passage. I'd lived in Portland for over 20 years yet had never driven there. It felt subtly wrong for me to be behind the wheel of a car in that city, where I'd been a pedestrian, bus rider, and bicyclist for so long. I felt like I was in the wrong half of the lane, driving streets long familiar from the passenger side of the car.

Though it meant giving up 28 hours a week to a job, I found working on-campus had its own benefits. I had no commute between work and classes, and I was doing a job I believed in, talking with prospective students about attending the Graduate School for Holistic Studies. For the first time in my life, I had medical benefits and paid vacation. And that tuition waiver benefit, which saved me nearly $2,000 per quarter.

I found it odd at first, working my first steady job since leaving Equity Foundation. I no longer gave passing a second thought. I had no idea which of my colleagues knew I was an FTM, and which saw me as a cisgender man. I certainly couldn't tell from their attitudes.

About half of my co-workers were fellow students, and some of them knew from class presentations. Others found out gradually as circumstances dictated coming out, or through the occasional indiscretion of a co-worker. However, given that most of my co-workers were either alumni or current students in holistic programs, their worldviews were sufficiently expanded that not one had any problem with my identity or slipped on pronouns.

Final Thoughts—For Now

I have never been a very politically active person and have always had a difficult time coming out to people. I am an introvert and a private person, and talking about myself for the sake of coming out is not easy for me. I have an easier time if I am a guest speaker, or talking on a panel, where the coming out is done for me in advance, as part of the context of my presence. I believe strongly in every individual's right to privacy about their various identities.

On the other hand, I also hold the somewhat incompatible belief that if all trans people remain closeted in the name of privacy, it remains impossible to educate the general population that "trans" does not equal "drag queen." At the time I was in grad school, the only people seen as trans were drag queens (who aren't really trans) and those MTFs who didn't pass well. Therefore, they were seen by the general population as defining what it means to be trans.

Until Hilary Swank won the Oscar for best actress (how ironic!) for her portrayal of Brandon Teena in the 1999 movie *Boys Don't Cry*, most people didn't even know FTMs exist, we blend in so well. This is a double-edged sword. We pass safely and are invisible, unless we are "discovered," as Brandon was. At that point, we can be in grave danger, for some people will feel betrayed and others deceived to the point of reacting violently.

At the Boston FTM conference in 1997, I attended a workshop in which a cisgender[28] woman tearfully proclaimed that she thought every FTM had a moral obligation to come out in every situation in which a woman was being harassed by a cisgender man. She put on us the burden of changing the masculine paradigm of U.S. culture.

I agreed with her belief that FTMs usually do have a more balanced view of women than many cisgender men do.[29] However, I felt overwhelmed by the burden she was placing on us. My own transition took quite enough of my energy, much less being held responsible for changing the behavior of all the cisgender men around me who don't act appropriately toward women!

I also resented her challenge and realized, after the workshop, that her argument was fundamentally illogical. On the one hand, she wanted cisgender men to treat her as an equal. On the other hand, she was expecting

---

[28]Cisgender is a recent addition to the lexicon. At the time I first wrote Volume I, "biofemale" was the most common term used for those assigned female at birth. I made this change as my internal lexicon has shifted.

[29] This is not always the case. Back in 1996, I corresponded briefly with a highly conservative FTM whom I met online. I forwarded to my e-dress list a joke post I received, an excerpt from a 1950's Home Economics textbook outlining for young women how they should behave to make their husbands happy. Full of absurd tips that clearly placed the husband at the center of the wife's universe and far above her in importance, I thought this excerpt was hilarious. This particular FTM, however, sent me a terse reply saying he saw nothing funny about the post at all, that this was the way he and his wife lived their lives, thankyouverymuch. Being trans is no guarantee at all of being liberal politically or even of being non-sexist.

FTMs to be her "knights in shining armor," her protectors, against cisgender men.

As several transmen pointed out in the workshop, it's a balancing act, deciding when to come out and to whom. Is it safe? Is it necessary in this situation? Will it help me, or other trans people? If I see a woman being verbally harassed by half a dozen cisgender men, is the situation such that they are likely to beat me to death or shoot me if I challenge them? Would it really help the woman in question, if I become a martyred poster child for the FTM community, as Brandon Teena has become?

Cisgender men do not tolerate arguments coming their way from other men to the same degree as they tolerate similar arguments from a woman. Cisgender men are taught not to hit women, period. The exception to this, illogically, are women to whom they are married. As a transman, I cannot argue with a cisgender man to the same degree I could when I was perceived as a lesbian, unless I'm prepared for a physical fight. I would like to think I would speak out in situations in which someone is making inaccurate or inappropriate comments about women or trans people (or anyone else, for that matter). But I have to be careful. The world is not a safe place to be openly trans, even in the Bay Area.

Also, at 45, I don't have as much energy physically as I did in my early twenties. I've never quite regained the conditioning and strength I had in 1996-7, when I was working out with a vengeance to produce those wonderful anti-depressant endorphins. Now that I'm no longer depressed, my motivation for working out has diminished considerably.

My physical energy level is simply not what it was earlier in my life. I guard my energy. I pick my battles, and my battleground is the therapy profession. We can't be all things to all people or fight battles in all arenas. I leave overt political activism to others with more charisma and a higher degree of extrovertism. My contribution will be as a therapist, a writer, and, occasionally, as a speaker.

I've begun seeing clients now at my internship site and know with absolute certainty that I've chosen the right profession. I am passionate about my work, I love my clients in all their diversity, and I can't wait for each new day.

It's hard to know when to end an autobiography. If anyone had told me five years ago where I would be today, I would have thought them crazy. God knows where (or who) I will be five, ten, twenty years from now. Well, that will just have to be Volume II of this work in progress, this growth process that is my life. God, I love it! I wouldn't trade places with anyone.

Volume Two
October 2021

Introduction to Volume II:
Reflections on the Wisdom of Time

I wrote Volume One in the winter of 2000-2001, stuck at home with a broken leg in a non-walking cast. I haven't changed much of what I wrote twenty years ago except…with some degree of pain, I changed tenses in referring to my mother, and my sisters and brother. They are all past tense as I write this twenty years later, now an oldest, youngest child, homebound now, not with a broken leg but with the forced seclusion of a pandemic.

As I re-read Volume One for the first time in many years, what I find interesting is the "voice" I used, the life I chose to relate, what I left out, what I thought important, how "young" I sound despite my chronological age. I wouldn't be quite so sociological if I were to write the first 44 years of my life now. I have always led with my heart, but now do so with a strong sense of interconnection and compassion for those I would once have dismissed out of disagreement.

I also found an interesting thread in my writing. I was explaining myself, bordering on justifying my transition. "See, look what happened way back here. See, I always was trans." In so doing, I left out any tone of joy in life. I made it work for me. And it did. Sort of. Kind of. Had I died before transition, my gravestone might have read: *She did her best.*

Another interesting effect of that thread is that it placed my trans identity front and center in explaining why I am who I am, also in service of justifying my transition. In fact, my family structure went a long way toward repressing my true nature as an extrovert. I didn't want attention drawn to me, as much because of my family structure as because of my gender dissonance.

My father's alcoholism was never acknowledged beyond medical facts, its effect on family members completely glossed over. The unconscious message my young self gleaned from this was, "Don't rock the boat by talking about anything real." My young self extrapolated that to include, "Don't rock your internal boat by *feeling* anything real."

I did make two substantive changes to Volume One. When I talked of my emerging sexuality, my relationship with Elena, I was originally quite explicit in describing my reactions to sex. It never occurred to me that in so doing, I was also describing *her* sex life.

Some years ago, Elena and I coincided (via Facebook) for the first time since the late 1970s. I sent her Volume One, which she read with great interest and was then furious with me. I re-read that section, cringing as I read with new eyes. I changed that section to be about *me,* not about her. Perfect example right there of the self-centeredness of early transition: I'd only ever intended that section to be about me. That it also included her didn't occur to me at that stage in my process.

The other substantive change I made to Volume One was in describing myself "in crush," meeting Katie through the GALA chorus' listserv. When I first wrote Volume One, she warranted an entire chapter, and I described her as my "first love." In re-reading Volume One, I just couldn't give it that much airtime. She *was* a first crush, not Reid's first love. Now that I live with Reid's first love, married for fourteen years, the difference is so clear.

I could have started from scratch, rewritten Volume One altogether, but have chosen to leave it (mostly) as I was then. The difference in voice between Volumes One and Two is an object lesson in early transition becoming late transition over time. Always a transman, never "just a man," but maturing into transition, gradually catching up to my chronological age (as much as a youngest child ever can!).

What was Missing?

And what did I leave out of Volume One? Much of the emotional content of my first years in transition. Though I wasn't conscious of it, I wrote from the perspective of the grad school therapist, psychologically interpreting my life rather than conveying my heart and true self.

In 2000, this passage is what I wrote about how transition was playing out for me in the fall of 1995:

> I found several online mailing lists for FTMs and developed some close online correspondents. I found this particular method of support most comforting. I was becoming increasingly self-conscious about my body as I became more comfortable with the degree of masculinity in my personality. I relished being able to sit alone in my room, out

of sight, sharing my turmoil and feelings with others in much the same situation. In hindsight, this was a much more useful source of support to me than a face-to-face group would have been. I highly recommend online support for those in the very earliest stages of figuring out who they are.

Were I to write about that time period now, this is what I would say:

That fall of 1995, I poured my heart out alone in my room, putting forth and responding to long emails, able to shed the binder and misgendering for the day. Part of the gift of that form of connection is that we seldom (if ever) saw each other. I never talked on the phone with any of the folks who I consider my litter mates, unwilling to speak to them in an alto voice. The "voice" they experienced in emails was the depth of a man. We met on occasion at FTM conferences, but our real soul connection was via email.

I consider myself blessed to have transitioned at a time when email was available to me, and social media was not. Facebook, FaceTime, Zoom—non-existent. We could share with each other all the more deeply for our lack of visual contact, while email connection meant we weren't isolated in our transitions as previous generations of trans people had been. Facebook seems so much more *out there* than I would have wanted to be in 1995.[30] Email was perfect, one-on-one support.

One evening kd Lang's "Constant Craving"[31] played on the radio, and I about jumped out of my skin. I hadn't heard this song in several years, and it took on new meaning for me in that moment. I have seldom heard a better description of what it feels like to need to transition.

---

[30] Now, I'm all over Facebook, but I'm also 25 years into transition.
[31] *Ingénue* (25th Anniversary Edition), kd Lang and Ben Mink (song writers), lyrics © Kobalt Music Publishing Ltd, Universal Music Publishing Group, 1992

Quite a different description of the same time period.

A New Family View

My perspective on family is different than it was in Volume One. As I wrote Volume One, two years into my counseling program, I was very good at analyzing my alcoholic family, recognizing family patterns accurately. But what of the alcoholic himself, the father I never knew?

My cousin, Dave, is the family historian, with a passion for genealogy. A few years ago, he remarked casually to me, "My dad always envied your dad."

"Why?" I queried, taken aback. I had never heard anyone say something positive about my father.

"Because your dad was a master fisherman," Dave said. I was astonished. Dave was surprised I hadn't already known this about my dad. Apparently, he was something of a family legend in the realm of fishing.

A simple statement—"he was a master fisherman"—making me realize I knew nothing about my father other than "alcoholic." What was his favorite color? Was he a morning person? What was his favorite dessert? I didn't even know he liked to fish.

Though I don't remember him, I have a feeling I am much like my father. I'm pretty sure that, like me, he was a 100% F on the Myers-Briggs[32].

My mother divorced him some time in the early 1950s, his alcoholism too much to bear. With my young siblings, she moved back to her own family on the Missouri farm. I can't imagine any of them had much good to say about my father, that staunch Methodist family, no-drinking-no-dancing-no-card-playing. This makes them sound like no fun at all, but I adored them all as I got to know them, years later, visiting every summer with my mother.

My father tracked her down a few years later to the bosom of her family, 1,800 miles from his California home, and got down on bended knee to beg her back. He swore he'd given up drinking, and I firmly believe he

---

[32] See http://www.humanmetrics.com/cgi-win/jtypes2.asp. The Myers-Briggs is a personality assessment allowing for self-examination on four axes: introvert-extrovert; sensate-intuitive; feeling-thinking; perceptive-judging. Note on that last, "judging," isn't judgmental. This axis assesses whether you take every life situation as unique, to be examined on its own merits, or do you have life rules you live by that you apply to each life situation.

thought he could. What a heart he must have had, taking that step. She went back to him, hence the age gap between me and my siblings.

And about that alcoholism… I know full well it runs in families. In my own family, my father was portrayed as the black sheep, an anomaly. Yet was he?

An amusing family story that doesn't stand up funny if taken a step further. My grandfather, my dad's dad, died the year I was born. A story about him, told as a family funny story. My parents inherited a mahogany dining room table from that side of the family. It had two leaves, made of plywood. The real leaves, the mahogany leaves, had been shattered by my grandfather putting the family car in drive rather than reverse when pulling out of the garage. Ha, ha. End of story. But this was the era of manual transmissions. Not easy to mistake reverse for drive. Unless, perhaps, he was drunk? Just a thought.

I wrote Volume One from the perspective of a young therapist, analyzing patterns and applying labels. Yes, these patterns are part of my heritage. And yet, having now interacted with several generations down the line from my father, I see the healing stronger in each subsequent generation. I now see the danger in labels such as "alcoholic family." It can be hard to recognize healing as it's happening.

How Could I Forget?

Also not mentioned in Volume One… When I talk of family history, I usually mention Jan and my mother dying in the same year (more on that later). It seems immediate to me. On occasion, another family member is nearby when I mention family deaths, and they will remind me, confused that I could forget, "What about David? He died before any of them." And always with a shock, I'll think, *Oh, yeah, David.*

There are certain events in my life that hold such significance that the time immediately preceding feels much further distant in the past. I graduated from high school in 1973. I came out as a lesbian a year later. Yet, the gulf between 1973 and 1974 feels like centuries. Realizing I was trans in 1995 created a huge gap back to the few years preceding. And that's when David died.

My nephew, David, Jan's youngest son. He was a sweet boy who turned into what seemed the usual rather surly adolescent, not speaking much, and off on his own a lot. None of us recognized that he had a serious problem.

As his adolescence progressed, he became increasingly quiet and withdrawn. As the oldest sibling, Jan didn't ask for help or share much of her immediate family's problems, including the fact that David was eventually diagnosed with paranoid schizophrenia. As with my father's alcoholism, this information was relayed to the rest of the family in clinical terms, without conveying the devastating effect this was having on Jan and Jere, constantly monitoring a son who was a danger to himself.

I'll never forget the Christmas before he died. Jan had to offer some explanation why she showed up without Jere or David, unheard of in my family. She told us that David had refused to come, and Jere had stayed home. They hadn't felt he should be left alone.

My sister-in-law, Ivette, Puerto Rican and with decided opinions about how families should behave, said to Jan, "You let me talk to him. He needs a good talking-to. He shouldn't be treating his family like that."

The look Jan gave Ivette spoke not just volumes but encyclopedias. She said simply, "Ivette, you have no idea what you're talking about." I've often wondered what Ivette thought when David killed himself less than a month later.

Though I was shocked and grieving at the time, the upcoming events completely overshadowed his death when I think of my family history—Heidi coming out to me as trans, and my own subsequent face-to-face with suicide. It's as if David's death was in the rain shadow, while I dealt with the center of the tornado that tore my life to shreds.

Family Reacting to My Transition

Rita was an old-school lesbian, opinionated and set in her ways. And her ways made no accommodation for transition[33]. My Oakland grad school apartment was about a mile from Susan and Rita's house. My mother had moved in with them some months prior to my move south for graduate school. The first day I walked over to visit, Rita answered the door. When she saw it was me, she was walking away from the door while it was still opening. She wouldn't acknowledge my existence.

My mother read Rita the riot act. Family always came first with my mother. In 1992, she astonished me and Susan both when she came to each of us separately and told us she was voting for Bill Clinton. This, from a

---

[33] This was to change as the years went by, but I'm talking now about 1998.

lifelong Republican! My mother used to blame the economic problems of the country on Roosevelt and the New Deal.

Watching on television, she had heard Pat Buchanan speak at the Republican National Convention, waxing eloquently about the homosexual agenda and family values. With incredulous anger she realized how far to the right her party had drifted on social issues, and she thought, *He's talking about my family!* She never voted Republican again. I admired her for having the courage to tell me and Susan.

Now, seeing Rita's treatment of me, she made it clear that she wanted me to feel free to visit any time. My mother, farm daughter from Missouri, Depression-era child, never wavered in her love and support for all her family, regardless of identity, religion, political views, or any other of the issues that so often divide family members from each other.

As I prepared to move back to Portland three years later, post-grad school, Rita said to me, "You're kind of a neat person," meaning she liked me better post-transition. I knew then that she had completed her transition of me. From that point, I never considered anyone hopeless. If Rita could transition me in her mind, *anyone* could adjust, was my attitude.

My siblings had interesting reactions to my transition. Susan told me she had spent her nine-year-old summer asking everyone to call her Steve. She had always interpreted that as a reaction to her twin brother John having much more freedom of movement as a boy in the 1950s. She envied his gender role, not his actual gender. Upon learning of my eventual transition, she revisited that interpretation, wondering.

Jan ruminated on her own gender identity, forthright and outspoken as she was, excelling in male-dominated realms. Neither Jan nor Susan had ever had such conversations with me before. They had never had such conversations with themselves until my impending transition put it in their face.

John had no such reaction, quite happy to welcome me to the club when he found out about my transition. He'd always wanted a little brother anyway.

I had sent a coming out letter to every family pod and was nervous at my first all-family gathering. My nephew, Erik, came up to me and stuck his hand out to shake mine, not a thing among the men in my family. He was welcoming me to the club. His was one of the few overt demonstrations of support in my family, and I've remembered it with gratitude as a result.

Most took their time and adjusted in their own way, with no conversation directly with me.

In the years since, having heard hundreds of family reaction stories, I've come to realize that I'm lucky and typical at the same time. No one outright rejected my transition, though my brother-in-law, Jere, misgendered me behind my back until his 2016 death. He was too big a Rush Limbaugh fan to do other than mock the concept of transition. The rest adjusted slowly to my new name and pronoun. It helped considerably in their adjustment once I started taking hormones. A deeper voice and some facial hair helped remind them!

As I used to tell clients, "Families generally adjust over time. Even those who are rigid in their worldview usually come around. You're all family to each other." I had Rita in mind, my nephew Erik as an example, my experience with Jere to draw on. Today, there is no one in my family, from my Pentecostal niece, Lisa, to my lesbian great-niece, Sophia, who has any difficulty with my transition. It took some years for them to all get there, and we are all family to each other still.

What Else Was Missing?

Leon... I finished writing Volume One with Leon on my shoulder. The last sections of Volume One are quite sociological, my reactions to a cisgender woman expecting certain behavior of transmen. By the way, I agree with her now. We transmen, of all people, should be allies to women in a patriarchal society. Choosing a sociological ending to Volume One left no place for Leon's story, which had no sociology to it whatsoever.

When I moved to the Bay Area in 1998, I discovered that most rental listings said, "Absolutely No Pets." My beloved Bear Cub having died the preceding spring, for the first time in my life, I was cat-less. I decided, with sad resignation, that I wouldn't be able to find a place that would allow me a cat. So, I took the apartment that suited me best, based on location and general ambience.

I lived on the top floor of my building, in an apartment at the back. In good weather, I sat on the back steps when I did my laundry, enjoying the backyard. The washer and dryer were in the basement.

One afternoon a few months after I'd moved in, a tabby cat joined me on the back steps, hanging out with me. He wanted to be picked up, so I obliged. He wasn't a lap cat. He was a shoulder cat, wanting to be held close to my heart. What a sweetheart he was! My assumption was that he lived nearby, an indoor-outdoor cat. We hung out together at laundry time for several weeks, enjoying each other's company.

Late one night, I heard a meowing outside my living room window, which faced the back steps. My laundry cat was prowling up and down the window ledge, meowing at me to be let in. Cats have no difficulty seducing me. Within minutes, he was in my apartment.

I looked at him, more puzzled than I'd been by his previous behavior. It's one thing for a well-loved, well-homed cat to hang out with me on the back steps in the afternoon while my laundry dries. It's quite another for that same cat to observe where I live, climb three flights of back steps at night, and yell from the window ledge to be let in.

Short story shorter… he never left. I went to the store, bought cat food and a cat box. Cat litter. A cat bed. Which he never used because his sleep perch was on the pillow behind my head. I half-woke one night to feel him grooming the back of my head. In the morning, I puzzled, *Was that a dream???* Next night, I woke more fully to realize, no, not a dream—a dream of a cat. I went out and bought a king-sized pillow.

I named him Leon. The sweetest cat I've ever lived with, and that's saying a lot. I was still puzzled. He was so well-socialized. Didn't have a collar, but also didn't look like he'd been living on the streets. What happened in his life that he re-homed himself?

It's hard to play a practical joke on a cat. But I managed with Leon. My apartment was in an old building, all the utility machinery in the basement three floors below me. My shower took forever in the morning to produce hot water. I took to turning on the shower, then going back to my bedroom to get my clothes ready for the day.

One morning, I started my routine. As I came back out of the bedroom to head for the shower, I saw Leon strolling in front of me toward the bathroom. I called his name and he jumped a mile, then glared at me. He thought I was already in the shower and was coming into the bathroom to greet me when I emerged. Gotcha! He immediately forgave me, sweetheart that he was.

I've rescued other cats, before and since, and have become resigned to not knowing the backstory. In this case, I was gifted with finding out.

A few weeks after Leon came to live with me, I flew to Portland for spring break. I'd made arrangements for this weeklong vacation long before Leon's arrival on the scene. I looked at this cat I wasn't supposed to have and didn't think it a good idea to leave him alone in my apartment. I could arrange for people to feed him, scoop his box, and such. My worry was he would yell loudly when they arrived, and even more loudly as they left, and my illicit roommate would be discovered by the property manager. I decided to board him.

A little online research found a place called the Feline Bed & Breakfast. I made the arrangements, dropping him off the day I left for Portland. I came to pick him up a week later, so happy to see my boy again, and the staff were so sorry to see him go. Such a sweetheart.

Next day, Leon disappeared. I never left him inside when I went off to school, for fear his presence would be discovered. When I came home that afternoon, he was nowhere to be found. I was beside myself! I scanned a photo of him and created a flyer, which I posted on every phone pole and bulletin board for a dozen blocks around.

Over the next few days, I received quite a few calls from concerned people all over the neighborhood, each saying they thought they'd seen him. None of the cats in question were Leon, however. I was desolate.

One evening, about a week after his disappearance, I received a call from someone who said, "I think your cat is in my building. He's meowing in the hall outside my door." Without much hope, having been disappointed a dozen times already, I asked her where she lived. I about jumped out of my skin when she gave her address—*my* address! He was downstairs!

I thanked her for the information and hung up to dash downstairs and grab that idiot cat, roaming a hallway he'd never been in before. Apparently, he'd snuck in the front door with one of the residents, rather than coming up the outside back stairs as usual. I carried him upstairs with much affectionate scolding while he purred as if he'd never been away.

Two days later, I came home to a phone message: "I saw your flyer about your lost cat, Leon. Did Leon adopt you about a month ago? Did he disappear about ten days ago and come back a couple of days ago?" I held the phone away from me and stared at it, as if I could ask the caller, "How do you *know* all this???" The voice continued, "I think that's my cat, Bogey." I called her back, and together we made sense of Leon's story.

Lauren had gotten involved with someone who had a cat and a dog. They all moved in with her. But, Bogey had been an only child for twelve years with Lauren, his entire life. He was not all about sharing her with another cat, much less a dog. He discovered me, and decided, "This would be a much better fit for me." So, he dumped Lauren and moved in with me.

However, I boarded him out for a week. He thought, *Hmmmm. That didn't work for me. Maybe that other place wasn't so bad after all.* So, he went back to Lauren. And the other cat. And the dog. For a week. And concluded, *Nope!*

Leon came home to me. Lauren and I agreed he'd made his decision, and that was that. She was sad and relieved he was well-loved and well-homed once again.

Unbeknownst to any of us, Leon had FIV (the cat equivalent of HIV). A routine vet exam turned into a prescription for a tablet I ground up in his wet food each morning. The vet told me, "This medication will keep him on an even keel. You'll know the end is here when he loses control of his bowels in a runny fashion and is yelling in pain." So, it proved to be a year and a half later. January 20, 2001. RIP Leon.

Processing Grief as a Man

Had I included Leon's story in Volume One, it would have ended here. Now, however... I am an ENFP on the Myers-Briggs assessment. Extrovert. Intuitive. Feeling. Perceptive. While all are undeniably me, the only one on which I score 100% is the F. I respond from my heart, not my head. Time was, the story would have ended without my sharing my heart, a family legacy. China changed all that *(much* more on that later). So, sharing my heart...

I was bereft when Leon died, with a loneliness unlike any other I'd ever experienced. This was my first real grief since transition, and I had no idea how to process it as a man. Not only was I now living a gender role with very different expectations of grief processing, but I also had testosterone as my dominant hormone rather than estrogen. Part of the definition of "early transition" is navigating familiar situations that are new all over again because of those two factors in combination, the social and the hormonal.

The closeness of a grad school cohort is profound, particularly in a profession such as therapist. We played therapist with and for each other, in group process class, in classes on effective communication, sexuality, addiction, in family systems classes. They all knew of Leon, from the time he adopted me until his death a year and a half later. Several had met him and come to love him as well.

They commiserated with me. They consoled me. And yet, it didn't feel like enough. Of course not! In the past, I'd had the consolation of lesbian community during times of sorrow, the intensity of all that estrogen surrounding and comforting me. No more.

I understand all this now. I didn't understand, at the time, why I felt so inconsolably bereft, so isolated in my grief. I didn't know how to accept or seek consolation as a man. None of my cohort had known me prior to transition. They knew no other me than "Reid, the guy." They consoled me in keeping with how one consoles white men in U.S. culture.

I hadn't even come out to them as a transman until December of 1998, three months after starting my grad school program. When I moved to the Bay Area, I was reveling in having escaped the fishbowl of early transition. By December of 1998, I was a year and a half on hormones and one year post chest surgery. From the perspective of having witnessed nearly 500 people undergoing transition, I was very early in my process when I moved for grad school.

What I wrote of my grad school cohort in Volume One had to do with coming out to them as trans and educating them, not anything to do with bonding with them. And yet, we became very close during our three years together. I have become Facebook friends with a few folks from that time, and it still makes me smile fondly when Donna, Lisa, Lon, or Amy responds to one of my posts.

Anything Else Left Out?

Well, how about the AIDS epidemic? Reagan's gradual dismantling of the public sector response to mental health or addiction issues? When I reread my journals from the 1980s, it would appear my life took place in a vacuum. The only way to hide my identity from myself was to live exclusively within the lesbian community and not participate in a larger life.

I had no straight friends prior to transition. My only male friends were in the context of Bridges Vocal Ensemble. Prior to the formation of Bridges, there were no men in my life except family members. I tried to adopt a separatist viewpoint, holding men at bay to avoid facing the male energy within.

Writing Volume I, how could I have left out Trent dying? Bridges was one of the hits of GALA IV in Denver in 1992. At that festival, each chorus performed twice, moving from one concert hall to perform in another. We were so high after our first performance—there is no audience like GALA, LGBT choral singers singing for each other—that our interconnection was palpable. Trent chose that moment to tell us he had AIDS. It may seem like horrible timing, bringing us down from the high of a wonderful performance as we prepared for another, but it was absolutely the right time. We were always family in Bridges, and the feeling was strongest in that moment.

A year and a half later, we got the call we'd been expecting and dreading. It was time. After rehearsal that evening, we all went over to Trent's house, surrounding the chair he seldom left at that point. We sang every song he knew, his lips mouthing the words with a little smile. He was beyond singing by that point. Trent died the next day, the first member of Bridges to succumb to AIDS.

Several people who read this autobiography in advance of its publication remarked, "I would never have known this book was about you until I got to your graduate school experience! Then, I recognized you."

Not only was my separatist viewpoint a surprise to them, but also my lack of self-esteem or sense of purpose in life. Re-reading Volume One, my biggest surprises are that: (a) it took me so long to understand such a fundamental component of my identity as gender, and (b) that I survived at all.

What Else?

So, what else didn't I mention in Volume One? In July of 2000, the GALA choral festival rolled around again, an every-four-year event. I doubt I would have made the effort to go had it not been in San Jose in 2000, fairly local to me. I hadn't missed a GALA festival since GALA III in Seattle in 1989.

For the first and only time, I attended a GALA festival as a singer but not a chorus member. I felt so left out! I sang in a festival chorus, but when I saw the Portland Lesbian Choir on-stage, it was quite painful to not be singing in a chorus of my own. I missed Chorus more than I was willing to admit to myself during that sojourn for grad school. I didn't feel like I really participated in that particular GALA festival, without a chorus to call home.

There are a number of GALA choruses in the Bay Area. I deliberately chose not to join one while in grad school. Being in grad school had nothing to do with this decision. I could have handled the workload. No, my reason was that I knew full well how profoundly and deeply I give my heart to a chorus I've joined. I knew I was coming back to Portland immediately after graduation and didn't want to have to "break up" with a chorus. The pain of leaving the PLC behind was too fresh. I couldn't knowingly inflict that pain on myself. I gave up chorus for three years rather than bond and then leave again.

These days, I would make a different decision. The pain would still be there, yes, but so would the knowledge that everything comes and goes in life. I would take the pleasure of three years singing with a chorus despite knowing I'd be leaving eventually. We all leave eventually anyway, right? One way or another? I would have enjoyed making a whole new set of friends for whom to cheer at GALA festivals down the road.

Also not mentioned in Volume One, because I was unaware… Unbeknownst to me, my own process, my own transition, took a back seat for the next nearly 20 years once I started grad school. It wasn't until Bus A in China that my own transition came to the forefront, and with such abrupt persistence that I was propelled back to early transition stages that I'd believed were long behind me. I'd always needed to feel the feelings of early transition and had put them on hold as I trained to become a therapist. I then helped several hundred other people deal with what I had parked in a corner.

But I'm getting ahead of myself by some years here. Let's get chronological again.

Chapter Sixteen

Transitioning to Therapist

The third year of my counseling program (2000-01) was focused on seeing clients in an internship setting. The only class I took at the university during that third year was group supervision, discussing cases and any personal difficulties we were having as "real world" therapists.

The real world. Those first two years in our counseling program, we had practiced on each other, read books about theoretical approaches to therapy, read books about various issues, read books about relationships and sexuality. Then, there's the first client. The person who probably never read a book about their own therapeutic issue. They don't care what a book says about their therapeutic issue. They're living it and want something to change. That's why they're there.

Pacific Center

My internship was at Pacific Center for Human Growth in Berkeley, an LGBT counseling center. The interns each year came from counseling programs around the East Bay—Cal State Hayward, UC Berkeley, and me from JFKU. They became my other cohort, the student counselors of 2000-01 at Pacific Center.

Half my JFKU cohort were interns at various counseling centers around the East Bay. The rest interned at our university's counseling center in Oakland. Susan, a seasoned therapist, some ten years into her practice at that point, was a clinical supervisor at the JFKU counseling center. She also supervised one of my Pacific Center cohort. It was an odd feeling, knowing my sister was the supervisor for some of my fellow students.

Most of the interns at Pacific Center were part of the LGBT community, though not all. In addition to seeing 8-10 clients each week, we also attended weekly trainings pertaining to various issues that might arise with our clients. Three local trans people came in to provide training on trans issues. It is a measure of how new it was to have an intern who was trans that it didn't occur to anyone at Pacific Center that they might have an intern who could provide such training from personal experience.

One transman involved in the training recognized me and told the others who I was. All three, good-humoredly, wondered why they were there at all. They were gratified for this visceral experience of seeing, for the first time, a trans person as a therapist intern. One of our own was on his way toward becoming a therapist for our own.

Grad School Therapy

Most counseling programs require their students to be in therapy while in grad school. Previous therapy doesn't count. If you take a family systems class, inevitably you will recognize your own family patterns and how they play out in you. If you take a class in addictions and there is a family pattern of addiction in your background, *something* will come up as your childhood experience is in your face.

Though it's never graded as other classes are, part of the education of a counseling program is to learn about oneself, one's patterns and family dynamics, all the various things that might be trigger points when clients bring things up that hit close to home. Therapy is the place for the budding therapist to process it all.

My grad school therapist was a woman who helped me shift from "Reid, the transman" to "Reid, the trans therapist." I wrote quite a few pieces as things came up for me in grad school, always bringing them in for Kim to read[34]. Kim was invaluable to me as I navigated the space between early transition and early therapist as co-existing identities and parallel processes. What I didn't realize then is that early transition was a problematic time for me to undertake that particular navigation.

I have helped advance the therapy profession in the direction of "useful" for trans clients. However, I did so at some personal expense. My work with Kim was focused on my development as a therapist, at a time when I would have greatly benefited from her expertise working with trans clients. Transition issues came up, but through the lens of becoming a therapist, not as issues focused on in their own right.

When I talked with Kim about family, I was dissecting the effects of having had an alcoholic father I didn't remember. Though important work for me to do, there was other important work that was more immediate. I had moved back to my family at a time when they were still going through their adjustment process to my transition.

---

[34] Kim was one who read Volume One, remarking that she didn't recognize me until near the end, the time at which she met me.

For instance, at one point during my first year in grad school, my mother and I were driving somewhere with Jan and Jere. We stopped for food, and Jere and I went in. We were the only customers at the counter. Jere was ahead of me, placing his order. Then, he said to the guy behind the counter, "I don't know what she wants," meaning me. The guy looked at me in confusion, and I hung Jere out to dry. I shrugged my shoulders in equal confusion, as if I hadn't a clue who Jere meant.

Many trans people go through similar irritatingly common early transition experiences. When I processed it with Kim, I turned it into another funny family story. This one at Jere's expense. I didn't process with Kim how it felt to be misgendered by this person who'd known me since I was five. Coincidentally, the same age Susan referenced when she told me, "Your name hasn't fit you since you were five."

Make no mistake, I made good use of my time with Kim. I developed stellar therapist boundaries and wasn't triggered by clients' stories. And my own early transition issues remained dormant until China in 2018.

Navigating the Boundaries

During the fall of 2000, I was introduced to *In the Family,* a magazine for LGBT therapists. I read a few issues and decided to submit an article about being a trans therapist. The thought crossed my mind, *Should I publish this now, when I've begun seeing clients?* Given the audience the magazine was intended for—LGBT therapists—I thought the likelihood of a client seeing it was small to none. These kinds of boundaries were the sort of thing I was processing with Kim.

When the article was published, I was horrified. I'd emailed two scanned photographs of myself: high school graduation, and current day transman. The publisher (Laura) hadn't been able to open the file containing my current day photo and had chosen to use only the high school graduation picture.

I was out of town on a road trip to the desert, mourning Leon's passing, as the publication deadline loomed. Laura was unable to reach me to consult. This was before cell phones were common companions. She couldn't understand why the use of just my high school photo upset me, given that it was a pretty stunningly beautiful picture. Nevertheless, this was the first article I'd written from within the therapy profession, coinciding with the time I began seeing clients as an intern. I felt on my way!

One of the most valuable lessons I learned in my internship concerned my personal identity coinciding with my professional self. Coming out. A lesson from the textbooks: it's all about the client, so don't make it be about you. Valuable—as far as it goes. There are times, however, when it's in a client's best interest to learn something about their therapist. This is one reason it's so important for a therapist to know themselves and their triggers as fully as one can, to discern when it's about the client, and when it's about the therapist.

I'll call him Peter. He was a cisgender gay man, 38 when I first saw him in early 2001. He had just passed an anniversary date—one year since his last friend from the AIDS epidemic had died.

As Peter put it, "I feel so isolated and cut off and alone. No one else in my life remembers that time. No one else remembers all my friends. We all knew each other, and now, I'm the only one left. I've tried every kind of grief group, every kind of self-help technique, and now none of them work anymore. So, here I am."

Peter was a gay, cisgender man. He never mentioned trans anything. So, I never told him I was trans. Why would I? Irrelevant.

Peter talked a lot about his grief but never truly expressed it in session—the same problem he was having in his daily life. I didn't feel that I was helping him, other than by giving him a sounding board. Useful, but perhaps not helpful.

Some weeks into our work together, Peter came into session and pulled a magazine out of his backpack, saying, "I'd like to talk about this."

Of course. *In the Family,* with my article. At first, I panicked, thinking I'd made a huge error in clinical judgment publishing the article.

Peter told me, "I was in an LGBT bookstore. I'm always on the lookout for new things to read about and saw this magazine. I looked at the table of contents and saw your name but only knew it looked familiar. I turned to the article and had to sit down before I fell down when I realized who you were, a transman and not a gay man[35]."

As we talked our way through it, Peter said, somewhat accusingly, "When I called for my first appointment, I told the person I wanted to work with a gay man. Who else would understand the AIDS epidemic the same

---

[35] To be clear, it didn't matter to Peter that I was a transman. It mattered that I wasn't a gay man.

way I do? And the person said, 'We have the perfect match for you.' So, of course, I thought you were a gay man!"

I filed away in the back of my mind to find out who had told him that.

However, at our next session, Peter brought in a huge binder filled with obituaries. He told me why he was bringing it in now.

"Last time I tried therapy, I worked with a psychologist who was gay and when I brought this binder in, he cried. He knew half the people in here himself."

And with that, Peter started telling me stories through the tears he finally shed. He had been protecting me from a grief he assumed I shared. Finding out that I was not a gay man had freed him up.

Lessons Learned

I came away from this experience with the valuable knowledge that self-disclosure is sometimes necessary to the work. I can't emphasize this enough: it's all about the client.

I also came away from that experience understanding that people hear what they want to hear. In looking at Peter's file after he'd brought the magazine into session, I saw that Tracy had done his intake. Never, under any circumstance, could I picture Tracy telling a potential client over the phone, someone she'd never met and had only talked with for five minutes, "We have the perfect match for you."

And yet, as it turned out, I *was* the perfect match for him. One of the most valuable aspects of our work together is that Peter learned that he could trust someone, open up to them, feel seen and heard, and then, find out the person he'd thought was "just like him" was, in fact, not a gay man. This helped Peter bridge back to a world larger than gay men his age who had lost everyone to AIDS.

The art of therapy is as much the timing of an intervention as the content. The right content at the wrong time doesn't help the client. If Peter had known before our first session that I was trans and not gay, who knows if he would have opened up as he did. He might not have brought in that obituary binder, assuming I wouldn't be able to go there with him because we didn't share a gay identity. Finding out when he did, after bonding with me, was perfect timing.

A New Companion

I was bereft and cat-less once again when Leon died in January of 2001. A few months later, I was passing by a pet store in Berkeley and, on impulse, went in to look for a cat. There were two to choose from, in cages, one on top of the other. The cat in the top cage hissed at me. I couldn't see the shy cat in the bottom cage, but when I stuck my fingers through the bars, she emerged far enough to lick my hand. I said, "I'll take that one."

I'd forgotten what young cat energy was like. Leon had been twelve when he came to live with me and was a well-behaved gentleman of a cat. This one…the energy! She climbed and burrowed everywhere. "Go and find out"—the motto of the mongoose—gave me her name: Rikki Tikki Tabby. Rita thought I was nuts to get a cat within months of moving back to Portland, but Rikki was a joy to have around, and I wasn't meant to be cat-less!

In June of 2001, I graduated from JFKU with my Master's Degree in Counseling Psychology. My internship continued on until August, as did my university job as outreach coordinator. By late-August, I was free to return to Portland!

Chapter Seventeen

The World Changed

Over Labor Day weekend of 2001, I flew to Portland to look for a place to rent. I stayed with my friend, Lisa. It seemed appropriate to stay with the friend who had driven the U-Haul to the Bay Area three years before, launching my grad school sojourn.

Life Falling into Place

It was synchronicity that the GALA Choruses leadership conference was being held in Portland that Labor Day weekend. All the Portland-area GALA choruses came together to perform a concert in honor of GALA. Of course, I went, reconnecting with so many old friends, all of us thrilled that I was returning. It was a wonderfully nostalgic experience to see the PLC perform, no longer bringing with it the same pain of loss I would once have felt.

And then, a nice surprise. A former Bridges member had formed a mixed chorus during my absence in the Bay Area. As I watched Confluence sing, I thought happily, *Thank you, Ray, for forming a chorus for me to join when I get back!* Bridges was on the verge of folding. The PLC could no longer be home. Interestingly, though I now had the vocal range to join the Portland Gay Men's Chorus, the possibility didn't occur to me. Over my eleven years in PLC, I had always viewed PGMC as "other," and it never would have occurred to me to participate as a singer. It still didn't occur to me.

I didn't know then that at least one transman had already participated in PGMC, nor did I know that not all members were gay men. I don't know that this knowledge would have made a difference to me. It was my own relationship to PGMC that was in question, and, to me, it had always represented the "other."

And then, another happy surprise. At concert intermission, I got talking with an old friend about how life was going. Upon learning I was moving back and needing a place to live, she exclaimed, "You should move into my house!" She had recently moved in with her partner and was about to rent out her own house. A win-win. I didn't have to look for a place to live, and she didn't have to go to the trouble of finding a tenant. My new life was falling into place without effort on my part. The stars were aligning with synchronicity.

And Then...
There are certain dates that change the world, living on in history (or in infamy, as President Roosevelt said of December 7, 1941, the day Pearl Harbor was attacked). 9/11 is one such, and it has always struck me as eerily significant that the date on my JFKU diploma is September **10,** 2001.

On September 11, 2019, it occurred to me that those born on 9/11 were turning 18 that day, eligible to vote. I thought about the continuity of history. People are always being born into their place in the web of connection between generations that we call history. No one comes in at the beginning or end of a story because there's no such thing. It's all the middle, with one thing born from another and then becoming something else.

I was born ten years after WWII, which had morphed into the McCarthy Era and the Cold War. Because the war itself happened before I was born, it had about as much personal significance to me as the Revolutionary War. As a child, both meant little more than dates and people to memorize for history tests.

Having lived through 9/11, I now understand the difference. My mother was a "Rosie the Riveter" during WWII. She welded ship bottoms in the Oakland shipyards. She had stories to tell. But for the Revolutionary War, there are no living relatives to remember even close to that time.

I asked my mother once whether 9/11 and Pearl Harbor were similar in their immediate impact on people. She said that 9/11 had a more visceral effect because it was on television, the images of those planes plowing into the World Trade Center seared in people's minds through replay after replay.

There were differences. 9/11 was an out-of-the-blue attack that struck at the heart and soul of the U.S., while Pearl Harbor was a wartime strategic attack among many in various parts of the world. Hawaii wasn't a state at the time of the attack on Pearl Harbor. It was a territory that many viewed in much the same light as Guam or Puerto Rico. And it wasn't near the mainland of the U.S.

Despite these differences, there were similarities. One similarity, my mother told me, was in the insecurity of not knowing what might happen next. The initial radio broadcast about Pearl Harbor made it clear that this attack came from Japan. The uncertainty lay in not knowing if this was the first in a series of attacks. Particularly on the west coast, the U.S. had felt protected from attack by the world's largest ocean, and now, here was this devastating destruction in Hawaii. If Japan could orchestrate this attack successfully, was the west coast *really* safe?

Another similarity. My mother remembered exactly where she was when she heard the radio broadcast announcing the attack on Pearl Harbor. She was eating Sunday lunch with my dad in their San Francisco apartment.

A Vivid Memory

On 9/11, I was packing up to move back to Portland. I had a U-Haul reserved for the following weekend. Mid-morning, I turned on a radio talk show I enjoyed. The radio came on in the middle of a sentence, my talk show pre-empted. An attack had occurred somewhere. While I don't remember the exact words, I do remember concluding there had been a major air strike somewhere, I assumed abroad. Americans have always felt safe from attack, oceans separating us from those we call enemies.

At some point, I thought, *This feels more immediate than I would expect.* There was an urgency in the tone of voice. It occurred to me that if this was on the radio, it was probably on television as well. I turned on the TV and had to sit down before my legs gave way. I had tuned in to see first one plane, then another, exploding into the twin towers.

In shock, I sat in front of the TV for an hour or so, turning it off when it was clear that I was seeing nothing more than replays of a few interviews and that footage, over and over, of the planes. There was no other information yet to broadcast.[36]

---

[36] In 2011, I traveled to New York City with the Portland Gay Men's Chorus to perform *BraveSouls and Dreamers* in commemoration of the tenth anniversary of 9/11. *BraveSouls and Dreamers* is a peace cantata commissioned by PGMC in response to 9/11. My wife, Cristina, and I wandered around Central Park and struck up conversations with various New Yorkers. When they learned why we were there, the stories poured forth, in great detail, as if it had happened the day before. We performed with a third of the New York City Gay Men's Chorus. The other two-thirds couldn't bring themselves to be in town on the anniversary. At the time of 9/11, I'd never been to New York City, and still, I was punched in the heart by what happened. How much bigger a punch for those for whom this was home.

Now What? What Now?

As I continued to pack boxes that day, uncertainty was prominent in my mind. I kept the radio on, listening to various tidbits of information trickling in. Some locales had already closed various roads that were near dams and major utility installations, in case they might be bombed. Would I be allowed to drive a truck over Shasta Dam, up I-5, the following week? (Yes.) Jan traveled to NYC regularly for work. Was she safe? (Yes.) Yes to both questions, but the answers were not apparent as I watched those replays that day.

No one knew what was happening, what was canceled. I had treated myself to a great seat at an Oakland A's baseball game that night, my last while still living in the Bay Area. I had no way of knowing, amidst all the confusion, would there even be a game? Along with hundreds of other fans, I showed up at the stadium that evening, all of us milling around with no one to turn to for guidance. No game. Osama bin Laden still owes me money for that prime ticket. I would no longer be in the Bay Area to take advantage of the A's offer to replace the ticket with one for a game later in the season.

Midday on 9/11, I received a phone call from the office manager I'd worked for at JFKU. I had left my job as outreach coordinator a week before, as I prepared to move. Nicole was calling with a question about a computer file they were having difficulty accessing. I went over to the school for a few hours, grateful for this reprieve to normalcy in the midst of a world in upheaval. Hanging out with Nicole was a nice gift that day. As I said goodbye, I had a sense of nostalgia. I knew I was saying goodbye to life as I'd known it in more than one sense.

Back North

On September 18, 2001, the U-Haul truck pointed north on I-5. Back in Portland once again, I spent the next week happily nesting, preparing my home not only for me, but for Rikki. I'd boarded my girl at the Feline Bed & Breakfast and left my car at Susan's house. It was time to fly back down there and pick them both up.

Rikki quickly explored our new home and approved. She discovered and made good use of the cat door in the back door. And I reintroduced myself to Portland. Again, early transition self-centeredness, I expected to pick up all my friendships just where we'd left off, without change to our relationship. Rather, I'd been gone long enough and undergone such profound change myself that all of my friendships felt new, while, at the same time, familiar.

Furthering the distance between us, my friends had undergone profound life changes in my absence. I knew of the changes, had kept in touch while gone, and still was surprised at how far our paths had diverged. We built new bridges back toward each other in the months after my return.

My best friend, Amy, from PLC days and her partner, Karen, had broken up. Amy was in a new relationship. All three were close friends. Lynda Garner had left the PLC. Bridges was on the verge of folding. Following my 1987 bicycle trip to Boston to visit Sylvan, she had since moved back to Portland, with her new partner, Pam. During my absence in the Bay Area, Pam had died of cancer. Sylvan had become deeply spiritual, and, eventually, became a Buddhist monk.

My close friend, Lisa, had set up a Christmas tree for me to come home to post-chest-surgery. She had driven the U-Haul truck to send me off to grad school. I had dinner with her shortly after my return, and she disappointed me deeply by her attitudes toward transwomen attending the Michigan Womyn's Music Festival.

"Why can't they just understand no means no?!"

My heart froze over as she said that. I withdrew from our friendship. She didn't seem to notice.[37]

Through my connections with other therapists, I began meeting new people, forming new friendships with people who only ever knew me as Reid, the transman. I met Andrew, a cisgender gay man in the early stages of a doctoral program in Human Services. We quickly became close friends and colleagues. Andrew would later be the best man at my wedding.

In mid-October, I decided it was time. I put the word out to colleagues that I was in the market for office space. A colleague told me of a space in an office suite of therapists, across the street from the library in downtown Portland. My first office had a view of beautiful large oak trees and the brick rooftop of a library. I was on my way!

---

[37] These days, 25 years into transition, I am centered sufficiently in my identity that I wouldn't withdraw from a close friendship on this basis; I would undertake to bring my friend along in broadening their understanding of trans identity. I would only withdraw if they refused the journey. At the time I'm writing about, however, I wasn't centered enough in my identity to feel able to defend it to such a close friend.

Chapter Eighteen

On Being Transtherapist.com

Right off the bat, a choice point: am I out, or not? Am I a therapist who happens to be trans, or a trans therapist? On a practical level, given how long I'd lived within the lesbian community in Portland, I saw little point in *not* being out. Too many people knew of my transition, and I would always be left wondering who knew and who didn't.

Further, the lesson learned working with Peter was fresh in my mind. Misassumption of identity doesn't always work out for the best. Most importantly, at that time, I would be one of the first (perhaps *the* first, not sure about that) trans people to enter the profession with a primary goal of serving my own. How could I serve my own if I wasn't open about being trans?

I met Tom through a colleague. A professional website developer, Tom was enthusiastic about helping me with my first website and designed it for me at little cost. My choice: did I want reidvanderburgh.com as my domain name? No, my name wasn't the point. The point was the domain name I ultimately chose: transtherapist.com.

Pursuing Licensure

I had attended JFKU in order to participate in the transpersonal psychology program. The university happened to be located in California. The powerhouse therapist license in California is Marriage and Family Therapist (MFT), and this was the licensure my counseling program was designed to support. I had taken all the coursework required for a California MFT license.

Oregon, however… The Oregon licensing board had never dealt with an applicant who had graduated from JFKU. The board required that I send a substantial package of information about my university program, including a syllabus and course outline for every class I'd taken, and a copy of my master's thesis. Ultimately, I was approved as a candidate for licensure in Oregon, except that I had to take a graduate-level course in research methods.

My JFKU program offered no such course because the state of California didn't require a research methods class for the MFT license. Oregon did. I fought this requirement, largely because I had taken a research methods class in obtaining my BA in Psychology at PSU. The PSU psychology program is research-oriented, leading to a mathematical approach that is foreign in a counseling program. I knew sight unseen that my undergrad research methods class was more rigorous than the graduate-level class would be through a counseling program. However, there was no budging the licensing board on this issue.

In signing up for the class, I found myself talking with Marian, whose responsibilities included overseeing the Continuing Education curriculum offered through PSU. Not being licensed yet, barely occupying an office yet, I was only vaguely aware of Continuing Education requirements for licensed therapists. Everyone with a license needs to take a certain number of credit hours of relevant classes each year, keeping abreast of new developments in the profession. It would be several years before I would accrue enough client-contact hours to be licensed and would need to take such courses myself.

My situation wasn't exactly Continuing Education, but Marian worked with me to get me into the research methods class, despite my not being a student in the counseling program. As we talked, I had the idea to ask her whether I would be able to teach Continuing Education classes through PSU, teaching licensed therapists what they needed to know to effectively work with trans clients. Why yes, I could indeed do that. Licensure wasn't required to teach Continuing Education classes. Subject matter expertise was the requirement, and I certainly had that.

Thus began a three-course-a-year venture with PSU, teaching CE classes to my peers. I earned nearly as much teaching my first all-day class as I spent taking my research methods class, which, as I had suspected, wasn't nearly as rigorous as my undergrad class had been.

As time went on, my own clients' stories informed my teaching, as I was able to discern what was a variation of normal and what might actually be a red flag. I am a storyteller at heart and heard hundreds of stories to illustrate the model of transition I'd developed while in grad school.

Making a Difference

I quickly got involved in helping various Portland agencies develop services to enhance the quality of life of trans people in Portland. I was part of an ad hoc group (including Andrew) that met weekly at a café to develop the Identity Project, a program to provide trans people with free legal name changes and gender changes on state ID cards and driver's licenses.

Outside In was the agency hosting this program, having written the grant that funded the Identity Project. Outside In exists to help homeless youth navigate their way off the streets. About half the youth they serve are LGBT+ in some way. Nearly half those are trans. The Identity Project served any trans person in Portland. In this instance, Outside In expanded its mission beyond homeless youth in recognition of how few services were available in Portland at that time to *any* trans person, regardless of age.

I conducted numerous trainings for various local social service agencies, all anxious to understand their role in serving trans people. I found that, quite often, agencies would approach me with the request that I help them understand current terminology.

I would respond, "Why yes, I'd be happy to come in and lead a staff training."

The actual event, however, had little to do with terminology and much more to do with education around the nature of gender identity, how it plays out in everyone's life, what transition looks like to various people, and dismantling stereotypes based on cultural misinformation. We would then have a discussion about the mission of that particular organization, and how best to serve those trans people accessing services. Then, we might talk about current terminology.

Families!

Andrew and I developed a presentation around the power of supporting identity actualization as an intervention, using the Identity Project as a model that could be implemented in other cities. We submitted our proposal to the American Public Health Association's national conference and were overjoyed when our proposal was accepted! My first professional conference!

The APHA conference was held in San Francisco that year. When Andrew and I learned our proposal had been accepted, he said, "You have family in the East Bay. Why don't we invite them to come into San Francisco to have dinner with us afterward, in celebration of your first professional conference?"

I laughed, and without having to put any thought into his proposal, said, "That will never happen!"

Mystified, Andrew queried, "Why not?"

I said, "Here's what would happen if I suggested this to Susan, because that's who we're talking about here—Susan, Rita, and my mom who now lives with them." And I related how the conversation would go:

> Me: Susan, my colleague, Andrew, and I are coming to the Bay Area to participate in the APHA conference, my first professional conference. How about you all come into San Francisco for dinner to celebrate with us?
>
> Susan: Oh, traffic is really bad coming into San Francisco [spoken in a tone that assumes I don't know that]. How about if you and your friend come over to Oakland on BART[38]? We'll pick you up at the BART station, and we can go to Little Shin Shin for dinner.

I then told Andrew, "Little Shin Shin is a Chinese restaurant in Oakland near where Susan, Rita, and my mom live. Susan and Rita have been going there often since they bought their house in the early 1990s."

I then went on to tell Andrew, "This is what will happen, because we will be expected to go. If we turn this down, that would be the height of rudeness, though I might be able to use you being too tired as an excuse. Easiest is, we go over there for dinner.

"They will be early to pick us up at BART, and we'll go to Little Shin Shin. Susan will look over the menu and say, 'If we're eating family style, I can't eat anything spicy.' And, by the way, there is no other way my family eats Chinese food. It would be seen as extremely antisocial to order something and then just eat your own plate and nothing else and not share. Rita will respond, 'You love their lemon chicken.' My mom will say, 'Would anyone care to join me in a glass of plum wine?' And after dinner, she will take the check, as if it's her birthright, and pay for the entire meal, in cash. At that point, they will invite us back to their house, and we can either accept or tell them we're too tired, and then, they'll drive us back to BART."

---

[38] BART: Bay Area Rapid Transit, a light rail system

Andrew digested this for a moment, and then said, "That's it? No acknowledgment of why we're there, that you've just had this big professional milestone?"

I said, "No. I'm so much the youngest, that's not how anyone in my family will ever view me. As far as they're concerned, I'm visiting and brought a little friend along with me to dinner."

After a pause, Andrew: "That's weird."

I said to him, "You have family down there too, right? What about them?"

Andrew waved his hand dismissively, saying, "Oh, that'll never happen."

Mystified, I said, "Why not?"

Andrew said, "This is what will happen in my family. I've got an aunt who lives in San Francisco. She owns a duplex that she lives in, and her son and his wife live in the other half. So, I'll send them an email to say we're coming down there. I'll tell them we don't know exactly what the conference schedule is, so we can't make a plan yet. I'm giving them a heads up that we're coming. I won't hear anything back.

"Then, a couple of weeks before the conference, when we know our schedule, I'll email again and tell them when we're free. I won't hear anything back. Then, about a week after our return, I'll get an email from my aunt saying, 'You were down here, right? Why didn't you get ahold of us? We were here.' So, we won't ever see them."

After a pause, me: "That's weird."

So, Andrew never heard a word from his family. We went to Little Shin Shin, my mom ordered plum wine, and Andrew nearly choked on his as Susan ordered lemon chicken.

I have often used this story to illustrate that families only appear weird from the outside looking in. My family's behavior seemed normal to me, as Andrew's did to him. And we both predicted precisely how our families would behave. And we each thought the other's family was weird.

I have also used this story to illustrate that families behave from habit just as individuals do. It's hard enough for me to see my sister ordering anything other than lemon chicken[39]. How much harder to shift her view of me from "Nancy, her youngest sister" to "Reid, her youngest brother?"

A New Chorus Family

After seeing Confluence perform over Labor Day weekend of 2001, I had decided this was my new chorus. However, having sung in one GALA chorus or another since 1986, I was cautious. Rather than coming to the first September rehearsal after moving back to Portland and jumping right in, I decided instead to nest a bit and then attend the December Confluence concert. Seeing more than a few songs amongst other choruses would give me more data points to make my decision. Was this my new chorus?

Confluence is a chorus rather unique in that it deliberately draws on LGBT+ folks from the entire Willamette Valley, rather than focusing its energy on Portland. The group rehearses in the state capital, Salem, some 60 miles south of Portland, and draws singers from up and down the Willamette Valley. The chorus produces three shows of each concert, performing in Portland, Salem, and Corvallis, the three cities that are home to most of the singers.

I attended the Sunday afternoon performance in Corvallis that December of 2001. I'd never been to Corvallis, some 75 miles from Portland; going to a new town was part of the adventure of it all. There were perhaps fifty people in the audience, so I was clearly visible to all the performers.

Confluence had become home to several former PLC members with whom I'd sung, and, of course, there was the director, Ray, with whom I'd shared Bridges. After the concert, Ray made a beeline for me and enveloped me in a bear hug. One former PLC member came up to hug me and asked excitedly, "Are you going to join Confluence?" I took a deep breath and said, "Yes."

My mother had attended many PLC and Bridges concerts over the years. She now shifted her allegiance to Confluence, attending at least one concert every year. After her first concert, we went to the after-concert party, hosted by a chorus member. The first reality TV show was popular at

---

[39] I spent a concentrated block of time with Susan in her Oakland home in the summer of 2019. I had to laugh to myself when we went to Little Shin Shin, and she ordered *orange* chicken. I thought whimsically that adjusting to my transition had broadened my sister's horizons.

the time *(Survivor)* and my mother was quite a fan. At one point during the party, I looked for my mother to see how she was doing. I was quite entertained when I poked my head in the door of the TV room to find her in the center of a group of about six or eight chorus members, all of them waiting with bated breath to see who would be voted off the island this time.

Compartmentalizing My Life

That was a rather abrupt shift from talking about establishing my therapy practice to talking about Confluence. There is no easy way to bridge these two aspects of my life as I kept them deliberately compartmentalized and separate from each other. One big attraction of Confluence, for me, was that the chorus rehearses in Salem. There was very little likelihood that a client would join. Leaving Portland once a week for rehearsal helped create a necessary gap between these two aspects of my life.

Chapter Nineteen

Equilibrium

Confluence was my self-care, being a therapist was my passion, and both brought great joy to my life. I carpooled on Sunday afternoons to rehearsal. The carpool was part of the fun of the whole experience. To this day, I play pinochle monthly with several of the people I met in the Confluence carpool, though none of us have sung in the chorus since the mid-2000s.

In establishing myself as a therapist, I used my background in typesetting and graphic design to market myself. I produced a professional newsletter every month, with a short article about something to do with trans issues. I learned to ruthlessly edit my own work. Each article had to fit on one side of an 8½ x 11 inch sheet of paper.

Not quite satisfied with the structure of my original website and wanting to be able to make changes quickly and easily, I took an online class in web design and created a fabulous website. I designed my own business card and flyers and created ads to run in *Just Out* (Portland's LGBT newspaper) and in concert programs. I had to laugh, putting to good use talents I'd used on others' behalf for years.

The "Go-to" Guy

The following few years were a balm to my soul. I was the "go-to" guy for anyone wishing to transition in this region. Or their partners. Or a couple wanting to work through issues related to one of them transitioning. Or a genderqueer (now non-binary) person wanting support navigating a culture that had no framework for recognizing or supporting their identity. Or a parent wanting reassurance after learning their adult child was considering transition. Or an adult child wanting to work through feelings arising upon learning their parent was embarking on transition. Or a parent wanting to know what their move was in realizing that their still-at-home child was trans. Or a sibling wanting to work through having their world rocked by a sister saying, "I'm really your brother." Or vice versa.

Everything became a variation of normal as I normalized their lived experience of gender for my clients. And everything became (anonymous) fodder for the CE classes I taught through PSU, workshops I presented at conferences, and presentations I gave for college classes and counseling programs.

On occasion, I experienced something new. Lori called me for an appointment, saying, "I need to transition to male." I said, "Okay," and we set up the appointment. But when Lori walked into my office saying, "I'm trans," I had the immediate and disconcerting thought, *No, you're not*.

And she wasn't. What emerged over a period of a few sessions was a discontent with the narrowness of the female role to which she'd been raised. Her mother had raised her to be feminine, to look to a man for self-completion. Lori rebelled internally, finally deciding through convoluted existential logic that if she transitioned to male, she'd be out from under her mother's expectations of her as a woman.

Problem is… Lori wasn't trans. I saw that, felt that, from the moment we met. For the first, and perhaps the only, time, I didn't agree with a client's self-definition. And I never said that to Lori! I got her talking about her mother, brought her rebellious discontent to the surface, and helped Lori draw her own conclusion about what was right for her. Which wasn't transition.

This experience brought to the forefront the idea that I did, indeed, have a sense of what gender "felt" like in a client. I have never been able to pinpoint exactly what this instinct is based on—an aura, a sense of self, a presence—I only know that I relied on my instincts heavily in my work with trans people and their families.

This didn't mean verbalizing what my instincts were telling me. Therapy isn't the same as giving advice. At the heart of my work with clients was the goal of helping them tune in to their own instincts. Only by taking seriously their own sense of self, their own presence, would they be able to know they were making the best decisions for themselves regarding their identity and what to do about it.

My Own Lack of Therapy

Occasionally, a client would call for an appointment who was ahead of me in transition. Wayne called me to process through how to tell a woman who "really mattered" that he was a transman. I was awestruck to learn he was *32 years* into transition. I was still in high school when he started taking hormones. I'd never met anyone that far along and felt that I was only barely helpful to him; I should be sitting at his feet absorbing wisdom.

This is the kind of dilemma that would be great fodder for a therapy session of my own. In establishing myself as the local expert and teacher on all things trans, I found myself faced with a conundrum. If a local therapist knew enough about trans issues to be helpful to me, it was quite likely they'd learned it from me, by taking a class or consulting with me. If we didn't already know each other, that guaranteed they didn't know enough about trans issues to be useful to me. Where else would they have acquired the requisite knowledge? What I was teaching in my CE classes was an entirely new way of looking at the therapist's role in transition, a new view of trans identity.

This dilemma would no longer hold true today. These days, far more Portland therapists are trans-knowledgeable and have moved here from other places. They wouldn't already have known me. And online therapy would be available to me today. At that time, however, I was ahead of my own field and had no one I could turn to for my own therapy.

Trans-therapist vs. Cis-therapist

I never doubted how right I'd been to advertise myself as transtherapist.com. My clients relaxed into telling me their story without hesitation or reserve, believing before they'd met me that I wouldn't be judgmental, negative, doubting, or any of the other reactions they expected from the cisgender world. Many had encountered such reactions from previous therapists (as I had myself some years before), only willing to try therapy again because they knew I was a trans therapist.

Therefore, I was quite taken aback to encounter a client whose reserve and distrust were palpable. I'll call her "Janey," a transwoman who had yet to begin any part of her transition process other than facing the need.

From the moment Janey entered my office, I felt at sea, unable to understand her reserve. Something was clearly going on here that I wasn't getting. In asking about her reasons for seeking me out, she said a trans friend had given her my phone number. Her entire demeanor was one of justifying herself to me. Initially, I wondered if this was because I had transitioned in the opposite direction, but that didn't feel quite right.

On occasion, I had bolts out of the blue in a client session, cosmic interventions that I recognized as "Truth." In Janey's case, the bolt hit me with a shock: "The friend who recommended that you call me, did your friend tell you that I'm trans myself?"

The change in Janey's demeanor was night and day. "Really??? No, I had no idea!" And her story poured forth, all reserve gone and forgotten. If I'd ever questioned my decision to be out as a trans therapist, that session would have laid all doubts to rest.

In that situation, my identity was a positive intervention unto itself. And how many trans therapists are there? Most trans clients are going to be working with cisgender therapists, some of whom question, "How can a cisgender therapist be helpful to a trans client, never having undergone transition themselves? Wouldn't trans clients automatically be better served by a trans therapist?"

I point out several things to cisgender therapists.

> First, no therapist shares all identities with a client. We might both be trans, and we might differ in every other way possible: race, ethnicity, religion, age, gender assigned at birth, etc. Some of those identities might feel crucial to a client to have in common with their therapist.
>
> Second, the therapeutic alliance is a connection between therapist and client that transcends identities. There have been some trans clients I just didn't "click" with, who went on to work with other (cisgender) therapists that fit them better. And I worked very well with some clients who were cisgender.
>
> And finally, cisgender therapists have an advantage I would never have. How powerful is it for a trans client to tell their story to a cisgender therapist, sharing their hearts and being vulnerable, and receiving unqualified and congratulatory support? The client may have their first experience of wholehearted joy in their transition coming their way from someone who is cisgender. They *expected* me to be supportive. A therapist's cisgender identity can also be an intervention unto itself.

Giving and Receiving Support

In establishing my practice, I had called and emailed dozens of Portland therapists, setting up a network of colleagues. In addition to introducing myself, I was also assessing licensed therapists in order to find the right match for me as a clinical supervisor. Annik Larsen was the one, and she happily agreed to spend the next few years signing off on my client-contact hours and helping me navigate the space between graduate school therapist and licensed therapist.

I presented at professional conferences around the country, taught CE classes locally, and made myself available for consultation to therapists from anywhere. Clients from all over the region sought me out, from Boise, Idaho to Coos Bay, Oregon. Many had been quite isolated in their identity, certain there was no knowledgeable therapeutic support closer than Portland. When I first opened my practice, they were right, though as the years went by, therapists in other parts of Oregon began taking my classes, wanting to serve trans clients that might live nearby.

Since I knew where they all lived, I offered several times to introduce clients to each other, knowing they lived in the same general vicinity. Some ended up carpooling to Portland together for various appointments, forming lasting friendships. Such introductions were interventions in their own right, lessening isolation and loneliness.

In addition to my work with clients, I derived great satisfaction from the work I did with Shellie, Kathy, Jorge, Caitlyn, Joe, Mark, Laura—therapists from various parts of the U.S., consulting with me on a regular basis as they developed their clinical expertise in working with trans clients. For every therapist I helped with hours of consultation, I was benefitting hundreds of trans clients they would work with down the road.

Life was good, fulfilling, productive… Then, there was 2004.

Chapter Twenty

The First to Go

I spent the week between Christmas and New Years of 2003 with my mother. Susan and Rita were taking a much-needed vacation and traveled I forget where. I stayed with my mother, putting Susan's and Rita's minds at ease so they could enjoy their break from caregiving. My mother and I had some family over a few times, went out to dinner once (Little Shin Shin, of course), and generally had a nice visit.

The Beginning of the End
The day before I was to leave, my mother fell. She hobbled over to her bed. She lay down for a while, then tried to get up. At that point, it was apparent that something was broken. I called an ambulance and off she went to the hospital. I flew back to Portland the next day, shortly after Susan and Rita returned home.

As it turned out, my mother never left the hospital. On January 21, she had surgery on her broken hip. The doctors had hoped her hip would heal on its own, but it became apparent that surgery was unavoidable. We were all advised (including my mother) that given her general frailty, she probably wouldn't survive surgery. But she did, to all our relief.

I took myself off to a movie in celebration, seeing for a second time the newly released *Return of the King*. One of the last scenes in that movie shows Frodo shipbound beyond the horizon, forever leaving Middle Earth. I choked up, so thankful my mother wasn't taking that ship just yet.

Next day, I saw clients as usual. Just before my last client, I got a call from Susan. Our mother had ended up in surgery again, and, this time, her systems were shutting down. She wasn't going to survive.

I was numb as I hung up the phone. I knew what I had to do. I opened my office door and ushered my client in. I then said, "I'm really sorry. I can't see you today. I just found out that my mother is dying." A personal disclosure absolutely, and absolutely necessary in that situation.

I stayed with Susan and Rita as we planned our mother's memorial service. Both were religious women and had accumulated, over the years, various bulletins from memorial services they had attended. Meaningful poems, quotes, Bible verses that held great meaning for them were all in one folder called "Memorials." One piece in particular resonated with Susan and I both, and I read it at our mother's memorial service:

> I am standing upon the seashore.
> A ship, at my side,
> spreads her white sails to the moving breeze
> and starts for the blue ocean.
> She is an object of beauty and strength.
> I stand and watch her until, at length,
> she hangs like a speck
> of white cloud just where the sea and sky
> come to mingle with each other.
>
> Then, someone at my side says, "There, she is gone."
> Gone where?
> Gone from my sight. That is all.
> She is just as large in mast,
> Hull, and spar as she was when she left my side.
> And she is just as able to bear her load
> of living freight to her destined port.
> Her diminished size is in me—not in her.
>
> And, just at the moment
> when someone says, "There, she is gone,"
> there are other eyes watching her coming,
> and other voices ready to take up the glad shout,
> "Here she comes!"
>
> And that is dying.[40]

At the reception following her memorial, I was touched to find Confluence members had all signed a card and had a large floral arrangement delivered. My mother had been popular with Confluence.

---

[40] "Gone from My Sight," also known as the "Parable of Immortality" and "What is Dying," was written by the Reverand Luther F Beecher (1813-1903).

The Continuity of Chorus

There is only one thread of continuity that has been a continuous backdrop to my life since 1986, and that is GALA choruses. July of 2004 was the GALA choral festival, held in Montreal that year. What a perfect city to host GALA! In walking through the gayest part of town, the thought occurred to me that if you combined Pride time in the Castro in San Francisco with the French Quarter of New Orleans, you'd have a fair approximation of how it felt for GALA to be in Montreal. This marked my fifth GALA festival.

My first two GALA festivals (Seattle in 1989 and Denver in 1992), I had no idea of Reid's existence within me. At GALA in Tampa in 1996, I knew transition was my path, though I was still a singing member of the Portland Lesbian Choir. I was Reid, but still living a female-bodied existence, the transman inside invisible though no longer dormant. At GALA 2000 in San Jose, I would have been a tenor or bass had I been a member of a chorus, but I was bereft of chorus family. I was lonely enough from that experience to be fairly oblivious of how it felt to be perceived as a man at GALA rather than as a lesbian. At GALA 2004, in Montreal, I'd been a member of the Confluence bass section for three years.

And it was at Montreal GALA that the sociological implications of gender within the GALA choral movement were laid bare for me through visceral experience. For the first time, I was a member of a tight-knit chorus while being perceived as a man. As a lesbian attending GALA, I had been able to give the lesbian nod of acknowledgement to other women: "I see you, sister." An unspoken commiseration for being surrounded by gay men, who we perceived to be oblivious to our presence.

Now, however, no more lesbian nod of acknowledgement. Accepted by gay men as one of them when I wasn't one of them. Completely invisible as a transman. Though lesbians have historically been marginalized within the GALA choral movement, they aren't invisible. As part of Confluence, I did at least have the acceptance of my choral family. No invisibility there!

At Montreal GALA, I participated in the first trans festival chorus. Once we'd had our first festival chorus rehearsal, I had the opportunity to spot my fellow trans chorus members, giving a nod of acknowledgement when we encountered each other. No, more like a bear hug of gratitude for our mutual presence, now visible to each other.

Really? Again?

In September of 2004, I got a call from my nephew. "I'm calling to tell you that my mom is in the hospital. And there is more probability under the curve that she might not be coming home…"

At that point, I interrupted to say, "John, are you trying to tell me I need to come down there?"

Pause. "Yes."

Once again, I had to open my office door to a waiting client, to say, "I'm really sorry. I can't see you today. I just found out my sister is dying." Existential eeriness. This was the same client I'd had to tell months earlier, "My mother is dying."

Jan had always been my take-charge big sister. She took over the role of family matriarch sometime in the early 1990s, hosting all-family gatherings and the like. To learn in 2003 that she had cancer was a shock, and she continued to downplay it until her condition was so serious that she could no longer keep the rest of the family out of that particular loop.

I stayed with my niece, Lisa. She went to the store after picking me up at the airport, leaving me alone in the house. As I unpacked my suitcase, I heard the phone ring, the answering machine picked up, and Jere's voice informed us that Jan had died.

I sat on the edge of the bed and cried. My beautiful, brave big sister. Later, Susan and I concluded that Jan had held off her decline long enough that she didn't pre-decease our mother.

Once again, at Jan's memorial, I read:

> I am standing upon the seashore.
> A ship, at my side,
> spreads her white sails to the moving breeze
> and starts for the blue ocean.
> She is an object of beauty and strength.
> I stand and watch her until, at length,
> she hangs like a speck
> of white cloud just where the sea and sky
> come to mingle with each other.
>
> Then, someone at my side says, "There, she is gone."
> Gone where?
> Gone from my sight. That is all.

> She is just as large in mast,
> Hull, and spar as she was when she left my side.
> And she is just as able to bear her load
> of living freight to her destined port.
> Her diminished size is in me—not in her.
>
> And, just at the moment
> when someone says, "There, she is gone,"
> there are other eyes watching her coming,
> and other voices ready to take up the glad shout,
> "Here she comes!"
>
> And that is dying.[41]

A Lonely Season

Jan and my mom were the social glue that held our family together. Both dying in the same year resulted in no holiday gatherings in 2004. Even when I couldn't attend, I always had an awareness in the back of my mind that my Bay Area family were together on Thanksgiving. Not this year. No holiday gathering in December.

Confluence was on break after our December concert. More from habit than necessity, I took a week off around Christmas time. But to what purpose? Christmas Eve was intensely lonely that year. It was on this day that my entire family would gather, during my childhood at our house, and as my mother aged, at Jan's house.

I didn't call friends. Sympathy would abound. If I went to someone's house, I would be surrounded by their loving embrace of each other, their pleasure in exchanging gifts, perhaps their joy in the season. And I would be grieving, out of step, and bringing a grim reality into their happy holiday.

For some reason, unbeknownst to me, I wanted to go to church. The only sense I could make of this was that nothing else was bringing me any solace or comfort. I knew some people get this from church. Maybe, there's some small chance, it might work for me. I went to a Unitarian service in downtown Portland on Christmas Eve. And got about as little out of it as I expected. Oh well. It had been a long shot.

---

[41] See fn. 37.

Chapter Twenty-One

New Directions

My mother was 86 when she died. Frail. Poor eyesight. Bad balance. A slow decline to a mercifully sudden death. Jan, however! She died at 62. She'd had in mind books to write. Poetry to share with the world. Travels to far-flung places post-retirement. Instead, she retired into cancer.

Get on it!
Prior to 2004, January 22 and September 15 held no more significance to me than any other day of the year. Now, they are family death anniversaries. It occurred to me after Jan died that some given day of the year would, one day, be the anniversary of my death.

I was galvanized: "I'd better not let fate catch up with me before I've said what I've got to say!" By that time, I'd worked with over 200 clients and was some nine years into my own transition. I could count on the fingers of one hand the number of clients who weren't dealing with some form of trans issue, either from personal identity or from a partner or family perspective. I had a lot to say about the subject, and it was time to say it.

I had a head start. All those professional newsletters provided me with chapter outlines. A developmental model of trans identity. Parallels between addiction recovery and transition. How young is too young to transition? Partners. Religion. Work. School.

I finished *Transition and Beyond* in 2005, then tried to find a publisher. One after another turned me down. One said, "We've already published a book just like this." The title was *Just Add Hormones,* and I thought, *Some other therapist beat me to it!* Then, I read the book. It was a transman's autobiography. He wasn't a therapist at all. I realized what the publisher really meant was, "We've published a trans book this year, therefore, we've filled that slot." I was in despair, wondering how I'd get my book out there.

A friend suggested a publisher she knew. One thing led to another, and the first edition was produced! The publisher had kept me out of the production loop. She was used to being micromanaged by authors who had no idea about book production. However, I knew a lot about book design, typesetting, and book production. Typos leap off the page at me. I lost faith in my publisher when she handed me four books hot off the press, tied with a ribbon and bow and, from six feet away, I saw my name misspelled on the spine of the book.

To this day, one of my pinochle playing friends, a fellow therapist, calls me Dr. Vandergurgle, poking fun at my name being spelled, for the first, last, and only time "Vandergurgh." After that debacle, I decided that since I could do better, I should take over publishing my own books.[42]

Transition and Beyond was well received, the first book about trans issues to be written by a trans therapist. Non-pathologizing, addressing transition as a process that changes everything, and addressing the nature of the changes as I'd observed them, both personally and through working with so many trans clients.

As I wrote, I'd had four people metaphorically looking over my shoulder, reading and learning along: my mother, my best friend from PLC days, a potential trans client, and a well-meaning therapist. I dedicated the book to my mother and to my sister, Jan. I'd written the book I wished had been available to me (and my therapists) when I transitioned.

Upping the Ante

Despite my mother dying, despite Jan dying, I never lost my sense of inner peace and equilibrium. Nearly ten years into transition at this point, I was still basking in the contentment of my own centeredness. I have a shelf full of journals from the 1980s, full of angst over one woman or another, the bottom-line issue underlying everything being, "When am I going to find the right relationship that will make me okay?" And now, I had—my relationship with myself.

In September of 2007, Confluence returned from summer break. The usual excitement, seeing my chorus family after two months of not. And then, she walked into the room. From the moment I saw Cristina, I knew she was "The One," despite the fact that she looked for all the world like a Mennonite when she walked into our rehearsal. If my fellow chorister, Clark, hadn't greeted her, I would have thought she'd wandered in by

---

[42] This book is my first to be published not by me. I don't have the bandwidth at this point in my life to do more than write a book! And now, there are publishers out there willing and eager to publish trans authors.

mistake. Long dark dress, head covering, long sleeves, clutching a folder across her chest. She looked so uncomfortable.[43] And she was "The One."

As Cristina recalls it: "Clark pointed people out to me helpfully, so I could get to know everyone more quickly. He pointed to you and said, 'That's Reid. He's trans.' And I thought to myself, 'What's that???' I had no idea what he was talking about. All I saw was this cute bass."

Feeling quite whole and content with myself, I wasn't looking at all, and here, out of the clear blue, was this Mennonite. Well, not Mennonite. Orthodox Christian. Devout. Orthodox.

Cristina had joined Confluence to learn to sing better, so she would be a better singer in her church choir. She had gone to an Orthodox church music conference, and one workshop facilitator had said that singers who want to learn to sing better would do well to join a community chorus. Church choirs were of necessity focused on what was to be sung next service and spent no time focusing on *how* to sing.

Cristina knew her co-worker, Clark, sang in a community chorus, so she asked him when Confluence rehearsed—Sunday afternoons, her only free time. I was to learn later that she spent upwards of 20 hours each week in church, in addition to working full-time.

She asked Clark for the rehearsal address, fully intending to join. Clark knew she was Orthodox, so said cautiously, "We sing about gay and lesbian issues. Is that okay?"

Mystified by the question, Cristina said, "Why wouldn't it be?" The Orthodox perspective on life, the universe, and everything is conservative, but it is so not conservative Protestant!

Cristina joined the soprano section of Confluence that fall, and we spent the next two months eying each other. She lived in Corvallis, and I lived in Portland, over seventy miles apart, so we had no opportunity to easily see each other outside of rehearsal without considerable orchestration on both our parts. We both carpooled to rehearsal from opposite directions, so couldn't even meet privately before or after rehearsal.

By early December, we had been circling and dancing around our attraction sufficiently that I was pretty certain our feelings were mutual.

---

[43] Cristina later told me her discomfort had nothing to do with joining an LGBT chorus, or with the fact that she knew only one person in a roomful of people joyfully hugging after two months apart. Her discomfort had to do with entering a Unitarian church. I had much to learn about Orthodoxy.

Pretty certain. Trying to get her point across, Cristina wore a nametag at a holiday party that year, one at which Confluence had been invited to perform, that said KISStina. I took it that the hint was aimed at me. We managed to circle around each other sufficiently to align for a coffee date in early January.

Arrrrgggggghhhhhh!
    Cristina went to visit her sister in Virginia for two weeks after Confluence's December concert, and I was on pins and needles awaiting her return. Our coffee date was set for January 4.[44]

    I was pretty sure our feelings were mutual. Pretty sure. I had dinner with a friend from Confluence over the December break from chorus. I told her of my feelings for Cristina, and she said, "Oh, but I think she's straight!" Rather offended, I responded, "I certainly hope so!" Which took her aback considerably.

    My friend's remark intensified my anxiety. Though I had been happily content to be single, whole unto myself, now that a relationship might be in the offing, I felt like a teenager in love for the first time.

    And from a transition perspective, that's exactly what was going on. Through beginning hormones, through my school adventures at PSU, and then on to grad school, through building my therapy practice, establishing myself as a trans therapist, writing my first book, through all that time, contentedly single, I never so much as went on a date. Reid had never been in love.

    While Cristina was in Virginia, I tried to do my homework, looking up Orthodoxy on the internet. I wasn't raised in a religion. My family was agnostic. My ignorance was complete. I found a website where there was passionate argument whether the sign of the cross should be made with two fingers rather than three. I didn't understand in the least what the problem was!

    I didn't understand what made this different from any other Christian religion, but clearly it was. I felt very much out of my depth, and a bit desperate. How could this possibly work???

---

[44] The 4th of every month is now our monthaversary.

We met at Peet's Coffee,[45] near my apartment. The place has since been remodeled, yet still, every time I go into Peet's, I glance over toward the window where we sat on that first date. For that is what it was.

We talked for some hours, then Cristina went off to Corvallis. She had come to see me directly from the Portland airport upon returning from Virginia. We arranged to get together a few days later for dinner at a restaurant across the street from Peet's.

I was floating on air as I walked home. Yes. It was all true.

---

[45] In early 2023, I learned that this location had been a lesbian bar for a year or so back in the early 1980s. With great amusement, I told Cristina our first date had been at a lesbian bar.

Chapter Twenty-Two

The First Relationship

Over dinner at McMenamin's, we began talking more earnestly. Cristina told me that she had had deep conversations with herself, boiling down to, "Would I give up my religion for love?" I was quite taken aback. Talking like this on our second date??? But, meeting her where she was, I said, "Would I convert to Orthodoxy for love?" For that had been on my mind.

I was to learn later that Cristina had asked her priest for a blessing to sing in Confluence. Sure, no problem. But a blessing to date me? A transman? No. Orthodox people are discouraged from dating anyone they aren't eligible to marry, as it would lead to either relationship or religious problems down the road. Her priest determined that a transman wasn't a candidate for marriage.[46] So, don't date him.

The root of Cristina's question, "Would I give up my religion for love"? She had already had to ask and answer that question before she kept that second date, based on the priest saying, "No."

She ignored my question, "Would I convert to Orthodoxy for love?" Certainly, my not being Orthodox was a sticking point in dating me, but not a deal-breaker as I could eventually convert. My being a transman led to her decision point, and she chose me, knowing it would eventually, inevitably, lead her away from the religion she so loved.

This date took place on a Monday evening in early January. As we ate, large numbers of men started entering the restaurant, obviously a group that knew each other well. With a bit of a shock, I recognized some of them. We were being joined by the Portland Gay Men's Chorus. One of them also sang in Confluence and, recognizing us, came over to our table. Daniel looked from me to Cristina and back again, and then said, "Are you two on a *date???*"

Busted! Our dinner date had inadvertently coincided with Chorus Night Out, a PGMC tradition after the first rehearsal of each month. Never having

---

[46] Transition is far too new a process for Orthodoxy to have accepted it as identity actualization, therefore, ours was seen as a lesbian relationship.

been to a PGMC rehearsal, I had never heard of Chorus Night Out, and didn't even know they rehearsed in my neighborhood.

And then, there was Nick…

Nick fell into my life at about the same time as my first date with Cristina. Our first conversation, Nick calling Reid the therapist:

"Hello, this is Reid."

"Hi, I'm looking for a doctor referral. I need to renew my hormone prescription."

"Okay, whereabouts do you live?"

"Ummm… I'm outside Corvallis. But I probably have to come to Portland for this. I need a doctor who'll write me the prescription without putting in my chart why I need it."

That got my attention. No one had ever made that particular request before. During the course of our conversation, it emerged that Nick had started taking hormones the year I was born. *1955.* I referred him to Dr. Sara Becker, a transwoman physician who had begun transition while I was away at grad school. I knew that if any doctor would be willing to accede to his request for identity anonymity, it would be someone who was also trans.

That was the easy part. Harder was to let it go at that, and as we talked further, I worked the conversation around to asking if I could interview him. His journey would be lost to history otherwise. We set a date, and he gave me detailed directions to his rural home. I could tell he was nervous, though the extent of why only emerged when I heard his story. Then I understood that the only reason he agreed to meet me at all was because I was also trans.

In mid-January, I drove to Nick's place, only making a few wrong turns as I navigated completely rural Oregon about thirty miles outside of Corvallis.

He was clearly nervous, and I understood why when he said, "You're the second transsexual I've ever met face-to-face that I know of, and I'm not sure the other one counts cuz we never talked about it at all. I've had to put a lot of thought into it to remember anything about that time in my life."

I recorded his story, then drove into Corvallis to spend an afternoon with Cristina, our first concentrated block of time alone together.

I have no idea what Nick said that day, and I have no idea what Cristina said that day. The content didn't matter (good thing that I recorded Nick), only the lasting impact. Nick gave me the backstory about transition in its infancy. Cristina gave me assurance that she was my future.

> Be patient toward all that is unresolved in your heart
> and to try to love the questions themselves
> like locked rooms, like books written in a foreign tongue.
> Do not now strive to uncover answers,
> which cannot be given you
> because you have not been able to live them.
> And the point is to live everything.
> Live the questions for now.
> Perhaps then you will gradually, without noticing it,
> live along some distant day into the answer
> ~Rainier Maria Rilke[47]

Religion to the Fore

Cristina moved in with me in the spring of 2008. As our relationship continued to develop, I felt increasingly at sea regarding religion, clearly the most important consideration for Cristina. My attitude at the time was, *Oh, that religion isn't welcoming and affirming? Oh, that religion won't accept our relationship? Well, let's just find one that will. There are plenty from which to choose!*

We tried different variations of Protestant services, choosing from among the many welcoming and affirming congregations Portland has to offer. UCC. Episcopal. Methodist. Lutheran. I didn't have any kind of spiritual experience in any service, except at one Episcopal church. For the most part, I was bored.

The one service we didn't attend was Unitarian. Not believing in the trinity at all was a deal breaker as far as Cristina was concerned and was the reason she was uncomfortable that Confluence rehearsed in a Unitarian church. She would have felt more comfortable in an entirely secular space.

We then went to MCC[48], "the gay church." While neither of us had a spiritual experience, we continued to attend MCC services for a year or so. MCC was a placeholder church as we sorted and sifted through existential confusion.

---

[47] Written in a letter to Franz Xaver Kappus, a 19-year-old officer cadet and aspiring poet, on July 16, 1903, https://www.mindfulnessassociation.net/words-of-wonder/be-patient-toward-all-reiner-maria-rilke/.

[48] Metropolitan Community Church, was founded in the mid-1960s as a haven for LGBT folks, who were not welcome in any Christian denomination at that time.

In 2009, our MCC minister was delighted to perform our wedding ceremony. Nathan had to look up the paperwork. He told us, "I've never performed a *legal* wedding before!"

As Cristina put it, "I didn't think I could take being married in a Protestant service, but I could reconcile myself to being married in the gay church."

Off and on, we attended various Orthodox services, especially on the high holy days. This was difficult for Cristina, reminding her of what she'd left behind in choosing me. She grieved her religion intensely. She was radiant during Orthodox services, clearly tapping into a fundamental power that had eluded me.

And yet, I was astonished to find I felt powerful spiritual experiences during Orthodox services, something I never felt in any other worship service, though Episcopal came close. Cristina took for granted an experience I'd never felt before.

Still on the Path

Eventually concluding that Protestant services just weren't doing it for either of us, we began attending Orthodox services regularly, while Cristina eagerly educated me during the week about the rhythm of living an Orthodox life. This is one tradition that centers daily life around a rhythm of worship that informs all aspects of life. This is not a two-hour-a-week-on-Sunday kind of religion.

And yet, despite the spiritual experience I had in services, I couldn't give my heart, for I knew it would be broken. This *wasn't* among the welcoming and affirming traditions. Welcome though we were to attend services, our relationship would be a deal-breaker for the church if I officially converted. Our marriage would not be recognized.

That wouldn't mean we'd be asked to leave or be made to feel unwelcome. We had become close friends with some fellow congregants. Judy, in particular, was a good friend, a fellow therapist who attended one of my CE classes. No, we would be welcome at services, but if we were Orthodox in good standing, we would be living as brother and sister rather than husband and wife. Without being in good standing, we wouldn't be able to take communion or sing in the church choir, for instance. We never took communion during the years we attended services at Holy Annunciation.

When I attended my first Orthodox service, the power of the Protestant Reformation was brought home to me. I felt I was stepping back 2,000 years and 5,000 miles from Portland each time I attended an Orthodox service.

And I loved it! I loved that the service was almost entirely sung, not spoken. I loved that there was no sermon tying religion to politics, no reference to current events. The whole service was geared toward making parishioners look inward, connect the spiritual lesson to their own lives, to become their best selves as a result. It was never about judging others, nor about judging ourselves in a guilt-ridden sense. Self-reflection, self-examination, was the goal.

Only once in the years we attended Orthodox services did I ever hear Father Matthew make any reference to a current event. At the Sunday service on June 13, 2016, he said, "You probably heard on the news that there was a mass shooting in a gay nightclub in Orlando last night. No matter who was in that nightclub, that was wrong. There can never be any justification."

I was so gratified he said that overtly. I had already discerned, through pretty good gaydar, that there were several gay men who were devout members of our congregation. And I had talked with Father Matthew extensively myself when we first began attending Orthodox services. I have never been one to be comfortable with the assumption of cisgender identity, and I wanted him to know me. I gave him a copy of *Transition and Beyond*.

He told me, "If it were up to me, you are a man, you and Cristina are married in my eyes. But it's not up to me."

I'm ahead of myself here...

Conservative Isn't Monolithic

As we got to know each other, Cristina told me she had converted to Orthodoxy in the late 1980s, and the one thing that gave her pause was that it wasn't a welcoming and affirming religion. She had a number of friends who were gay or lesbian. Little did she know that this issue would one day be of personal relevance to her.

I came to discern between conservative religions. As Cristina explained to me, within her religion, it was a more heinous sin to discriminate against someone based on race than it was to be gay. According to Orthodoxy, being gay was between you and God, and not anything that should involve others.

Further, *being* gay wasn't the issue. Acting on being gay, being sexual, was the issue. The only sex that was considered okay in Orthodoxy was that between husband and wife. Other forms of sex were considered sin, regardless of the gender of the partners. Being single, having sex outside your marriage, these were sins no more or less serious than having gay or lesbian sex. None of these were considered huge, big-deal sins, however. Discriminating based on race had real-world negative consequences for another person and, hence, was the more grievous sin.

Though I didn't agree, I did see the distinction between the Orthodox view and that of Westboro Baptist Church.[49] You will find an Orthodox person praying for the soul of someone who is in a gay relationship, and you will not find an Orthodox person picketing the funeral of someone who was gay, as Westboro Baptist might.

Cristina put it well: "Orthodoxy isn't welcoming and affirming—yet. Give it 500 years. That's the church's biggest strength as well as its biggest weakness, the slowness of change. On the one hand, it doesn't change as fast as it should on issues where it's right to change. On the other hand, when it *does* change it's because it's lived its way into the answer. No change is at the whim of politics of the day."

Looking at it from a therapist's perspective, Orthodoxy will change at the pace of families, which is the slowest pace of social change. The point at which a clear majority of families in Orthodox countries accept their gay and lesbian children's relationships as valid is the point at which the Orthodox church will be performing same-sex weddings.

This is one church that sees change as not only coming from the top down, God, on high, making His will known to the people via a priest or minister. God's will can also make its way known through the people, from the bottom up, so to speak. As I said…very different from Protestant (or Catholic) religions.

On Hiatus

In the fall of 2016, we stopped going to church at all. We'd reached a crossroads: Was I going to convert to Orthodoxy, or not? I couldn't quite go there. When I claim membership in anything, I do so with my whole heart and being, and I just couldn't claim Orthodoxy because I knew it could not accept me precisely as I am, as a transman. I missed it intensely, while

---

[49] Westboro Baptist Church is located in Topeka, Kansas. Their *only* mission in life is opposing homosexuality. They travel around the country picketing various venues and events that seem to support LGBT people.

Cristina grieved with an intensity she feels to this day and perhaps always will.

    And yet, she has never once said, "I'm sorry I chose you instead."

Her love reminds me of a poem by Hafiz, a 14th century Persian poet.

> Even after all this time
> the Sun never says to the Moon: "You owe me."
> Look what happens with a love like that—
> it lights the whole sky.
> ~Hafiz, written approx. 1350

Chapter Twenty-Three

A New Equilibrium

After seven years of giving my all to Confluence, I was ready for more challenge musically. After seeing the Portland Gay Men's Chorus perform at GALA in Miami in 2008, Cristina suggested I join PGMC instead of Confluence.

My initial reaction was a kneejerk, "I can't do that!"

Cristina's mystified response, "Why not?" brought me up short.

"Huh…I didn't know why not. "

A New Chorus

I auditioned for PGMC in the fall of 2008. I wasn't nervous. PGMC's artistic director Bob Mensel sang in Confluence for several years, and I'd sung next to his powerful bass voice. Confluence only ever had six or seven basses, and Bob was 2/3 of them. I knew he would support my membership in PGMC. I'd proven myself to him in Confluence.

It's a big adjustment, switching choruses. From the family feeling of 50 voices in Confluence, with a membership spread across the entire LGBTQ+ acronym plus a number of straight singers as well, I joined a chorus of almost entirely cisgender gay men. Over 120 members at my first rehearsal. I knew a dozen or so from my PLC and Bridges days, and there were a few who also sang in Confluence. By and large, however, I'd never met any of them before.

PGMC now has an organized system of mentors who befriend new members, and two section reps per section. At the time I joined, there were no mentors and only one section rep per section. I felt thrown into the deep end of the pool without certain knowledge that I could swim. And I loved it! For me, the chorus was the right balance of camaraderie and musical excellence. I knew I wouldn't tire of this organization any time soon![50]

---

[50] In 2019, I passed a milestone. My membership in PGMC is the longest of any chorus of which I've been a member, including my original beloved Portland Lesbian Choir.

Settling into Change

After moving to Portland in 2008, Cristina looked for work. She had been working in the field of internet security for as long as there's been an internet. Her first job in Portland was a temporary contract at Nike. She kept searching for a permanent position, but jobs at her level don't come open often. In 2009, she was hired at Columbia Sportswear. We were both over the moon.

That year saw more change. Shortly after we married, Cristina's fifteen-year-old daughter decided she'd like to live with her mother and me. I'd never lived with a child before, and mid-adolescence was a challenging time to start. We navigated the challenges as a family. Maggie had her pet rats and loved Rikki and living in Portland. Maggie is an artist, with a dreamy temperament and a heart of gold. I felt honored that she joined the GSA at her high school, in honor of having a trans stepdad and a best friend who was bisexual.

In the spring of 2010, sadness. After ten years, my sweet companion, Rikki, developed kidney problems and died. Some months later, Cristina was passing by a pet store near our home. She saw that the Humane Society had brought several cats to the store that day with the intent of promoting pet adoption.

She came home saying, "We have to go get this cat. He looks depressed." We went over to the pet store, but the cats had gone back to the Humane Society for the day.

On a mission now, we drove to the Humane Society and asked after this cat. His paperwork said his name was Figaro, and he had been brought in some months before with his brother, Mr. Elvis. We intended to take them both, as the paperwork said they weren't supposed to be separated. However, no wonder Figaro was depressed: his brother had been adopted without him a month before. He was four years old. They had been together since birth.

We met Figaro in a small greeting room. He was a friendly, gentle giant of a Siamese cat, so well socialized that I knew there was a story here. How did a pure-bred Siamese and his brother end up in the Humane Society? In Figaro's case, I wasn't gifted with knowing the backstory, as I had been with Leon.

Cristina had the brilliant idea of asking, "Is there another cat in the same situation? Brought in as part of a bonded pair and weren't supposed to be separated, but now they are?"

Why yes. There was one other cat in that situation, named Winken. (I never could decide whether her bonded pair companion had been Blinken or Nod.) Figaro and Winken had never met before, but we brought them both home, hoping for the best.

Once out of his cat carrier, Figaro was not shy, happily understanding that he was homed once again. Winken promptly hid under the bed. We coaxed her out with cat treats provided to us by the Humane Society. Figaro had started to eat the treats when Winken emerged shyly. Figaro backed away from the treats to let her have them, and I thought, *This is going to work!*

I had lived with various combinations of cats over the years, most of whom stalked away from each other, tolerant of each other's presence but no more than that. We renamed Winken, deciding her name wasn't sufficiently proud for a cat. Of course, we named her Susanna, in keeping with Mozart's opera *The Marriage of Figaro*. The two quickly became inseparable, and I lived with a bonded pair for the first time.

Bolt Out of the Blue

In the midst of this happy family existence, my therapy practice was thriving, and I continued to attend conferences, presenting workshops, and doing book readings. At one conference, after a powerful question and answer session about my book, a bolt out of the blue entered my mind: *I became a therapist to write this book.*

Over the next few months, that thought grew in my mind. I found the therapy profession feeling increasingly isolating for me. The weight of all the stories I'd heard was taking its toll on me, despite the fact that my clients generally blossomed through transition. My own lack of therapy was increasingly problematic for me. I would have felt better about my work if I were part of a team. Had the OHSU Transgender Health Program or the Kaiser Gender Pathways program existed at that time, I would have found a way to work in a team setting rather than remaining in private practice.

I was part of an ongoing therapist consult group and had been for about five years. All of us worked with trans clients to some degree or other, though I was the only one whose practice focused entirely on trans clients and their families. We would talk about challenging clients (anonymously, of course), giving input and our different perspectives. Our monthly meetings were a joy to me, yet not enough to alleviate my isolation.

In the summer of 2009, with Cristina now employed at Columbia Sportswear and providing considerable income, I decided it was time to retire as a therapist to focus on writing and teaching. Given the nature of my work, I knew I'd have to give clients a lot of notice. Early transition is a time of such major upheaval and change, the last thing a client would need is to have to switch therapy support systems. I decided to give clients two years. However, I didn't tell them that. Rather, I stopped taking new clients. I didn't tell anyone (other than Cristina and my consult group) why.

In July of 2011, I told clients I would be closing my practice in six months. In October, I gave them a January date. In December, I told them they had thirty days in which to see me for a final appointment. In January of 2012, I was done.

Reinforcement for Leaving
In the week after my last client session, my relief in leaving the therapy profession was jarred when a former client (I'll call her Liz) informed me via email that she had lodged a complaint against me with the licensing board, based on my having not responded adequately to her feeling suicidal at the time I'd seen her. She felt lucky to be alive still.

I still remembered that last session with Liz, a day when I was feeling particularly isolated and overwhelmed by stories. I leaned against the door after she left, feeling I hadn't been useful to her. Part of the therapeutic alliance is the energetic effect client and therapist have on each other. Had I felt a better energy within myself, I might well have been more useful to her that day, possibly alleviating her suicidal feelings. I was so depleted emotionally that I didn't recognize her feelings for what they were.

I didn't do anything about it with the licensing board. Any resolution of the complaint was predicated on my remaining a therapist. My feeling, at the time, was that Liz's complaint reinforced why I was leaving the profession. In retrospect, it also reinforced why I needed my own therapist!

Shifting my Life
By the time I retired from my therapy career, Maggie was launched and living on her own, a student at the University of Oregon in Eugene. I became a househusband, rising every morning to make Cristina breakfast, and then lunch to take with her to work, kissing her off to work each day to earn our living. I cleaned house, took over all the cooking, shopped.

And I wrote. I was asked to write a commentary for Oxford Dictionaries on shifting gender terminology. I was commissioned to write an encyclopedia entry about working with trans clients. I was asked to write a book chapter for the first edition of *Trans Bodies, Trans Selves.* I was invited to write a number of book chapters, or to submit writings for anthologies. And I was a bit at sea about my own writing project. What's my next book about?

I was struck by something Helen Boyd once told me, that her first book *(My Husband Betty)* practically wrote itself because she needed to say it. The second book *(She's Not the Man I Married)* took more effort and was a bigger deal when it finally came together. My first book certainly wrote itself. Now what?

I thought to write about mid-transition issues, as no one had written much beyond the tumult of early transition. I talked my idea over with Cristina.

She said, "Is that it? Maybe you could contrast mid-transition with the experiences of older gay men and lesbians." Though that didn't seem like quite *it,* I did interview several older gay men and lesbians. I began gathering stories before I understood exactly what this new book was about.

With my days all my own, I started having lunch here and coffee there with various friends and colleagues, hoping someone would say something that would spark my second book. One day, over lunch with Stacey, it happened. A transwoman who worked at Q Center,[51] Stacey remarked casually, "Here I've been working at Q Center, and I've met all these different people. Every now and then, someone will say something that takes me completely by surprise, and I'll realize I just don't understand gay men!"

My second book crystallized in that moment.

Excitedly, I said to Stacey, "Why would you? You never were one!"

Journeys of Transformation was born in that moment. I had the temerity to try to explain that whole, big, long acronym to each other, knowing from personal experience of having lived several of those identities how little understanding there is across the gulf of L to G to B to T, etc.

I spent much of that next year writing, sometimes not leaving my computer all day beyond a reluctant dashing into the kitchen to make a PBJ

---

[51] Q Center is Portland's LGBTQ+ community center, https://www.pdxqcenter.org/.

for lunch. I put the call out to various friends and colleagues, seeking people across the acronym, across geography, across ages, races, religions, and ethnicities, gathering stories.

And I asked Nick, "Can I share your story with the world?"

Finally, a venue.

And Always, There was Nick…

I had recorded Nick in 2008 for posterity, not for a project. As Cristina and I settled into living together in the spring of that year, we talked more about Nick. It seemed to both of us that he was lonely and might welcome a visit. I called him and made the arrangements and thus began a routine of visiting monthly. We would call and get his grocery list, shop for him, get his favorite fast-food meal, and head over to his several acres of mountaintop. His dogs barked in joyful warning as we unfastened the gate. We spent several hours with Nick of a Sunday afternoon.

I told Nick's story in great detail in *Journeys of Transformation.*[52] But this is *my* story…

Nick was an irascible lonely old man. As a therapist, it was clear to me that his loneliness was entwined in his lifelong "just a man" existence. The only people he ever came out to were the few women with whom he'd formed sexual relationships.

All he ever said to them was, "I was supposed to be born a boy and that's why I have these scars on my chest and why my sexual equipment looks like it does."

Nick's internalized transphobia was complete. He had no practice coming out to cisgender people and experiencing support. His 1950s automatic assumption was that if anyone found out he was trans, they would reject or kill him. He could not understand why anyone would choose to live as a "transman" rather than as "just a man." I was an essential enigma to him. He so looked forward to our conversations yet couldn't fathom why I lived as I did.

Nick had a degenerative muscle disease, requiring a walker to get around his house. His wall calendar only had us on it. He spent most of his time watching television, ranting against Republican politics. Nick never

---

[52] Nick was still alive when I wrote *Journeys of Transformation.* I gave him the pseudonym "Joe." He died in 2017, and it has since seemed appropriate to use his real first name in subsequent writings.

quite knew what to make of us. Cristina and I talked of trans issues, lesbian and gay issues, as if it was the most normal thing in the world. He was existentially confused by Cristina, this devout Orthodox woman in love with a transman and not seeing the least bit wrong with me or our love. She loved me for who I am, not in spite of my identity. Nick adored her.

Though he wanted to be "just a man," he had so many questions for us about LGBTQ issues and identities, and derogatory comments in response. We never talked of anything else. When I joined PGMC a few months after our first visit, he had such difficulty wrapping his mind around a transman singing in the chorus. It was hard for him to believe that other Chorus members knew who I was and accepted me. And I wasn't even gay. When the first cisgender woman joined PGMC, his head exploded at the idea. He was speechless (a rarity!) when Cristina sang with PGMC as we traveled to New York City to sing *BraveSouls and Dreamers* for the tenth anniversary of 9/11.

When Caitlyn Jenner's transition was front-page news, Nick was beside himself with conflicted views. He recognized Bruce Jenner could never have transitioned privately. At the same time, he found it impossible to understand how Caitlyn could have lived within Bruce all those years, presenting such a happy, successful face to the public. He was incensed to learn Caitlyn was conservative in her views and deeply religious. Nick had, at one time, been religious himself but had turned his back on God after his wife divorced him some years before we met.

It would be more accurate to say Nick believed God had turned His back. Nick claimed to be an atheist, but Cristina and I both recognized the pain and anger behind his atheism. It's not that he didn't believe in God. He was *mad* at God. Mad because God had made him trans. Mad because he had this muscle disease. Just *mad*.

Over time, as we made the journey to his house each month, various of our friends learned of his existence.

Many a trans friend would say, awestruck to learn Nick had transitioned in the 1950s, "I want to meet him!"

I think they had in mind sitting at the feet of a guru, a font of trans wisdom. Ruminating on Nick's outspoken and judgmental irascibility, his deeply entrenched transphobia, his very odd ideas about gay men and lesbians, I would think to myself, *No, you really don't!*

One Sunday in 2015, we let ourselves in the back door as usual, corralling the excited dogs and calling out, "Hey, Nick, we're here!"

As we moved through the kitchen into the living room, a sight met our eyes that changed our relationship to Nick permanently. He was on the floor, looking simultaneously helpless, relieved, and scared. He was long past embarrassment. He had fallen over 24 hours earlier. Now, we were caregivers.

Part of the new equilibrium of our lives became weekly visits to Nick. Shopping. Bringing in his mail. Cooking so he would have leftovers. Laundry. Sweeping and vacuuming. Feeding the dogs. Bringing in huge bags of pellets to feed the woodstove.

Cristina and I would take turns at the chores, one of us visiting him while the other worked. We occasionally spent Saturday night at his house. Our weekends revolved around his care. The dogs were thrilled to have regular visitors. Given Nick's trans identity, he was adamant in his refusal to employ caregivers. *We* were his only option, as far as he was concerned.

The Rest of Our Life

Though we were central to Nick's life, his only contact with the outside world, we had full lives in Portland. Cristina enjoyed her work at Columbia Sportswear, and we became friends with some of her co-workers, all of whom were originally from various parts of India.

Through her co-workers, I was introduced to Indian cuisine, immediately embracing it with the thought, *Where has this been all my life!?* I began experimenting with cooking Indian food at home. I would send leftovers with Cristina to work, and she would test her lunch out on her co-workers. They would send advice home for me, suggesting tweaks to the dishes I'd made. When she came home with the response, "Just like mum!" I would know I had that recipe down.

The first time I made a curry dish, I scanned the list of ingredients, making sure I had everything I needed to hand. I was increasingly puzzled. *How can this be a curry dish when curry powder isn't listed as an ingredient?* I was a bit embarrassed that it took me some many seconds to consider: cumin, coriander, turmeric, ground chilies, these are the spices of curry powder. How typically American. I felt provincial.

The first time we had Rakesh and Nithu over for dinner, a couple who had lived and worked in the U.S. for nearly ten years, we were amazed (and honored) to learn they had never been to a non-Indian household for dinner. Nithu was quite skittish around Figaro, who insisted he was our ambassador, always the first to meet and greet visitors. Nithu had no idea what the boundaries were with a pet cat, which is not a thing where she grew up. Would a cat bite if petted? Does it like to be picked up? What does it mean if it rubs against your legs? Is this a sign of aggression or danger?

I contemplated this as I put the finishing touches on dinner. What if I were to visit a country where raccoons were pets? Or a mongoose? I would have no idea what the social boundaries would be with such animals.

Over dinner, the four of us had a wonderful discussion about cultural exchange and the beauty of learning from each other. In honor of cultural exchange, I hadn't made Indian food for our guests. Instead, I made them homemade macaroni and cheese, potato salad, and collard greens. Americana. And pecan pie for dessert.

Giving Back, Being Honored

In 2014, I was invited to join the board of PFLAG[53] Portland. I had always had a soft spot in my heart for PFLAG. Lon Mabon was the chief organizer of the Oregon Citizens Alliance's anti-gay ballot measures of the 1990s. He once said that the only organization the OCA had no answer for was PFLAG. There is no way to successfully challenge PFLAG on a platform of family values. To be invited to join the board was an honor, and I've been there ever since.

Not long after I joined PGMC in 2008, Bob encouraged me to consider submitting workshop proposals for the GALA Leadership Symposium, held every year in different cities in the US or Canada. GALA eagerly accepted my proposal for a workshop discussing how to best support trans singers in various kinds of GALA choruses—men's, women's, and mixed.

The 300 or so in attendance at the symposium were executive directors, board presidents, artistic directors, and various other staff and high-level volunteers within many different GALA choruses. I began attending the symposium regularly, always presenting one or two workshops about trans identity, later broadening my focus to workshops about intersectionality of identities. In addition to presenting workshops at the Leadership

---

[53] PFLAG used to stand for Parents, Families and Friends of Lesbians and Gays. In 2014, the national PFLAG board voted to change the name. The acronym PFLAG now *is* the name, but it doesn't stand for anything. This change reflected a recognition that the acronym has expanded far beyond the L and G that existed in the early 1970s when PFLAG first formed. Most of the parents that access PFLAG these days have trans or non-binary kids.

Symposium each year, I also began presenting similar workshops at the GALA choral festivals.

In the spring of 2016, Cristina and I spent a few vacation nights at a peaceful cabin up in the mountains. The first morning we were there, I took a walk for coffee. Waiting for my latte, I checked my email and came across one from Bob titled, "Something to share with you." I was completely unprepared for what I read and blurted out, "Oh. My. God!" into the quiet of the coffee shop.

Bob wrote: "PGMC, PLC, Bridging Voices[54], and Confluence united to nominate you for a GALA Legacy Award, and you have been selected to receive the Distinguished Services Award. This will be presented to you in Denver on Sunday, July 3 at 5:30 at the Legacy Awards reception!"

One GALA chorus or another has fed my soul since 1986, and to be recognized by GALA Choruses remains the most powerful honor I've ever experienced.

Cristina hadn't gone to the coffee shop with me. I went back to our cabin to share this exciting news with her, only to find that she'd known for some time! Bob had consulted her for details about my involvement in various choruses over the years.

---

[54] Bridging Voices is Portland's LGBT+ youth chorus. I was on the board as the organization was founded in 2013.

Chapter Twenty-Four

Out of Balance

In 2015, Cristina began experiencing odd symptoms that defy diagnosis to this day. Balance issues. Headaches that occasionally are migraines. Dizziness. Problems with depth perception and memory. Uncertain vision. Her cognitive and math abilities became suspect. At first, the symptoms were slight enough to nearly escape notice, more in the category of, "That was odd." She continued to work, but with increasing difficulty. One neurological test after another didn't result in diagnosis, but in elimination of one possibility after another.

She had several surgeries—kidney stones, gallstones, patching a minute hole in her inner ear. Everything seemed related in some way to calcium levels, but no one could figure out exactly how. Her symptoms gradually grew more severe. By 2016, she was home on long-term disability. She never did go back to work. Eventually, Columbia Sportswear was forced to let her go. They needed her job done, and she clearly wasn't going to be able to do it.

We had been living in a beautiful 1890s duplex, up eighteen stairs into an apartment with floor-to-ceiling windows all around. Cristina's disability was such that this particular apartment couldn't be more unsuitable. Eighteen stairs up and down, for someone with bad balance and poor depth perception? A recipe for disaster.

Thank You, Jan

In the fall of 2015, my nephew, John, sent out an email to the entire family. Jere, left a widower by Jan's 2004 death, would be entering hospice imminently, approaching the end of his life. John had taken on the task of emptying his parents' house and preparing it for sale. Among many items on offer were two vehicles—Jere's pick-up truck, and a Toyota Avalon that had been Jan's. I immediately put my hand up to claim the Avalon, responding to John's email within minutes of him sending it out.

I had to laugh, remembering back to Christmas of 2003. Jan had been furious with Jere because he had totaled her Avalon a few weeks earlier. Trying to make it up to her, he had bought her a brand-new Avalon with all the bells and whistles he could find. Heated leather seats. All the connectivity and sound systems available in a 2004 car. A car that I was now about to inherit, seldom driven since Jan's death.

To this point, Cristina and I had not owned a car, relying on Zipcar and Car2Go for transportation. With Cristina's increasing disability, however, we needed our own. And now, here was Jan, providing from beyond the grave.

All-family gatherings are no friend to introverts when it comes to forming relationships across extended family. If I'd seen my cousin, Dave, on the street, I would have recognized him, and yet I knew nothing about him. He was always in the woodwork at family gatherings. I put out the call to my family that I needed some transportation, flying into Oakland and from there heading up north of Sacramento to pick up Jan's car at their home. Cousin Dave offered to drive me.

On that drive, we became fast friends. It was on this drive that Dave informed me that my dad had been a master fisherman. On this drive, he told me of a close friend whose 20-something offspring was in the beginning stages of transition; I offered to send Dave a copy of *Transition and Beyond* for the family to use in navigating the process. We compared notes about our experiences of family. Before we knew it, we'd made the 90-minute drive. As I drove Jan's car back to Portland, I was thankful to have the family I do.

Recalibrating Life

In 2016, we moved to a beautiful apartment in a 55-and-older complex. One of its main attractions was wheelchair accessibility. I qualified for the apartment based on age, but it was Cristina who benefited from the accessibility. Through her work with various neurologists and physical therapists, we had acquired two walkers and a cane. I surfed the Internet and found a $50 used wheelchair. Though Cristina could walk, we wondered if she might have more independence wheeling around rather than expending all her energy trying to figure out where vertical was.

Our goal was to determine which mode of mobility suited her best when out and about—walker, cane, or wheelchair? The answer was apparent quickly. The wheelchair was it. Cristina uses her cane if we're heading to a crowded event, but for getting about on her own, the wheelchair is the vehicle of choice.

Our apartment complex was in a beautiful location a few hundred feet south of Portland. Trees all around. A nice view of Mt. Hood in the distance from our balcony. Our hilltop apartment building was so convoluted to navigate, we never locked our front door unless we were going to be gone for days. We met friends in the parking lot when they first visited, so difficult was our place to find.

Cristina had happily worked in the field of internet security ever since there was an internet, and this gradual shift into disability left her feeling at sea and purposeless in her life. Her feeling of purpose in life had been wrapped up in her career. "Who am I now?" is a question she has struggled with since her forced retirement into disability. She has taken classes here and there at one or another of our local colleges, alternating between studying music theory and Chinese. Yet, to this day, she has a feeling of continually living her way into the answer.

Her disability insurance eventually paid for a custom lightweight wheelchair, leaving her with the feeling that she had taken the training wheels off and was now driving a Ferrari. Nevertheless, we lived on a hilltop she could not navigate by herself.

She signed up for Lift service, our bus system's solution for people with disabilities. Making a reservation at least a day in advance, the Lift bus would come to pick her up and drop her off at her intended location, later bringing her home again. Either that, or I drop her down the hill at the nearest bus or light rail stop. No opportunity for spontaneity all on her own. No "all on her own" at all. She gave up her driver's license not long before our move and hasn't driven since.

The Clock Ticks

It was a hassle and a half to officially lay claim to Jan's car. Not exactly a hoarder, more of an accumulator, Jere had stashed and stored things in a fashion that defied interpretation; John hadn't been able to find the title to Jan's car.

Jere died not long after my taking possession of the car, unable to give any information about the whereabouts of the title. Sometime caregiver, sometime writer, sometime presenter and trainer, sometime chorus member, the last thing I needed was the hassle of trying to register an out-of-state car without title in hand.

I'm not one who deals well with bureaucracy at the best of times. I spent some phone hours on hold with the state of California. I spent some time at the Oregon DMV. No one quite knew what to do with my situation. I finally gave up and drove around with California disability plates. Which expired. I drove around still, holding my metaphorical breath, parking and driving *very* carefully to avoid tickets of any kind.

In the summer of 2018, a year after the plates expired, one of the license plates was stolen while the car was parked in our apartment-assigned spot. I was rocked with anxiety. During Pride season that year, I had put a postcard advertising PGMC's concert on our communal bulletin board, next to the apartment complex mailboxes. Several of our neighbors were long-time chorus supporters. The day after I put the postcard up, I found it in our mail recycle bin, torn in half. When Jan's license plate was stolen the next day, I immediately connected the two incidents and wondered if we were experiencing anti-LGBT harassment. Crime of any kind was virtually non-existent in this apartment complex.

On the other hand, even expired and out-of-state, a disability license plate might be worth something to someone and the two incidents might have no connection at all. I continued to drive with the remaining plate. I was done in when that plate, also, was stolen. I realized the time had come. I had run out of license plates.

The Kindness of Strangers

I put some thought into how to handle the situation. Clearly, I needed to go to the California DMV in person. My first thought was the Bay Area. However, an urban, busy DMV? An extremely non-standard problem? Seemed a recipe for frustrated disaster to me.

I decided I'd do better at a small-town DMV, and chose Yreka, the first town over the California border from Oregon. I called and made an appointment. I made a hotel reservation, sure and certain I wasn't making this five-hour drive down and back in one day. I went to the Oregon DMV and acquired a temporary permit to drive the car, the kind of thing ordinarily issued for new cars that have yet to be registered. I taped it inside the rear window for the drive south.

John had been unhappy that the car situation was unresolved, the last unresolved remnant of his parents' life. Completely distrustful of bureaucracy, he put together a huge file of documentation of the car's history, proving beyond a shred of doubt my right to the car. He included notarized death certificates for both of his parents, as well as any paperwork Jere had ever signed related to this car. As the executor of the estate, John wrote a letter stating in no uncertain terms that I owned this car. He had that notarized as well.

I walked into the Yreka DMV armed to the teeth with paper. I threw myself on the mercy of the woman behind the counter. That saint, I wish I remembered her name.[55] She barely glanced at the mound of paperwork I'd brought. She spent 45 minutes jumping through computer hoops for me.

She'd never encountered this situation before. Several times, she consulted the other clerk staffing the DMV that day. At one point, she explained to me, "We're trying various options, hoping when we click 'ok' that the next screen isn't grayed out as 'not an option.'"

Fifteen minutes in, she came over to me and said, "Look me in the eye and tell me this car has been 'garaged' in California. Not driven in California." Which, quite truthfully, I was able to tell her.

As she worked, we chatted. She and her husband had bought a boat via Craigslist a few years earlier, from someone in the same town where Cristina and I lived. We talked lakes and boating. We talked about her living near Lake Shasta. Of my family renting houseboats for a week one summer when I was a teenager, puttering around Lake Shasta.

Finally, she went over to the printer and came back to hand me two pieces of paper. A car title and a California registration for one Toyota Avalon. Both in my name. I nearly cried. Because the car hadn't been driven in California since Jere had died, the fact that the registration had expired carried no penalty. Instead of $585, my total cost was $76.

As I was heading out the door, she called after me, "I'm sorry for the loss of your family."

Oh Nick...

Adding to the complication of our lives, we received a phone call that Nick had fallen again, breaking his leg. He was in the hospital awaiting surgery. This time, he had fortunately fallen near enough to his landline phone to be able to call for help.

We dropped everything and made the 75-mile drive, only to find visiting hours over for the day. We spent the night at his place, feeding his dogs. The next day was spent tracking him down. Surgery complete, he had been transported to a rehab facility in the next town over. Midafternoon, we were face-to-face. Desperately mouthing the words so his roommate wouldn't hear, Nick silently screamed, "Get. Me. Out. Of. Here."

---

[55] I may not remember her name now, but I did fill out a form I picked up on my way out of the DMV, a "How Did We Do?" opportunity in which I gave her a glowing review.

But we couldn't. Physically unstable and feeble under the best of circumstances, living alone on a mountaintop ten miles from the nearest hamlet, here he was with his casted leg suspended above a hospital bed. With a roommate. In a small-town rehab facility.

I read the poster on every other wall of the facility: "Having a problem? Contact an Ombudsman. An Ombudsman is an advocate who serves to protect the civil and human rights of elderly and disabled residents living in long term care facilities."

Did the Ombudsman know a damn thing about trans health care? How to help the trans person who doesn't want anyone to know he's trans? Nick had just had surgery on his broken leg. How could the hospital staff have *not* noticed that he's trans? Had they noted the information in his chart? Did everyone in this facility already know he's trans? And what if they didn't by some chance know, and I told them by asking questions? What's our move here????

Cristina and I talked it over in the car, the only place we could be certain of a private conversation. We decided our move was to visit Nick regularly. I was reminded of a family story about my Aunt Janey in Missouri. In the mid-1990s, she developed Alzheimer's and spent her last years in a memory care facility. My Uncle Jim visited her faithfully several times a week until her death some years later.

Some time after, the facility made the local news. There had been a widespread pattern of elder abuse occurring over a period of years, spanning the time of Aunt Janey's residence. My family was shocked and surprised. Aunt Janey had always seemed quite content and well-looked-after. Then, we realized that, of course, she wasn't abused. She had regular visits from her husband, who most certainly would have noticed any form of abuse.

Taking our cue from this family experience, Cristina and I visited Nick several times a week during his two-month stay in rehab. We were there when he was transported back home, making sure his hospital bed was in place, his dogs looked after. We visited regularly as he began a program of home health care with visiting nurses. He no longer had a choice about that.

We visited until he made it clear that he didn't want visitors, didn't want anyone to witness his helplessness, his sense of degradation. Our last phone call, as he turned down our visit, we told him to call us when he was up for a visit. Nick died in late 2017, two months after we'd last seen him.

Cristina and I had a conflicted mourning process. Thank God, he's out of pain, out of his misery, which was considerable. Thank God, we had him in our lives, and thank God, he had us in his.

Nick lived at a time when transition was only barely possible, for the narrow few who had sufficient access to services and came across the right information at the right time. He may have been lonely in his "just a man" existence, his end of life may have been miserable, but it's sure and certain he would have committed suicide in the 1950s had he not transitioned.

Here's to a pioneer.

Chapter Twenty-Five

And Then There was China

In 2016, the Chorus announced to members that an exciting opportunity was on the horizon. In September of 2018, PGMC would be the first LGBT chorus to tour mainland China. There was no question that I would go!

I took a class on China's history at a local community college, free to me because I was over 62. I hung out with some of our friends who had emigrated from China. And my own transition process told me that no matter how often I talked with people from China, no matter how many books I read, nothing could fully prepare me for the reality.

The trip became real to me in March of 2018, as the Beijing Queer Chorus came to Portland and performed a joint concert with PGMC. A former member of PGMC was from China and hosted a welcome reception. A bus transported our visitors to the reception, and, as they emerged, exhausted from their long journey, we gave them a prolonged standing ovation.

Various members of PGMC and PLC hosted the BQC, showing them Portland and the surrounding beauty of the Pacific Northwest, giving them rides to rehearsals and to the performances. Lasting friendships were formed. We weren't in a position to host anyone but did enjoy various social events that brought the choruses together. And as we watched them depart, the countdown began. We will see them again in six months!

And then there was China...

And Then There was China

As I said earlier, there are certain events in my life that hold such significance, the time immediately preceding feels much further distant in the past. Going to China in 2018 had a similar effect on my life. The gap back to 2017 feels like an eternity. We took off on August 30, returning September 9. I was agnostic when we left and deeply religious when we returned. It took me nearly a year of puzzled processing to come to a centered equilibrium once again: *What just happened here???*

Chorus members had been told in advance that neither Facebook nor Google would be available to us in China. I had anticipated being able to check in with Cristina by email while I was gone, not quite connecting the dots to realize "Google" and "Gmail" were linked.

Cristina had told me, "Don't contact me while you're gone. *Be* in China."

So, realizing it would require jumping through technological hoops to make it happen, I let go of my Portland life while in China, trusting Cristina would find a way through any emergency, knowing that, if necessary, she would find a way to contact me. I let go. As a result, I let God.

One member of our chorus ended up in the hospital, very dehydrated and disoriented. Fellow singer Sue stuck with Daniel that day, giving up a day with the Terra Cotta soldiers in Xian. These side trips into tourism were all voluntary, and I didn't realize until the next day as we flew to Shanghai that Daniel hadn't been to see the soldiers because he was ill. He was being wheel-chaired through the airport to our waiting tour bus, Sue carrying his things. I could see how tired she was, so I took Daniel's carry-ons from her.

She said in a low voice, "I'm exhausted."

The next day, I sat by Sue on the tour bus and that was the final catalyst for a soul-deep journey I may never fully understand. Daniel's experience had brought my transition to the surface, all those early and mid-transition issues I'd parked in a corner while I helped others. Without having to focus on clients or Cristina or conducting activities of daily living, I focused on myself.

Here was this gay man, hospitalized in China, with doctors and nurses who spoke no English. Thank God, Sue was with him. She didn't speak Chinese, but she was not the one who was ill. She advocated for him, found the people who spoke some English, and never left his side. It didn't take much imaginative leap to contemplate: What if that had been me, *a transman hospitalized in China???*

For the first time in years, I felt vulnerable in my identity. In Portland, I'm well known. I have many people I could call on to be at my side in a medical emergency. In China, I knew I'd have some chorus member at my side, just as Daniel had. Nevertheless, the idea of being a transman, helpless in a country that doesn't recognize trans identity, brought forth a vulnerability that I hadn't felt in years. All this came to the surface, and Sue heard it all.

And what does this have to do with the emergence of my religiosity? I have no idea. I only know what happened, not why. Hand of God stuff. Sue is deeply religious herself, allowing me to talk about spirituality, trans identity, vulnerability, linking my identity with my profession by being a "transtherapist," all linked, all me, all the time. She has a trans son. She is religious. She is a singer in PGMC. Intersections of experience such that I felt seen, validated, understood, and invited to emerge in all my newfound vulnerability.

I'm What?! Religious?!

Upon our return from China, still reeling with a fundamental challenge to my self-concept, I began processing through what had happened to me with various people. Sue became my spiritual mentor and sounding board, taking long walks with me as I allowed my cognitive sense of self to catch up to the fact that I now believed in God.

I developed an email correspondence with my cousin, Mary, in Missouri, also a religious woman. We had never been regular correspondents before. Now, I looked forward tremendously to seeing her name in my inbox.

Susan had taken refuge from our alcoholic father in a nearby church when she was 15. She had been a deeply religious woman since the 1950s, leading to a faint scorn on the part of the rest of us. Including me. Until now. Susan was delighted to hear of my spiritual emergence. We had a fine correspondence throughout that winter and into the spring.

And, of course, I talked with Cristina, bemused by the fact that I came back from China as religious as she is. We didn't seriously revisit Orthodoxy. The same reasons we'd stopped going some years before would still apply, perhaps more so. I was ready to give my heart to some brand of Christianity, but only as a full participant.

Cristina would have supported whatever religion I chose. I had a dim memory that the only Protestant service that had even come close to giving me a spiritual experience during our time of exploration had been Episcopal. Sue was Episcopalian, but it was my own vague memories that were driving this bus, not Sue's affiliation.

Agnostic to Religious

After PGMC's first rehearsal back from China, the chorus celebrated at Hobo's. A local gay-owned restaurant and piano bar, Hobo's had hosted various chorus events for years[56]. The place noisy with the boisterous energy of our tour well-done, I found myself standing alone for a moment, and Robert came up to me.

Robert had been a PGMC member longer than I had. He was also the rector[57] at St. John the Baptist Episcopal Church. He looked uncomfortable approaching me, and said, "Sue told me you and Cristina were looking for a new church home, and that I should invite you to come to St. John's."

Though I'd already talked it over with Sue and planned to try St. John's, I was taken aback at Robert's unexpected and out-of-context invitation. I made some response about considering it, not knowing what we were doing religiously. I don't remember exactly what I said, but he went away again. I was still pretty uncomfortable talking about my religiosity, even with someone who had made it his life's work.

The following Sunday, we attended services at St. John's for the first time, and Robert said to me afterward, "Episcopalians just don't invite people to church, maybe once every 27 years. I was so uncomfortable, and I walked away at Hobo's thinking, *Well, that went over like a lead balloon* and here you are!"

I replied, "Not to burst your bubble, but we were planning on coming anyway!"

Robert laughed uproariously, relieved he hadn't offended us.

I was still reeling from finding myself religious, still coming to terms with embracing traditions I'd kept at arm's-length since the anti-gay ballot measure era. I was putting a toe in the water, but wasn't ready to dive right in. Sue suggested I join the church choir, but I wasn't ready to give my heart.

In solidarity with me, Cristina joined the church choir. I drove her to rehearsals and spent choir rehearsal time in the extensive church library, reading and absorbing and letting it sink in that I was now deeply religious.

I knew nothing about joining a church. What does that even mean? Passing an exam? An initiation rite of some sort? Turns out, it means filling out a form, so they know how to spell your name for a nametag. Giving

---

[56] Hobo's has been one of the casualties of the Covid quarantine, closing its doors permanently in the fall of 2020.

[57] Various denominations use various terminology—rector, priest, minister. It's the same role, leading a congregation in worship.

your address, so they can send you newsletters. Making a pledge of some sort, if you can afford it.

Rather than reinvent the wheel, I am copying and pasting some of my blog entries from that time period, chronologically, writing about coming to terms with this huge shift in self-perception, agnostic to religious.

I chose not to rewrite Volume One of this memoir, to provide the striking contrast between the voice of then and the voice of now. By the same token, I have not made mention, during the course of Volume Two, of the ways in which I now perceive the hand of God playing out in my life. I didn't perceive it at the time.

Nov. 3, 2018 blog
Finding Peace

In September of 2018, with 80 or so of my closest friends, I had the honor of traveling to China with the Portland Gay Men's Chorus—the first LGBTQ chorus to tour mainland China. It was an intense trip. Ten days, four cities, four concerts. And, in between concerts and rehearsals, about twice as much tourism as you might think would fit our schedule. It was exhilarating. Inspiring. Exhausting. And one of the finest experiences of my life.

One gift of this trip was the opportunity to form friendships with various chorus members I'd seen across the room at rehearsal for years. "Hi, how are you?" during a fifteen-minute break at rehearsal doesn't allow for close connection. Sitting together for four hours on a bus? Yup.

Among the people I connected with on this trip were several members of the Portland Lesbian Choir. They weren't singing with us. They were along because they thought touring around mainland China with PGMC for ten days sounded like fun. I had never met these women before, and we had a great time getting to know each other.

This hanging out with the PLC had a familiar feel to it, reminiscent of concert tours from twenty-plus years ago. In 1986, I was a founding member of the Portland Lesbian Choir. I had come out as a lesbian twelve years before and was ensconced in the Portland lesbian community. I had no idea "transman" was a more authentic identity for me. The

Portland Lesbian Choir quickly became home to me, the only place I felt truly centered and at home in lesbian community. Singing has always been central to my spiritual self-care. The PLC gave me the space to take care of myself sufficiently to continue to live as a lesbian.

Until 1995. A partner came out to me as a transman, stripping away any possibility of my avoiding the self-knowledge, "Me too." I fought as long and as hard as I could against the truth of me. I didn't want it to be true, and wailed to the Universe, "Why does it have to be my *voice*???" I knew I was fighting a losing battle. Authenticity finds a way.

I left the Choir in 1997. Choir members were upset about my transition, not because I was trans. They were upset because I was leaving. I left with a hole in my heart. Over time, that hole healed, but I retained a bit of nostalgic grief over what I'd lost. Nothing ever replaced what that group had been to me.

In China, bonding with PLC members once again, I felt a bit of that grief in my heart heal.

A few weeks after my return from China, a friend of mine asked me to sing back-up vocals on a song she was going to record. Naomi was a lesbian singer-songwriter here in Portland during the 1970s, '80s, and on into the '90s. Iconic. In certain circles around the world, her music is still iconic. Would I sing backup vocals? Did she have to ask? Of course!

At one early October rehearsal, we were standing in a circle in Naomi's kitchen, singing to each other. Several younger PLC members, several older lesbians, and me, the only person in the room with a testosterone-influenced voice. As we sang in unison, me in the same octave as everyone else, I closed my eyes and felt the love. I was singing with the Portland Lesbian Choir again. And another bit of that nostalgic grief in my heart healed.

Toward the end of the rehearsal, one of the older lesbians referred to me as "she." I was more bemused than anything else. There is a milestone of transition that I passed long ago, an anniversary I wish I could toast every year, but

I have no idea when it actually is—the last time a stranger called me "she." How could I ever know when it was the last time? I can venture a guess, based on when I started introducing testosterone into my system. I'd say, mid-September-ish of 1997.

I'd been out to coffee with this woman (I'll call her Pam) the week before. At Stumptown Coffee, I was "Reid, he." What just happened in this singing circle to turn me into "Reid, she?" I puzzled through this on the way home from rehearsal. It wasn't long before I knew.

Pam and I are of a generation. Her lesbian community and mine intersected for years, this tight-knit circle. About half a degree of separation between any of us. She and I hadn't been friends, exactly, but we knew each other's names. A good friend of mine had once been Pam's partner.

Inside that lesbian community circle, in the heart of it, the ONLY pronoun is "she." Though Pam called me "she" unconsciously in that singing circle, she did do so intentionally. Her intention was this:

> I see you. I honor you. I trust you. I invite you back into the circle. You belong. In this space, in this singing circle, in this moment in time, you are an honorary lesbian.

In that moment, I felt my transition circle around back to my Portland Lesbian Choir roots. I felt my 19-year-old self, proclaiming in 1974, "I'm a lesbian!" enfolded in the circle of my heart. My life became a seamless thread, no longer "pre transition" and "post transition" but simply me. All of me, enfolded in the circle of my heart. I am an honorary lesbian transman married to a woman and singing baritone in the Portland Gay Men's Chorus. All me, all the time, without contradiction of identity. How can there be a contradiction when all are me?

Welcome, my friend. Sing with us.

And, in that moment, my heart was healed.

Dec. 17, 2018 blog
Like Night and Day

In May of 1995, my then-partner said to me, "I've always felt like a man inside." This revelation from a partner of seven years rocked me to the core. I was a founding member of the Portland Lesbian Choir, and that group was the center of my life. My spiritual self-care has always been connected to singing. Beyond singing, my family of choice, all my close friends, the structure of my life, my social center within lesbian community, the PLC was all that. I had never needed the Choir more than at that time, and it was devastating to me when June came, and Choir was on summer break.

During the course of that summer, I experienced what I later learned to call "the dark night of the soul." I was depressed, paralyzed by dread and self-doubt, bordering on suicidal. Along about August, I made an attempt to better understand my partner, tired of the repetitiveness of my thoughts spinning down into the same depression and recrimination. Breaking the cycle, I asked myself one day, "What *would* it be like to walk around in the world as a man?" Far from dread and self-doubt and anxiety, that question brought to the surface a most-unfamiliar feeling of excitement and a giddy exhilaration, startling me no end. From those feelings emerged the now-inevitable realization: "OMG! Me too. I need to transition too."

September... back to PLC. In June, I was "Nancy, a founding member of the PLC." In September, I looked the same. I sounded the same. And no one yet knew that I had become "Reid, the guy who is eventually going to transition." It was a surreal experience. I had changed so much that I felt like a new member, yet everyone was treating me as they had in June, having no idea anything had changed.

September 2018... long living as a transman. Settled into Reid. Settled into baritone in the Portland Gay Men's

Chorus, now a member nearly as long as I was a singing member of the Portland Lesbian Choir. Married. Over 21 years on testosterone, the same amount of time I had lived in the lesbian community. What could possibly change now?

Then, I went to China. My dark night of the soul is easily explained. I know precisely why I cycled downward in 1995. I have no idea why I cycled upward in 2018. China exploded my heart open to life, the universe, and everything. I came back looking the same, sounding the same, as I did when I left. And yet, as in 1995, changed to the core. Spiritually awakened. Energized. In the three months since my return, I have processed and puzzled and written reams, seeking the same level of understanding as 1995. And not getting it.

I have now blessed and released the question, "What just happened here???" I have adopted instead a new mantra, the closing line of the iconic lesbian novel *Patience and Sarah*. "You can't tell a gift how to come."[58]

---

[58] Alma Routsong, writing under the pen name Isabel Miller, McGraw-Hill, 1972, p. 213.

Chapter Twenty-Six

And Then There was China
Take Two

I tend to view life from deeply personal and sociological perspectives simultaneously. My work as a therapist reinforced this life lens, seeing my clients as individuals with deep psyches while keeping an eye out for how life was treating them in the "real world." It was several weeks after finishing writing this memoir, at the stage of tweaking what I'd already written, before it occurred to me that I'd neglected to mention the trip itself, with its profound sociological implications. That is a measure of how deeply personally this trip impacted me. The sociology of it all paled in comparison. So now I'm adding a completely new chapter.

PGMC's Finest hour

We took off for China on a Thursday. The preceding Saturday, we had a four-hour rehearsal scheduled. We were reconvening after summer break to brush up on our music, all of which was chosen from our spring concert nearly six months earlier. We also had a goal of gelling as an ensemble half the size of our usual chorus.

When I walked into rehearsal, I was surprised that Bob wasn't there. He was usually the first to arrive. At the appointed time, our associate conductor, Mary, stood on the podium and said, quite calmly given the circumstances, "Bob went to the emergency room last night with back pain so intense he couldn't stand, lie down, or sit. We don't know with certainty what this means regarding our trip to China."[59]

I knew full well what it meant—Bob wasn't coming with us to China. We spent that four-hour rehearsal scrambling. Several chorus members are artistic directors of other GALA choruses in the region. Erik and Evan stepped out of the chorus to become PGMC conductors, ostensibly "just in case," but we all knew...

In one four-hour rehearsal, we gelled as an ensemble, brushed up on our music, and became used to singing under three directors unfamiliar to

---

[59] What it ultimately meant is that Bob underwent back surgery a few months later, after hobbling his way through our holiday concert in December.

us while they switched gears to direct music they had learned as singers. In Mary's case, she didn't even have the head start of a singer's memorization. Her usual role in the chorus was directing our subgroup, Cascade.

We flew to China and performed four concerts in ten days without our artistic director leading us. Mary, Evan, and Erik spent the flight learning the music as directors, not as audience or singers. Mary directed half the concert, and Evan and Erik each took a quarter. Our concentration was sharpened, working with unfamiliar conductors, and our concerts were stellar as a result.

While we felt bad for Bob, we also knew we were doing him proud. At times, over the years, when he knew we could do better, he would scold us by saying, "Always remember, each of you individually, you *are* the Portland Gay Men's Chorus."

In China we lived up to his expectations of us.

Complete Uncertainty…

The Chinese government had required the chorus to send copies of each song we were going to sing, subject to approval. We were bringing Broadway to China, singing musical theater pieces. Not only did this present a bit of "Americana" to China, we also weren't going to be singing any overtly LGBTQ+ music (Bob coined a term some years ago: "affinity music") that might be too controversial to be approved by the Chinese government.

We each had to submit our passports and a small mound of paperwork. These were sent off as a group to the embassy in San Francisco. If one of us had filled out anything wrong, the entire group would be denied visas. We had folks at rehearsals, vetting our paperwork so each of us would be sure we wouldn't be the one to jeopardize the trip for the entire chorus.

In the back of my mind was the question, "Will I be the one to jeopardize the trip for us all?" My passport gender marker has never matched my birth certificate. I'd had a passport with "M" on it since 1998, had never had one with "F" on it. My birth certificate wasn't among the required documents, yet I wasn't sure how far this vetting process extended. Those looking over our paperwork had no answer for me. My situation was unprecedented.

The tour company we had contracted with told us, "We have no idea what to tell you. No LGBT chorus has ever toured mainland China before. We don't know if you'll have any audience, or if people will be too scared to attend, or if there will be some security issue that prevents a particular performance from happening at all."

This, from a company that specializes in facilitating international tours for musical groups. They had worked with musical groups touring China before. It was the LGBT bit that had us all wondering.

As we took off for Beijing, I'm sure I wasn't the only chorus member to wonder, "Will they really let our plane land???"

I'm Really in *China*

When I was a kid in the 1960s, the Soviet Union and China were considered to be "Evil Empires." Either would destroy us at the drop of a hat (especially the Soviet Union). Hence, the need for missiles poised to be deployed at any moment. In school, we learned about the history of Great Britain and Europe. We learned some about Africa. A bit about South America. And we learned nothing about Russia or China beyond "Evil Empire." It was the era of the Cold War. As a child, the words "cancer" and "communism" evoked equal dread in me, though I hadn't the least idea what either word meant.

There was no component of questioning reality involved for me. This was how I grew up. I could have experienced some cognitive dissonance. My best friend in high school was from a Chinese family. Her parents were first generation. She told me once that she was taking a class in Chinese on the weekends and couldn't get together with me. I asked her why, and she said she wanted to be able to hold conversations with her grandmother, who spoke no English. It didn't occur to me to connect Janice with "Evil Empire," hence my lack of cognitive dissonance. Growing up in San Francisco, I wouldn't say I was exactly surrounded by Chinese people, but they were part of my city, my world, and in no way part of an "Evil Empire."

Our first tourist excursion came the day after we landed in Beijing, a trip to the Forbidden City and Tiananmen Square. As our tour bus maneuvered its way through Beijing, I was surprised by how surprised I was. The city was crowded, yes, but I wasn't surprised by that. Eventually, it came to me. I was surprised by how relaxed and generally happy folks looked, going about their business.

Unpacking these feelings further, I realized that for me, "Evil Empire" had been coupled with the largely-unconscious attitude that folks in China and Russia *must* be completely unhappy with their lives and *of course* they would want to leave their country if given the slightest opportunity. The thousands of people I saw happily going about their business as we rode buses through various Chinese cities belied these attitudes I'd internalized as a child.

Coinciding with our visit was an economic summit[60] between China and various African countries. During such events, Tianan-men Square was closed for security reasons. Our group of 80 was funneled along a walkway around the Square to reach the Forbidden City, walking pretty much single file along the pathway.

I was toward the end of the line. As we passed by a row of booths selling various touristy items, a middle-aged woman approached me, all smiles. She stopped me and took both my hands in hers, speaking to me in a gentle voice, her face beaming. I tried to tell her I didn't understand Chinese, but she just talked on, eventually, patting my hands and allowing me to proceed.

As I walked on, I puzzled, *What just happened here???* It wasn't long before I understood. Her body language and tone were easily interpreted. She and I were of an age, learning as children that our respective countries were the "Evil Empire." She had just witnessed possibly the longest line of American tourists she'd ever seen pass by her booth. She had stopped me to say, "I'm so glad you're here! Welcome to China!"

Communicating in China

We may not have had Facebook or Gmail, but we did have a means of communication available to us: WeChat, an app that provided a powerful means of sending messages to individuals or groups. We could chat amongst ourselves, and we were kept apprised of details of our trip, such as, "The buses will be parked on the east side of the parking lot. Be back by 2:00." I had wondered, *How will audience members find out about our concerts if everything LGBT is so hush-hush and unspoken?* Turns out, WeChat plays a crucial role. Rather than a flash mob, our performances were flash concerts, news spread via WeChat.

I had met Ray, the first person to transition to male in China, when he visited the U.S. in 2016. He had written a memoir *(Life Beyond My Body)*

---

[60] It turned out to be a good thing, this intersection of our tour with an economic summit. China had shut down all industry near Beijing to clear the air (so to speak) for this international summit. We had been quite worried about air pollution affecting us as singers, and it turned out the air quality was just fine.

and was on a book tour. His co-author, Lura, was local to me, and contacted me in advance of his arrival. Cristina and I had him and Lura over for lunch, introducing him to various local trans people.

I tried to get in touch with Ray when I was in China but didn't know about WeChat in time to arrange the connection before we left. Once in China, I had no way to contact him via Facebook or through my Gmail account, so we missed each other. The mechanisms of keeping in touch are enough different that it's easy to miss connection, as I did with Ray.

He lived near Beijing. Before the trip, I had told him our itinerary while in that city, hoping he could come meet me for breakfast. I didn't know in advance that one can't just walk off the street and meet someone in a hotel dining room. No, I had to show my room key in order to enter the dining room. Even had we been able to communicate, Ray could not have joined me for breakfast quite that easily. There is a heightened awareness of security in China that is normal to the Chinese and literally foreign to Americans.

Conversations About China

We spent hours on our tour buses. Several hours there and back to climb the Great Wall. Several hours there and back in Xian to see the Terra Cotta soldiers. We moved about our buses, chatting with each other, sitting with different chorus members each day. And we chatted with our tour guides.

Our tour company employed local tour guides in each of the four cities on our tour, people raised in that particular area and who spoke the language of the group on tour. Michael[61] was our guide in Beijing. On our bus ride to the Great Wall, I said to him, "When I was a kid, we were taught China was an Evil Empire and that communism would destroy the U.S. if we weren't constantly vigilant. What were you all taught about us?"

Michael got this little quirk of a smile on his face, and I thought, "Uh oh, I don't think I'm going to like this…"

He replied, "Have you heard the term 'paper tiger'?"

I thought back to learning that Chairman Mao had referred to the U.S. as the paper tiger. I remembered Ronald Reagan so angry when he heard the term applied to the U.S. Essentially, China viewed the U.S. in much the

---

[61] Each of our tour guides had taken an English name for themselves when they started working as guides for those whose native language was English, making it easier for those of us who didn't speak Chinese.

same light as adults view a toddler. You have to take them seriously as they can do a great deal of damage when in a tantrum. And you can't take them seriously as people because they're babies.

Beijing is considered the new capital of China. The original capital was Xian. Beijing is new because it's only been the capital since 1420; Xian was the capital over twice that long. How can a people with this continuous history possibly take seriously a culture that considers the Revolutionary War a long time ago?

And yet, the Chinese are quite pragmatic and have formed economic ties with the U.S. This is a country that will do what it considers best for its people. If that means dealing with the U.S. economically, so be it. Economic ties, however, don't automatically lead to cultural admiration.

During my conversations with Michael, it occurred to me for the first time that there is an advantage to a single-party system of government. How commonplace is family fracturing, distrust, and demonization in the U.S. over Republican vs. Democrat, conservative vs. progressive? How to find common ground? Increasingly difficult, especially after Donald Trump's presidency. The problem predates him. He just hasn't helped matters.

A single-party system has no such issues. Others, yes, but not that one. I realized that my childhood teachings portrayed communism as entirely negative, without any advantages, just as our capitalist system was portrayed in an entirely positive light, leading to "the greatest country in the world." I had a lot of brainwashing to undo.

Tourism in China

Each of our tour buses had two guides, one employed by the tour company and the other supplied by China. We weren't being spied on. We were being "handled." The Chinese government wanted to make sure the country was presented in the best possible light. We were told in advance of our trip that only one topic of conversation was off limits, even in the confines of the tour bus—the 1980s uprising at Tiananmen Square. Challenges to communism were not sanctioned topics of conversation with either of our tour guides.

Some of our excursions into tourism struck me as quite light and rather wasteful of time and energy, given how much was already on our plate during this ten-day trip. A tour of a silk making company. A brief class in calligraphy. I found out long after our trip that the government offered the chorus discounts on the cost of the overall tour for each such optional venture offered to choristers. Not only did these activities present Chinese culture to us, but they also gave us an opportunity to spend money. As I said, a pragmatic culture. Tourists spending money on silk goods or calligraphy is part of boosting the economy.

One venture into tourism that I greatly appreciated was our lunch in a Beijing *hutong*, or neighborhood. Dating back to the 1400s, the *hutong* concept is that of intentional, enclosed neighborhood pods. Each neighborhood contained its own class, from the richest of the rich *hutongs* to the poorest of the poor.

As China emerged from dynasties into communism, many *hutongs* were demolished to make way for a new way of life. Belatedly, the government realized that a centuries-old way of life was being destroyed and began deliberately preserving them. These days, living in a *hutong* is a form of employment in the tourist industry. We were transported into the walled *hutong* via bicycle-drawn two-person carriages. Small houses ringed an open square, in which a group of older men and women were gathered in their daily Tai Chi ritual.

Incongruously, there were small cars parked here and there in the alleyway cobbled streets. I envisioned a weekly itinerary sent to residents, outlining when tourists would be present, all residents understanding that they would not be moving their cars during a tourist visit. Either get out early in the morning, or you're not driving your car that day.

We were served lunch in a home, eating at one of several large round tables. I haven't much to say about the food, as was true throughout our stay. We were mostly served Chinese food cooked for Americans, not much different than one would find in a Chinese-American restaurant in the U.S. The highlight of that day wasn't the food, but the atmosphere, as close as one can come, in this day and age, to experiencing ancient Chinese ways of life.

Me and The Terra Cotta Soldiers

In the mid-1990s, Portland had the honor of being one of a handful of cities in the U.S. to host an exhibit of a few Terra Cotta soldiers that were touring the world's museums, on loan from their home in Xian. I didn't see the exhibit at the time but did have a tangential experience of the event.

At one point, I was walking through the northernmost section of downtown Portland and glanced east toward the Willamette River. The typical view would be not of the river itself, but across to the east side. That day, it appeared that a building was suddenly blocking my view. Curious, I walked down to the waterfront only to see a huge cruise ship in our medium-sized river.

It seemed this was an arts cruise, and part of their itinerary had been to float their way up first the Columbia River, then into the Willamette River, south to Portland and the Terra Cotta soldier exhibit.

Unfortunately, the Willamette River is not of a size to accommodate a cruise ship. As the ship continued south, the river narrowed and the effort to maneuver it became increasingly perilous to the fate of several of Portland's bridges. The ship finally gave up a bridge or two north of its intended stopping point, parking itself alongside Waterfront Park. The passengers were then brought to the Portland Art Museum by bus.

Such was the extent of my interaction with the Terra Cotta soldiers. Until 2018 and my trip to China.

Me and The Terra Cotta Soldiers (Again)

The Terra Cotta soldier museum outside Xian is reflective of the intensely practical nature of Chinese culture. The museum is a building erected over the archaeological dig. Once in the museum, a walkway around the perimeter allows a view down into the dig itself, with archaeologists hard at work.

The people I encountered in China uniformly admired the life work of Mao Tse Tung. And, to a person, they blushed when talking of the Cultural Revolution, in tacit acknowledgment that they viewed that idea as one of Chairman Mao's less-than-ideal attempts at redirecting a several-millennia-old civilization in the direction of fair play.

The idea of the Cultural Revolution was to level the playing field. Take academics out of their rarified atmosphere, move professors to the countryside and elevate the working classes to on par, everyone suddenly equal and physical labor exalted. As I've said before in this book, the pace of change is slowest at the family level. Sociological changes as sweeping as the Cultural Revolution are bound to fail, as they don't allow people time to catch up and change ways of thinking instilled through dozens of generations.

And what does this have to do with the Terra Cotta soldiers? Throughout time, Chinese farmers often found shards of pottery and the like in their fields. To a farmer, these remnants of the past fell into one of two categories: (a) something useful that could be repurposed in present time, or (b) garbage, toss it out. During the Cultural Revolution, academics were sent to various rural parts of China to learn "real work." On one particular hillside farm, an archaeologist was sent to live as part of the toss-up of society. The farmer found a bit of pottery in his field and had the idea, "Let's see what my new guest makes of this."

The upshot was this. The "natural hill" on the farmer's land was anything but. In 246 BCE, an emperor ascended to the throne at the age of 13. He spent the bulk of his life's energy constructing his own tomb, much like the Pharaohs of Egypt. His plan was to build a palace complex, with terra cotta residents, which was then covered with earth and plantings. The soldiers were the first discovered, but the area contained all the residents one would expect in a major complex: terra cotta cooks, families of servants, gardeners, and soldiers to guard all.

Upon completion, the emperor had all the planners, builders, artisans—anyone associated with the project—killed so no one would know the location of his final resting place. And until the Cultural Revolution, no one did.

Beginning to dig into the massive site, the paint on the first figures unearthed promptly dissolved upon contact with the atmosphere. Archaeologists have the technology to accurately map what remains underground, which is most of the tomb, and also know that they don't yet have the technology to preserve anything exposed to air. They are waiting for future generations to develop the necessary technology, unwilling to risk destroying anything further. I had a feeling many Americans would react more along the lines of racing to be first (Indiana Jones-style). The patient "let's wait a few generations" illustrated to me the difference between our cultures.

I could only imagine how various government officials and scholars felt when they understood the magnitude of what had been lost to history for over 2,000 years. Farmers throughout China are now encouraged to bring forward anything they find in their fields, with promises of a reward if it proves valuable. How many history books must have been replaced after this discovery! How many discoveries are waiting their turn to be unearthed?

Xian, the old capital. The capital until 1420. The implications of this longevity of place are staggering and fairly incomprehensible to an American. Had something like the tomb of the Terra Cotta soldiers been discovered buried in U.S. soil, in no way would we Americans connect the builders of 2,000 years ago with U.S. culture.[62] The builders of the Xian tomb undoubtedly had descendants living in the area, quite possibly including the farmer on whose land the tomb was unearthed.

A Musical City

I had an open mind when I went to China, knowing I knew nothing. Turns out, Xian was my favorite city. We sang in Beijing and Shanghai in part because they had LGBT chorus presence and are two of the most influential cities in China. We sang in Suzhou because it is Portland's sister city in China.

In the 1990s, artisans from Suzhou came to Portland and constructed the Lansu Chinese Garden. During our trip to China, I learned the meaning of the name for the first time—PortLAN and SUzhou. The Chinese have some difficulty with the ending consonant "d" and our city is pronounced Portlan by many whose native language is Chinese.

I asked our tour guide, "Did we send artisans to build a garden in Suzhou, a Portland Garden to match our Chinese garden?" I was entertained imagining what a Portland Garden might contain to best reflect Pacific Northwest culture. A McMenamin's pub was my best guess. McMenamin's is a regional icon, noted for their great burgers, excellent relaxing atmosphere, and craft beer. But, no, we had not reciprocated with a garden for Suzhou. I'm sure national politics was the only reason, either ours or theirs or both. I know my city well enough to know we would happily have sent folks to Suzhou to construct a gift garden.

And then there was Xian! Hands down my most beloved memory of our side trips into tourism was wandering around a park that used to be palace gardens. I have never before or since used my phone to record so many videos.

We visited on a Tuesday midmorning. Everywhere we turned, there was something musical going on. A band playing a song apparently quite popular, as many dozens of people were singing along. A few hundred feet away a flute quartet was playing classical music. In a formal square, several dozen couples waltzing along to recorded orchestral music. Up a flight of stairs to a platform with several dozen people participating in a Tai Chi ritual.

---

[62] The exception to this generalization would be those of indigenous culture descent, whose ancestors were very much a presence on this soil 2,000 years ago.

As I walked alongside a lake, I saw a group of some twenty older women in what looked like a ceremonial procession, moving in time to recorded Chinese music. They caught my eye because they were hardly dressed for any kind of occasion, let alone something as ceremonial as their movements would indicate, and there was no audience. This was clearly a rehearsal.

The entire park had a festival atmosphere, but not the atmosphere of a special occasion. "Festival" is the everyday atmosphere of the park. I took several photos of the lake, with ancient palace structures alongside, and, in the background, high rise modern apartment buildings that would almost certainly be where I'd choose to live if China was home. Walking distance to this park.

Modern high-rise apartments, walking distance to a park preserving palace grounds dating back to the eighth century. As the original capital of China, there is more ancient history to preserve in Xian than anywhere else. The unearthing of the Terra Cotta soldiers was just one example. Though trying to bring China into a more egalitarian mode through the Cultural Revolution, the government now also recognizes the power of preserving the past, nowhere better illustrated than in Xian.

PFLAG China

In viewing PGMC's online "photo album" of our trip (you can see the photos on Facebook), there are several photos showing a group of women in formal Chinese garb. How profound their presence was. These are PFLAG moms. In one city, several PFLAG dads joined them. These PFLAG parents had traveled from various parts of the country to participate in our concerts, contributing to a historic event.

They performed a ritual procession during the intermission of two of our concerts, every gesture and movement proudly owning several millennia of tradition. Their presence made a statement: "We are Chinese. We are traditional. And we support our lesbian and gay children by our presence." The T of the acronym isn't yet on the radar in China for them to add "trans" to the list of children they support.

In the U.S., PFLAG is involved in activism—supporting the legalization of same-sex marriage, laws protecting trans youth, and the like. PFLAG chapters are a major presence in Pride festivals. In China, PFLAG activism takes a different form—providing a means for parents to connect at all, to know they are not alone. WeChat proves invaluable in this effort, allowing connection without requiring people to meet in person on a regular basis. China PFLAG parents aren't quite ready for that yet, illustrating the bravery of the parents who participated in our concerts.

PFLAG Portland hands out thousands of "PFLAG Loves Me" stickers every year at Pride. I informed the Portland chapter that I was cleaning us out of those stickers, taking every roll we had with me to China. I gave a roll of stickers to PFLAG folks in each city we visited.

It wasn't until some months after our return, still talking about the trip amongst ourselves, that I mentioned how much I enjoyed the trip to the park in Xian.

Frank, a fellow traveler, said, "Wasn't it great to see the PFLAG moms rehearsing before our performance?"

My face must have registered confusion, as he added, "Down by the lake. There was a group of women…"

I suddenly understood that group of women doing a ceremonial procession and not dressed for it. That was PFLAG, in a final rehearsal!

The Power of Music

Never Ever is part of a song cycle *(Naked Man)* commissioned by the San Francisco Gay Men's Chorus in 1996. Part of the permanent repertoire for PGMC, this song has become a GALA anthem over the years:

> Never will there be a moment, ever
> When we all will be together, never
> Never such a moment,
> Never will we look around
> And see these faces, all these faces never
> Will we hear these voices,
> Never, ever hear this sound.
> No never, never will we have that first time
> Or this last time, or just this time.
> Never get to live our lives all over, never, ever
> Oh life will take us where it will
> New beginnings, ends
> Take each moment as a gift,

> Give it back—give it back again.
> ~Philip Littell and Robert Seeley[63]

If you search YouTube for "PGMC Never Ever China," you will see a compilation of every performance we did of this song during our ten days in the country, beginning with singing on the plane to Beijing. The PFLAG parents are part of this compilation performance. It was the encore of each concert. We performed this song with the Great Wall of China as a backdrop. And we performed this song in the Forbidden City in Beijing.

As we rode our buses to the Forbidden City and Tiananmen Square, we were warned by our tour guides: "Don't congregate in large groups." Back stateside, larger groups represent safety among LGBT folks. In China, particularly in the capital Beijing, larger groups draw the attention of authorities, still cognizant of the uprising in Tiananmen Square in the late 1980s.

The size group permitted in The Forbidden City is that of a tour bus, with a Chinese tour guide alongside at all times. PGMC had two tour buses, each with its own tour guide; we were instructed to stick with our bus group on this particular day. One of the most dangerous things we did in China was to come together as one large group to sing *Never Ever* in the Forbidden City[64].

If you search YouTube for "PGMC Never Ever Forbidden City," you will see that one performance, rather than the compilation. Toward the end of that performance, you can see a security guard approaching Mary as she conducted us. You can also see a hand reaching out to draw the guard back. That was one of our tour guides, assuring the security guard we were almost finished. As instructed, we scattered again quickly upon finishing the song. Remaining as one group would have led to trouble.

---

[63] San Francisco Gay Men's Chorus, music by Robert Seeley, lyrics by Philip Littell, permission granted by Mitch Galli, Associate Director and Outreach, SFGMC, email January 9, 2023.

[64] What a great birthday that was for me! I was so jet-lagged that day after our arrival, and we had crossed the International Date Line, I had no idea what day it was. I didn't realize that it was my birthday until I returned stateside and watched the performance on YouTube, which indicated the date of the recording.

About that Music…

As I watched the Beijing Queer Chorus and the Hyperbolic Singers in Shanghai perform, I felt like I was watching classical choirs. Tuxedos and long black gowns. Music folders. No choralography. Focused on the director and their music folder, not the audience. Their very presence onstage as openly gay and lesbian people is enough to powerfully impact their audiences.

I understood then that the Chinese government had misunderstood the power of what we do in GALA choruses. They had assumed choral singing meant in GALA what it does in classical choirs. Rather, we perform from memory, allowing us to engage with the audience through the music, our very presence fulfilling PGMC's mission to "honor and uplift our community and affirm the worth of all people." We also incorporate dance and movement, reinforcing the lyrics. Our performances take LGBT stage presence to the next level beyond being on-stage at all.

Yet, despite Broadway, despite *Never, Ever,* the most powerful piece of music we performed was a setting of *Night Mooring on Maple Bridge,* a song iconic in China. Every schoolchild learns this song, as ubiquitous as singing "happy birthday to you" is in the U.S. Singing this quintessentially Chinese song, in Chinese, seeing the audience singing along with us, was the most powerful cultural bridge we could have offered.

Everything else we offered was of our own culture. I have yet to understand why the Chinese government allowed us to perform *My Shot,* from the Broadway musical *Hamilton.* Performed by three choristers as a rap trio, this is a song of revolution, of taking a stand against the powers that be, of taking our shot.

China is at a stage of identity emergence such that the very presence on stage of an openly gay and lesbian chorus makes a statement, regardless of what they sing. This is the power of the Beijing Queer Chorus and the Hyperbolic Singers. I'm reminded of the first performance of the Portland Lesbian Choir. At International Women's Day 1987, we were announced to an audience of perhaps 400, who gave us a standing ovation before we'd sung a note. We were taking our shot, performing for and on behalf of our community, as the lesbian and gay choruses in China are.

And that is the energy we brought to China.

China is Changing

PGMC made history touring mainland China. And yet, the Beijing Queer Chorus was ten years old at the time of our tour. The BQC formed in 2008—not coincidentally, the same year Beijing hosted the Olympics, opening China to tourism on a larger scale than ever seen. Opening China to the world.

The demographics of the BQC, and of the Hyperbolic Singers in Shanghai, are such that there are no members over about 30. The same was true of our audience—no older gay men or lesbians. There is good reason for this. Until the last few years, China has had a one-child policy per family. It's not that families were prohibited from having more than one child. With over a billion people, how could any government expect to enforce that? No, what the one-child policy meant is that only one child per family would receive government support, as in attending school for free, receiving government aid in times of crisis, etc.

With one child per family, the pressure on that one child to marry and carry on the family name and tradition is tremendous. Openly living gay or lesbian identities was insupportable in a society where marriage is not only expected, but essential to keep the country going. Now, however, the policy has changed to three children per household, in recognition that the math just doesn't work. One child per family does not lead to sufficient workers to carry on and support the economy, or those now retiring.

With a three-child policy, it matters less if one of those children happens to be gay or lesbian. A younger generation is feeling freer to come out and live in authenticity. All the lesbians and gay men in China who are out of the closet are young, with no examples of older generations living openly to inspire them. Rather like the experience of coming out in the U.S. in the first moments post-Stonewall.

One song in our concert set was *Can't Help Loving that Man.* The solo was sung by a 40-something PGMC member. Balding, bearded, a bit pudgy, wearing a wedding ring, this man sang from his heart about loving a man lifelong.

I sought out Thom after one of our performances and told him, "You singing that song is the most ground-breaking thing we're doing for our audiences, an older gay man standing, unashamed, in the spotlight, singing about loving another man."

One audience member told a chorister, "I couldn't imagine what life would be like when I got older. Now, I see that I can be happy when I'm older. Someday, I will be that person."

On tour with us were half a dozen women from the Portland Lesbian Choir. They had hosted some of the lesbians from the Beijing chorus during their Portland visit the previous year. They got together as a group during our China trip, the women from the BQC and the PLC women on our tour. One PLC member told me later, "It was so heartwarming to feel like a role model. Just being there, with my partner of over 30 years, meant so much to them."

Also on tour with us were several parents of PGMC members, retired and taking advantage of a once-in-a-lifetime tourism opportunity. Their very presence sent a message to the Chinese singers, "If your parents aren't supportive yet, if you haven't come out to them yet, have courage. This can happen for you, too." The presence of Chinese PFLAG parents reinforced this message.

While in Beijing, we participated in a "meet and greet" that included not only members of BQC but also representatives of some fledgling LGBT+ organizations, perhaps the first time they had all been in a room together. I made a presentation about trans identity, coming out to the audience at the end of my talk. The audience had no idea that I was trans (except half of PGMC), and immediately came to attention when they realized why I was the person doing the presentation. In addition to never having seen older lesbians or gay men, they had also never seen an openly trans person before. A fellow PGMC member told me later that a young person sat in the back of the room, weeping and taking copious notes as I spoke.

We were allowed to make this trip. There are PFLAG parents in China. There are lesbian and gay choruses in China. China is changing. Slowly. One of our tour guides pointed out a fundamental difference in perspective between England and China. The English sought to colonize the world, from India to North America. China had a different attitude. We have everything here that one could possibly want. Why should we go anywhere? Let the world come to us and learn. Now, the world is coming to China, and China is learning from the world, absorbing that which is useful and shedding the rest.

I had such difficulty shifting my equation: socially conservative = religious. The objection in China to LGBT identity isn't based in religious beliefs. It is based in a several-millennia-old harmonious structure of "family," and the roles within a family. Again, the Chinese government policies are in service of supporting a population of 1.4 billion people. If something will be helpful, let's do it. If it upsets the balance of society, let's *not* do it. We have a huge society to consider.

Incorporating lesbian and gay identities as part of the fabric of society does represent fundamental change. It will take a while. As in the case of unearthing the Terra Cotta soldiers, "Let's wait a few generations and not move too quickly." China is changing. Slowly.

Outreach Concerts

In non-Covid times, PGMC performs like clockwork—a holiday concert in December, some kind of themed concert in March (growing up LGBT, a retrospective of Cole Porter music, etc.), and a Pride concert in June. The weekend after each concert, we take it on the road, performing in some small northwest town far from Portland.

Outreach concerts are local fundraisers. PGMC partners with a local organization that provides the legwork in their community, finding the performance space and advertising the concert. The organization then receives all the concert proceeds.

Not long after I joined the chorus, we traveled some 200 miles east to Pendleton, in support of the local PFLAG chapter. We performed to an enthusiastic audience of several hundred. I'd been through various parts of eastern Oregon before and had never thought an LGBT organization would be so celebrated among such conservatism.

I came to find out that the chorus was also surprised. Turns out there was backstory. The chorus had been to Pendleton for the first time a few years before I joined, in support of the formation of their PFLAG chapter. On that visit, only one business in town would post a flyer advertising the concert, and the chorus outnumbered the audience three to one. No wonder PFLAG was so badly needed in this community!

On our second visit, the president of the Pendleton PFLAG chapter spoke to us as a group, thanking us for coming. Many of us had come into town the day before, spending the night in hotels or with local hosts. Everyone, from hotel reception clerks to waiters in restaurants, had been excited upon finding out we were part of PGMC, saying either, "Can't wait for the concert!" or "Sure wish I could come, but I have to work." This time around, only one business in town refused to post a flyer advertising the concert. The concert itself was standing room only.

Bob said all this to our PFLAG host and then said, "That's *so* different from our first visit a few years ago. What made the difference?"

Our PFLAG host replied simply, "You did."

We had a similar catalytic effect in China. When we arrived back stateside, Bob had people stand up in rehearsal and tell snippets of stories to those who hadn't made the trip.

One member got up and said, "After one concert, a woman came up to me, all energized by our performance. She told me, 'I'm a student at the university. I have some friends who are gay, and they were too afraid to come tonight. I'm straight, so I'm here for them. I'm going to change China!'"

See What I Mean?

And all I said about China in the initial writing of this book was about my spiritual emergence, talking with Sue on Bus A. This chapter is the backdrop of my own intense process. I have never in my life undergone such a profound personal process while in the midst of a profound historical event.

To this day, I have problems with my right knee, a legacy of not being able to drink enough water while in China. My feet swelled so from dehydration, I was unable to wear my walking shoes and was forced to climb the Great Wall, walk the cobblestone alleys of the hutong, etc., in sandals. It was an effort to force my feet into my performance shoes.

Another artifact of a huge population—China doesn't have nearly the infrastructure to treat water for 1.4 billion people to potability. Each home has one tap with a water filter, providing drinking water. Laundry, washing dishes, etc. is done with untreated water. We were warned to only drink bottled water for this reason but didn't have quite enough bottles available for us each day.

Despite the knee pain that plagued me after our return, [65] I wouldn't trade that trip to China for…well, all the tea in China. There was a magic about this trip that led to the kinds of connections only possible among those who share a life-changing event. I've done a lot in my 37 years singing in

---

[65] I finally had a total knee replacement in the spring of 2022.

GALA choruses, and I'm fairly confident saying this trip will never be surpassed as my finest hour as a chorus member.

Chapter Twenty-Seven

Change is the Only Constant

In December of 2018, three months after our return from China, I got word that John was in the hospital with kidney failure. My big brother, dying. I hadn't seen John in years. Guam is a long and expensive trip from Portland. I'd last seen him at our mother's memorial in 2004. That was also the only time I met his second wife, Jenny.

John had been living in Guam since the mid-1990s, heading the local social security office. At one point, he had mentored a young woman, named Karen, who had since moved up in the organization. She took the reins of local support as my brother's kidneys were failing and his health became precarious. Jenny by his bedside, Karen took on the responsibility of communicating with family back stateside.

Wanting Memories

I lit a candle on the Orthodox altar we still maintain and put his photo next to the candle. I sat in the living room, playing Sweet Honey in the Rock's *Wanting Memories* on an endless YouTube loop. I had sung this hauntingly beautiful song in every GALA chorus I'd ever joined, but now it took on a personal and poignant meaning as never before.

> I am sitting here wanting memories to teach me
> To see the beauty in the world through my own eyes
>
> You used to rock me in the cradle of your arms
> You said you'd hold me 'til the pains of life were gone
> You said you'd comfort me in times like these
> And now I need you,
> Now I need you, and you are gone.
>
> I am sitting here wanting memories to teach me
> To see the beauty in the world through my own eyes
> Since you've gone and left me
> There's been so little beauty
> But I know I saw it clearly through your eyes.

Now the world outside is such a cold and bitter place
Here inside I have few things that will console.
And when I try to hear your voice above the storms of life,
Then I remember all the things that I was told.
I am sitting here wanting memories to teach me
To see the beauty in the world through my own eyes

I think on the things that made me feel
So wonderful when I was young,
I think on the things that made me laugh,
Made me dance, made me sing.
I think on the things that made me
Grow into a being full of pride—
I think on these things, for they are true.

I am sitting here wanting memories to teach me
To see the beauty in the world through my own eyes
I thought that you were gone
But now I know you're with me,
You are the voice that whispers all I need to hear.

I know a please, a thank you, and a smile
Will take me far.
I know that I am you and you are me and we are one.
I know that who I am is
Numbered in each grain of sand.
I know that I've been blessed,
Again, and over again.

I am sitting here wanting memories to teach me
To see the beauty in the world through my own eyes.
~Dr. Ysaye M. Barnwell, 1993[66]

Karen called me later that afternoon. John had unexpectedly pulled through and wasn't dying just yet. I cried, thanking God. Still not used to

---

[66] Permission received from Dr Ysaye M. Barnwell to reproduce the lyrics from *Wanting Memories*, email June 7, 2023.

being a religious person, I was taken aback when Sue said, "Your prayers are very powerful." Of course. Playing *Wanting Memories* for hours on end had been a prayer. Asked and answered.

Jan. 27, 2019 blog
There's No Place Like Home

1976. I turned 21 on September 1. On that date, I registered for classes at Pacific University in Forest Grove, Oregon. A few weeks earlier, I had left the cocoon of the San Francisco house where I grew up, moving 700 miles to attend college. A fateful decision, Pacific University. I could've gone to Hofstra University. I could've gone to the University of Iowa. I could've gone to UC Berkeley. All had accepted me. But I chose Oregon.

Two years later, I moved the thirty miles from Forest Grove into Portland. With the exception of three years away at graduate school, I have never lived anywhere else. At an age when I could not be expected to know any better, I had happened upon the place that is "home" to me.

1997. Another 21 years have gone by. On June 20 of 1997, I experienced my first injection of testosterone. My physical transition had begun. By late summer, I was a baritone, my voice an octave lower. I was giddy as a 14-year-old boy usually is. Exhilarated. A bit terrified, having no idea how to live as a man. And, at the same time, knowing that I could not continue to live as a lesbian once I realized I had misunderstood my identity all those years. Onward and forward, without the least idea what the journey would look like. I had happened upon the place that is "home" to me.

2018. Another 21 years gone by. 21 years living as a man. Comfortable now living as a man, understanding better how to navigate the world and relationships with others as a man. Embracing the identity "transman." Happily married for 10 years. Happily singing in the Portland Gay Men's Chorus for 11 years. A stable life. Then, I went to China, on tour with PGMC. On September 1, I celebrated my 63rd birthday by singing with PGMC in the Forbidden City in Beijing's Tiananmen Square.

I don't think I will ever be able to convey in words why China changed me to the degree it did. The change was every bit as profound as every other 21 year change I've experienced in my life. I came back spiritually woke. I feel a sense of connectedness to life, the universe, and everything and everyone in it that I have never felt before. I have happened upon the place within that is "home" to me.

OK. What does 2039 have in store for me, I wonder? I will turn 84 that year. And I fully expect that year to contain a change in my life every bit as profound as the previous three "21 years" have done. Where will "home" be?

A rather abrupt ending to this blog. Might as well. How could I possibly have written my other "21 years" in advance of their unfolding? Moving to Portland? Transitioning? Becoming religious? And at 84? Becoming… All I can safely say is, I will be "home."

Finding Home

Cristina and I became official members of St. John's in mid-December of 2018. Robert had joked, "Episcopalians invite others to church about every 27 years." So, of course, we asked Robert to present us to the congregation for membership, a role typically undertaken by a parishioner who has brought someone with them to services.

Usually this is someone who is already Episcopalian, recently moved to the area, and membership to them is a nice formality. Robert's invitation was much more significant to me, joining a church for the first time in my over 60 years on the planet. I wasn't just being welcomed to the congregation. I was being welcomed to Christianity.

Cristina remains Orthodox in her heart, but also recognizes that we can't really live Orthodox. As she said long ago, "Give it 500 years and Orthodox will be performing same-sex weddings." In the here and now, however, we can't go there because Orthodoxy can't. Now, we both sing in the choir at St. John's and have made a place for ourselves in this most-welcoming parish[67].

---

[67] What a difference two years makes. In the fall of 2020, I was elected to the vestry, the church equivalent of a board of directors. I was astonished to be enthusiastically invited to accept the nomination.

In honor of Pride 2019, I was asked to participate with a commentary on how trans inclusion has progressed in the Episcopal Church. I wrote the following piece, which I read at the Sunday service of Pride weekend. If anyone in the congregation didn't already know I'm trans, this piece took care of that!

1969, a time of fundamental change within the Episcopal church, tackling head-on issues of racism and social justice. Though it would be another seven years before the Church would begin ordaining women, that conversation was also well underway. Let's look at 1969 from the point of view of a transgender parishioner, someone living a more typical experience than those who participated in Stonewall.

I'm a storyteller, so let me make up a story for you. Joan is new to town. She finds her closest parish and as she expects, she's welcomed nicely and settles into regular church attendance. The choir director approaches her at one point and asks if she'd like to sing in the choir, but she just laughs him off, saying she can't carry a tune in a bucket, and it wouldn't help her be worshipful to try. He laughs supportively and encourages her to sing along with the hymns anyway.

End of story.

This could be a typical story of someone new coming to St. John's today. But what if I tell you Joan used to be Kevin? That Joan transitioned a few years before and moved to Portland to start a new life? That her real reason for not joining the choir is fear that her voice, well controlled when she speaks, would give her away if she sang? No one in her new church has any idea Joan once transitioned and it would never occur to her to tell anyone. Every use of the name "Joan" and the pronoun "she" affirms her identity. Why come out?

Flash forward now to 2019…

Many who transitioned in 1969 are quite happy living private lives and have no desire to come out. How to support those who are invisibly already present in our parishes? How to support those claiming newly emerging non-binary identities, or the long-time parishioner who transitions? There are some practicalities up for discussion. Conversations around labeling bathrooms, or gendered nomenclature in services and hymnals. There may not be easy or quick solutions, but the main point is taking gender identity seriously enough to have the conversation in the first place.

Transgender identity is more visible in the larger culture these days than in 1969. Many a trans person is a bit uncomfortable with this, as Joan would be, still preferring a private life. Some may feel gratified to hear their parish addressing such issues and may come out in order to be of service. Hearing their issues taken seriously affirms the journey they had to go on to become their true selves. Knowing that the Bishop led the Episcopal contingent in the Pride Parade enhances a feeling of being safely home in their church.

And these days, some who transition never desired privacy, affirming, "Yes, my name is Reid. And I was given the name Nancy at birth." My trans identity has given me the gift of a deeper understanding of gender, a gift I share with others in service of creating community. If I don't come out, how can I properly use this gift God has given me? The church has expanded in the past 50 years, giving me the gift of being able to stand before you in authenticity, an opportunity not available to transgender people of 50 years ago.

Time to Go

In March, I got another call from Karen in Guam. John was back in the hospital, the prognosis more serious and definitive than in December. This was it. Knowing Karen was holding a phone to his ear, I called John. He and Cristina met for the first and last time; we talked for fifteen minutes or so, until he tired and had to rest.

March 13, 2019. RIP John Vanderburgh. I read a eulogy via Skype at his memorial service the following week. His ashes are interred at a military base on Guam, in recognition of his early 1960s service in the Army. He was 75 years old. Though Jan was the first to go, her death seemed premature. She wasn't old. John died at an age on the young side of old. My own mortality became a more prominent feature in my consciousness.

Now I get it!

A month later, Easter, my baptism. April 20, 2019. Sue sat next to me at St. John's. Also a member of St. John's, Bob had attached himself to my baptism process some weeks before and became my second baptism sponsor. The two of them laid hands on me as words were spoken over me, and I was anointed with holy water, affirming my process.

Sue later told me, "I've never seen anything like it. You were glowing. The veil was thinned, the Divine shining out."

That day shines out in my memory as an intersection of aspects of my life that had never before been in the same room. The PFLAG board was there. The congregation of St. Johns, my newfound church family. Good friends from PGMC.

And Judy was there, my closest friend from our Orthodox days, delighted that I was now a religious person. Her take on my being Episcopal rather than Orthodox? "I don't think God cares at all what we call it down here." I was so delighted to introduce Sue to Judy.

About a month after my baptism, still mystified about my spiritual awakening, I re-read Volume One for the first time since I wrote it, looking to the past for clues about "What just happened here???" ***And I found them.*** I was galvanized into writing:

May 29, 2019 blog
A 24-Year-Old Epiphany

It's been about 9 months since my return from touring China with the Portland Gay Men's Chorus. How appropriate. Long enough as a gestation time. In the first few months after my return, I attempted to make sense of the spiritual awakening that came my way during that 10-day trip. I have never in my life had such an intense experience in such a short period of time, changing me to the core.

Given that I include transition in the mix, that gives an idea of how life-changing this trip was for me.

I puzzled and wrote and processed with several helpful friends during the fall of 2018. I came away from all that conversation with a much more centered perspective on my identity. I am an honorary lesbian transman, happily married to a woman, singing baritone in the Portland Gay Men's Chorus. All me, all the time. I was at peace with my identity, though still mystified by the speed of my spiritual emergence. I didn't yet see that there was a connection between these various processes.

After my April 20 baptism, I extended my introspection about identity. I became more introspective about the history of my spiritual identity. My curiosity was aroused.

During the summer of 1995, as I have written in several blog entries recently, I experienced a breakdown of self and identity unlike any other that has ever come my way. However, sometime during the winter of 1995, my life did an abrupt about-face. I went back to school, got my bachelor's degree, went off to graduate school, got my master's degree, became a therapist, wrote two books, numerous book chapters, and built a life for myself. Oh, and, in the midst of all this change and growth, I transitioned. So, I went from a complete breakdown of identity and sense of self to a jubilant sense of renewed purpose and joy in life? Why? What just happened here??? I came back from China asking that same question.

Recently, I re-read some of my writings from my grad school days [aka Volume One], and therein lay the answer, not only to the mystery of why my life did an abrupt about-face that winter of 1995, but also a new explanation for China:

> "I still had periodic bad times, particularly on Friday nights. Sundays had structure because of evening choir rehearsals, but Saturdays had no structure to them, and a structured schedule was much of what held me together that fall and winter. I

dreaded Friday nights, always followed by a day with no structure. Whenever I had bad nights, I would wake from a crushingly depressing dream, always, it seemed, at 3 AM. I came to dread 3 AM, a time when I felt no one else existed in the world.

"One such night I woke and was so depressed and in such despair that I just said through my tears, to no one in particular, "Help me. I can't do this anymore." And suddenly I felt... lighter. I would not describe it as the presence of God, or any other deity known (or unknown) to humanity. I just felt a release from the sense of isolation I had lived with for so long. I no longer felt alone and knew I had come through a darkness that would never be quite so overwhelming again as it had been in recent months. I later learned to call this "the dark night of the soul," and to realize that I had survived a spiritual emergency. All I knew at the time—I was through the worst." (see Chapter 11 of this memoir)

When I re-read this passage, describing a night I had forgotten, I laughed at myself. These days, spiritually woke, I would totally call this "the presence of God, or any other deity known (or unknown) to humanity." Before this visitation by Grace, I was a complete mess. After... well, the rest is history.

After. There were clues along the way that my real spiritual awakening began not in China, but on that winter night in 1995. Here are just a few examples (among many that may be found reading this memoir).

- I chose a graduate school that focused on a holistic view of people as a mind-body-spiritual whole.
- My mother and sister both died in 2004. I was alone on Christmas Eve, and overwhelmingly lonely. What did I do? I took myself off to church. I looked to religion for solace. I didn't

find it. I wasn't ready to be open enough for that. Nevertheless, church is where I went.
- When I met Cristina in 2007, a devout Orthodox Christian woman, I investigated converting to Orthodoxy. If this tradition were already welcoming and affirming, which some generations from now it will be, I would have converted happily. My deepest spiritual experiences have been in Orthodox services, long before the trip to China that turned out to be the last step on my journey. (Or perhaps, the first step on the next stage of my journey)

China was not a 10-day experience that resulted in a spiritual emergence. China provided the last bit of catalyst needed to allow me to recognize my 1995 spiritual emergence for what it was. China provided exactly the right factors:

- We were in a country where I saw no churches for 10 days, allowing me to experience my spirituality without external influence. Back in the 1990s, I was deeply and negatively affected by the anti-gay ballot measures put forth by a few fundamentalist Christians. I had never realized how much those experiences affected me until I didn't see a church on every corner.
- Traveling about all day, every day, by bus, we were in a country where not only did we not understand the language, but we also couldn't even read the signs out the bus window, forcing us to interact all the more deeply with each other. I had long conversations about transition, religion, and my history, revisiting my early transition time for the first time since I experienced it. One of my bus mates, Sue, was a deeply spiritual person, affording me an opportunity to talk about trans identity in the

context of my emerging spirituality, for the first time ever. I needed that witness, a non-judgmental person who was wholly supportive of my process and would later become my baptism sponsor.

I have noticed a striking parallel between my transition process and my spiritual emergence process. In 1995, asking the simple question, "What would it be like for me to walk around the world as a man?" changed my self-perception forever, in the realm of gender. It had taken me three months of angst and a breakdown of identity to reach that simple question.

China provided a confluence of conditions balanced and poised in such a way that they provided the final catalyst, allowing my spirituality to emerge in its fullness, ready to be labeled accurately. Perhaps because it was my second go-round with identity questioning, and I was starting from a more centered place to begin with, it only took 10 days in China for me to come back with a new self-perception, that of a religious person. Ten days—and 24 years.

Prior to my spiritual emergence, I often used the words "fortunately" and "synchronicity" in describing the course of my life since that 1995 visitation by Grace. Now, I more accurately recognize the hand of God in my life.

Life Goes On Around Me

And, of course, life went on while my world rocked and reeled with my disequilibrium of identity and my brother dying. After 26 years as PGMC's artistic director, Bob announced that the June 2019 concert would be his last. Chorus and audience alike gave him a thunderous ovation as he said farewell from the stage that June night. Only the desire to gift our audience with song gave me the ability to sing the last song of that concert without breaking down completely, participating in the end of an era.

Chapter Twenty-Eight

Summer "Break"

In mid-July of 2019, Susan said something in an email that set off alarm bells in my mind. Rita had fallen, fortunately not breaking anything, but needing more care than my 75-year-old sister (still a practicing therapist) was able to provide. Now 85, Rita was also declining mentally, diagnosed with dementia. Susan was about to engage home health care workers to be with Rita 24/7.

I said to Cristina, "I think I'd better go down there and check things out!"

I called Susan to let her know I was coming. I drove south the next morning, intending to make a ten-day vacation of it. Little did I dream I wouldn't see Portland again until mid-September, and that this would be no vacation.

Shifting Gears

The sight that met my eyes when Susan opened the door to welcome me led me to surreptitiously text Cristina a photo of their kitchen with the message, "How can I possibly leave???" Piles of unopened mail on the kitchen table, a table ordinarily immaculate. Dirty dishes piled and stacked everywhere. Two house-proud women owned this house. A house in which I'd be worried that if I left a mug on the table while I went to the bathroom, it might be washed and put away before I returned.

First things first, I went upstairs with Susan to see Rita. Bedridden, a shrunken shell of her former self, it was clear she wasn't long for this world. It was also clear she didn't recognize me.

Susan and I helped Rita sit up, swing her legs over the side of the bed, and make her way a few feet to a commode. We then helped her reverse back to bed. That sentence took about 10 seconds to type. The actual event took 45 minutes to accomplish.

That done, Susan sat in a chair by the bedside. Her head fell back a little as she slept. I took another picture for Cristina, of Rita lying in bed, asleep, and Susan in a chair next to her, also asleep.

I went back downstairs, bringing my things in from the car and unpacking. Tired though I was from my trip, I rolled up my metaphorical sleeves and went to work. But first, I called Cristina, filling her in.

She said, not joking, "You'd better plan on being there through Christmas."

I was appalled at the prospect and filled with anxiety. In the blink of an eye, this trip had become one-way without a plan for reverse.

When stretched too thin, it's easy for items to fall off the radar without consciousness. Susan had little idea that I took over shopping, laundry, cooking. She had received a notice that her car needed maintenance. I took it in for her. I gave the kitchen a much-needed scrub. I made an appointment for carpet cleaning. And I took over cat care.

Rita had always been a cat whisperer. Their household had never lacked a cat or two in the thirty years they were together. Ten years earlier, Rita had participated in rescuing a household of cats from a precarious life and probable death, an old woman with a few cats who multiplied into dozens of unsocialized creatures. The old woman died, the cats were primarily feral, and Rita took two of them in, naming them Bessie and Kiko.

The two cats lived under Rita's bed for the next ten years, with their food and litter box in her room. Bessie had since died, and Kiko wasn't on my radar at first, well-hidden somewhere around the house.

It took me a day or so to adjust to what I was seeing. Rita far along in dementia. The day after my arrival, a new service—24/7 caregivers in her room. All. The. Time. With a feral cat who knew no other place to sleep, eat, or go to the bathroom. Poking around the house, I found a pile of paper grocery bags in the laundry room. Kiko had turned them into a cat box.

I marched upstairs and hauled Kiko's cat box down to the laundry room. I took her food bowl, washed it, and created a "food corner" of the laundry room. Cats do not enjoy spontaneous breaks from routine. They like to know their litter box and food are always going to be in the same place, and that there is a predictable rhythm to their day. I established a new rhythm for Kiko. She never went upstairs again.

At first, my only glimpse of her was out of the corner of my eye, a gray streak dashing from one hiding place to another. I had to laugh, in a macabre kind of way. Cristina and I had met Bessie and Kiko some nine years previously, on our first trip to the Bay Area as a couple. At the time, our attitude was, "We'll take your word for it that those two shapes under the bed are cats." Who knew I would one day turn into caretaker for Kiko?

Caregiving at a New Level

A few days into my stay, Susan received word that insurance had approved a home hospital bed for Rita. She had little strength, and a great deal of pain in her back and knees, the main reason it had taken so long for Susan and me to help her to the commode and back on the day of my arrival. We felt a hospital bed that raised to a sitting position might help.

Susan was seeing clients at the time the bed was scheduled to arrive. I hung around downstairs, ready to take delivery. I was appalled when the bed was brought upstairs by a driver who set it up in the correct room, then said, cheerfully and not at all facetiously, "Have a nice day," and was gone.

What? The caregiver Dee and I are supposed to get Rita transferred to this new bed by ourselves? Really??? I called my cousin Dave and Susan's oldest, Kathleen. Despite Bay Area traffic, they both arrived within half an hour. We eyed the situation from various angles, planning logistics. Finally, we each took a side of the blanket Rita was lying on, Dee cradled Rita's head, and on, "1...2...3!" we went heave ho. Fortunately, we succeeded. Nothing broke, Rita was transferred smoothly, and we felt blessed.

Susan and I bonded profoundly with the four caregivers assigned to Rita's case. Dee, JoJo, Lish, and Vasthi were dedicated women with a passion for their chosen profession. Dee and Vashti had helped elderly relatives approaching end of life and felt a spiritual calling to be involved in home healthcare. Lish loved the patients she cared for, always ready to listen to the same reminiscences, day in and day out, from people suffering from memory loss. JoJo was a deeply religious woman. Susan and I had long conversations with JoJo, of an evening, when Rita was long since deeply asleep.

Impressed though we were with our caregivers, the company that sent them cut corners in ways we found unacceptable. Dave, Kathleen, and I felt fortunate that, despite our general lack of knowledge, we were able to successfully transfer Rita to her hospital bed. And we agreed we should never have had that responsibility!

The next day, I brought Rita her lunch. She looked long at me, and then asked, "How's your honey?" Her nickname for Cristina. So, Rita now knew who I was. I began spending time with her each morning and afternoon, until she tired of laughing and slept.

I enjoyed having a captive audience, and I read her every pun I could find on Facebook. I've become known as the "Punster" and "Uplifter of

Spirits" to quite a number of followers on Facebook. We watched multiple episodes of *The Golden Girls,* Rita's favorite television show. I played her YouTube performances of PGMC and told her stories of China. She was living completely in the moment by that time and was a joy to be around.

In the Midst of Uncertainty

During the next few weeks, I took care of myself by having long phone conversations with Cristina. She was holding down the fort at home via grocery delivery, friends dropping by to help out, and the occasional GrubHub. This was a hard time for Cristina, needing some daily care herself and yet wanting to support family. She felt she was doing her part by letting me be gone when she needed me herself. As she put it, "This is my contribution to the family."

Long phone conversations with Sue helped ground me spiritually. I was visiting the bosom of my family for the first time since God had emerged from my heart. As was true when I realized I was trans in 1995, my self-concept was so new that I was experiencing my family in an entirely new way. I was more open, more forgiving, less abrasive. And I stayed, going the distance in a way I might not have done at any prior time in my life. My boundaries had shifted considerably. I was finding the spiritual space between caregiving and caretaking.

Every morning, I took myself off to Piedmont Avenue, a block away, then down to Gaylord's for coffee. I became pals with the barista I saw each morning. I became friends with some of Susan's and Rita's neighbors, occasionally going to lunch or dinner with Alan and Julie, or MaryAnn and Kerry.

I contacted a number of therapist colleagues in the Bay Area, arranging coffee dates. A Godbolt out of the blue, I remembered Shane, a psychologist who had once lived in Portland. He had moved to Santa Cruz some ten years previously.

Shane had taken several of my CE classes and had become a good friend to both Cristina and me. I found his website and contacted him, taking a pleasurable day off to drive to Santa Cruz and lunch with him. On Shane's website, I happened upon a link to the Myers-Briggs Personality Assessment and, on a whim, redid it for the first time in several decades. The result astonished me.

Blog 9/10/19
I Before E. Take 2!

On June 5, 2019, I published a blog entry titled "I Before E."[68]. In it, I wrote the following: "Looking at myself through the Myers-Briggs lens, I am an INFP[69]. The N and F and P are clear and beyond debate. (i**N**tuitive, **F**eeling, **P**erceiving) The I (**I**ntrovert)? Not so much!"

In fact... The introvert? Not anymore!

I was first introduced to the Myers-Briggs assessment while in college. I don't remember the exact class or the exact year, but it would've been sometime in the late 1990s. At the time, I scored undeniably INFP. I was not near the middle of the spectrum on any axis of the assessment.

In August 2019, I visited my home territory of the Bay Area. I made arrangements to get together with various friends and colleagues, one of whom is a psychologist. I looked for his phone number on his website and happened upon a link to the Myers-Briggs assessment. Having just written the piece "I before E," the Myers-Briggs had been on my mind. On a whim, I clicked on the link and redid the assessment. Much to my astonishment... *E*NFP. Once again, the N and F and P are clear. No surprise there. But... *E*??? By a wide margin, E.

Over the years, my identity has found itself challenged multiple times. In 1974, falling in love with a woman, I concluded I was a lesbian. It had never before occurred to me to question my identity, and my world was rocked upside down. In the mid-1990s, my identity was shaken to the core again upon the realization that I am a transman and not a lesbian. With my first assessment proclaiming me INFP, I read about this personality type. I felt a sense of coming home to myself. I have embraced INFP as my identity for over 20 years.

When did I become an ENFP?! How does this even happen?! My self-conceptualization is turned on its head

---

[68] https://reidvanderburgh.com/2019/06/05/i-before-e/.
[69] https://www.humanmetrics.com/personality.

once again, visioning myself as an "E" instead of an "I." And yet, re-reading "I Before E," my extrovert nature is so clear! I love teaching, speaking with groups of people, and meeting new people. I most enjoy myself when I'm with others, not when I'm alone. Sure, I need my down time, but too much of it drains me, rather than recharging me as it would a true introvert.

How does an introvert become an extrovert? Answer: when the introvert never really was an introvert because of personality type. Of all the scales on the Myers-Briggs, I believe the range between I and E is the most heavily influenced by social factors. At earlier times in my life, repressing my trans identity from my own awareness had the social effect of introverting me.

I have spent the past seven weeks living with my sister. I have never before lived with my sister as an adult. I was seven years old when she married and moved out of our family home. If the Myers-Briggs assessment was not enough of a clue to me, living with someone who is a true "I" tells me all I need to know about myself as an "E."

My sister much prefers being by herself to being in the company of others. She needs a great deal of alone time. I find myself leaving the house in order to be with others, even if they are people I don't know. If I have been alone too long, particularly if I am not focused on a project, I find myself reaching out to others for connection, preferably in person or by phone. In retrospect, I hid behind the identity of "I," and now feel much more at home embracing myself as "E."

There is a lot of power in labels. I encourage all of us to reflect on the various labels that others have put on us, and that we have put on ourselves, at various times in our lives. If you used the Myers-Briggs assessment at one point, do it again; if you have at one time or another needed to use repression or denial as a defense, if you have since centered more fully into who you are, your Myers-Briggs type may have shifted as well. The capacity for surprising ourselves is infinite.

This trip was, obviously, giving me a great deal of food for thought!

I had lunch several times at Little Shin Shin, of lemon chicken and plum wine fame. From the time they'd moved to the neighborhood 25 years before, Susan and Rita had had a good rapport with Dennis, their favorite waiter at their favorite restaurant. I filled him in on how things were going. He hadn't seen Susan and Rita for some time and had been concerned.

I looked forward to church each Sunday with Susan, attending services with that very sweet family of a congregation, Good Shepherd Episcopal Church in Berkeley. I became friends with Pam, Bill, the other Bill, and Lauren, friends to this day. Rita had been a long-time congregant and one-time deacon at Good Shepherd. Susan had become beloved as well, accompanying Rita to Good Shepherd when it became difficult for her to manage alone. Prior to that time, Susan had gone Baptist and Rita Episcopal on Sundays.

Susan hadn't been going to services for some weeks before my arrival, not wanting to leave Rita alone for that long, and the congregation had worried. With 24/7 caregivers in the house, Susan felt able to return to church of a Sunday.

During coffee hour at our first service together, I filled various people in on what was going on and solicited their help. Lauren came over and helped Susan process mail. A bookkeeper, she was invaluable in sorting through what needed payment and what was outdated. Pam came over several times to visit, her sunny personality brightening the household.

Nurturing through Cooking

Rita was largely beyond regular food by the time I arrived on the scene. Homemade chicken soup mushed in a blender was about as adventurous as her system could tolerate. I made her tapioca pudding from scratch, and when I brought it to her, she startled Susan and I by smiling broadly and eating every bite with delight. I kept a batch in the fridge at all times after that.

Rita had run their household and done all the cooking. With her gradual decline into bedridden, Susan had been living for some months on the healthiest version of TV dinners Safeway had to offer, supplemented by granola bars and energy drinks. I started making homemade stews, homemade pesto, homemade Indian food. Without having to expend energy on shopping or cooking, eating homemade food, Susan's energy levels rose tremendously.

Just as well. She was ending her thirty-year therapy practice at the end of August and needed all her energy for saying goodbye to her remaining clients. Her office lease was up at the end of August. She had decided in August of 2018, long before Rita was bedridden, that she would retire from her practice the following August rather than renew her lease. Over the course of 2019, she had said goodbye to one after another of her clients and was now down to four or five sessions a week. Now, here was Rita, at the beginning of dying as Susan's practice was ending. Coincidence? Hand of God?

Getting to Know My Sister

Susan and I were gifted with the opportunity to spend hours in conversation about everything, for the first time able to get to know each other as adults. We talked for hours each day. Religion. Identity. Family. Family history. Family future…

Rita was a bustling extrovert with decided and very vocal opinions about how the world should work. Rita didn't like children. A place for everything, everything in its place, and children had no place in Rita's life. One by one, Rita had alienated those members of my family who had small children. Susan recognized what was happening over the years, but didn't, couldn't, do much about it.

By 2019, however, the "children" in question were all in their early twenties, our great-nieces and nephews. It had been so long since Susan and Rita had seen these particular family members, they wouldn't have recognized their young relatives if they saw them on the street. This felt wrong to me, given they all lived within ten miles of each other.

I determined that when the time was right, I would begin helping Susan build bridges back to her own family. I didn't have in mind "once Rita has died." If she lived long enough, some of those same delightful young relatives might become family to her in a way they never had before. She was quite pleasantly living in the moment. Laughter was her best medicine.

It was a fine moment when I orchestrated Susan having lunch with our niece, Lisa, brother John's oldest daughter. I took a picture of the two of them having lunch in a nearby restaurant, building a bridge across the most estranged relationship in my family. Lisa's three children had been the most boisterous, resulting in the most outspoken criticism from Rita. I looked forward to facilitating further bridges, perhaps including Rita.

I had never gotten to know my great-nieces and nephews. They had all been born long after my move to Oregon, and I had never visited for longer than a weekend at a time, focusing my visits on my mom, my siblings, and possibly my nieces and nephews, rather than the generation down the line. I enjoyed spending time with various great nieces and nephews during the course of that summer.

One had recently come out as a lesbian, to the distress of some of her religious relatives. I, on the other hand, was quite pleased to discover more queer presence in my family.

I told Sophia, "If that girlfriend of yours doesn't treat you right, you tell her she has to answer to *me*!"

My great-nephew David had fallen in love with a young woman, and with her religion; he had converted to Mormonism. We had excellent discussions about religion and identity. His mother is married to a woman. I'm his trans great-uncle. His cousin is a lesbian. It's all good to him. And to his Mormon-raised wife.

Delightful, thoroughly nice people, my young relatives.

Work-life-work Balance

I continued to work during this holding pattern. Awaiting Rita's death, supporting Susan, running her household, my Portland life on hold—and at the same time, receiving an email asking me to write an encyclopedia entry on affirmative therapy with trans clients. Receiving back my rough draft of a major book chapter, with feedback to incorporate. My work was a haven, a reprieve back to normalcy. I thanked God that I'd had the foresight to bring my computer. Given that I'd thought I was only going to be gone ten days for a vacation, it wasn't an automatic decision to bring it.

Recognizing Rita's death was on the horizon, Susan had begun making vague plans for a future that included moving into a retirement center within sight of their house, downsizing to an apartment. With that in mind, I considered her future living space while she sat with Rita or sat with clients.

I began going through files and boxes of papers, organizing and making "to shred" piles. I spent some hours each day shredding paper. Tax returns from the 1980s, a will leaving our mother a substantial amount of money (in 1982), various real estate transactions from 40 years earlier. I burned out two shredders, ultimately giving in and having family members haul 120 pounds of paper to an office supply store to shred.

I found a useful file: "Rita's Memorial." Rita had gone so far as to create the actual bulletin for her service. I could have added a death date to the front cover, and it would have been ready for copying. I took this with a grain of salt. There was no date indicating when she'd created the bulletin, and the folder contained a number of quotes and such that weren't part of the bulletin. I began preparing a new bulletin, as I knew it would be used soon.

I was face-to-face with mortality on a daily basis. I created a folder on my computer titled "Reid's Memorial." I added to it various quotes and readings I came across. I chose which songs I'd like to have sung. I made a list of people I thought might like to do a reading at my service. I wasn't trying to micromanage the event, as Rita had in creating a bulletin, but to smooth the path for those wanting to honor me, grieving as they planned my memorial. When I finally got back to Portland, I chose a few people and shared the information with them, how to access the folder on my computer, and what it contained.

Cat Comfort

I wanted the comfort of a cat and tried coaxing Kiko into my room, which was adjacent to the laundry room, to no avail. I was her source of food now, and she would follow me from the laundry room into the kitchen, meowing around me as I washed her food bowl and filled it again. Then she would follow me back to the laundry room; we would do a little dance as I reversed directions, and she shot past me to her food bowl.

At one point, while getting her food ready, I looked down at this cat at my feet, waiting to be fed. Rita had always referred to Kiko and Bessie as feral cats. Here was this cat, prancing around me and meowing like any other, and on a whim, I reached down to pet her, certain of rejection.

A feral cat would have been out of the room like a shot, hissing all the way. Kiko butted her head up against my hand and purred like she'd never stop. From that point, she wanted to be petted at any opportunity, conditionally. Never on my lap. Never in my room. And *never* picked up.

I wondered about this creature. *What will become of her?* Susan looked for all the world like a cat lady but wasn't. She barely registered that there was a cat in the house. I put out feelers among friends and family members that I had a formerly feral cat to rehome at some point.

The End Inexorably Approaches

About a month after I arrived, Susan came downstairs and told me, "Rita waited until JoJo was out of the room and then said, 'One of these mornings, you're going to find me dead.'"

Susan replied to her, "Yes, I know," and went on to list for Rita all the names of beloved family members who had gone before her. She made clear to Rita that it would be a joyous reunion, and that the time was coming to make that journey; she had Susan's blessing to go on ahead.

The next day, I was in Rita's room. Lish took advantage of my presence to go down to the laundry room.

Rita said to me, "I want to talk to you." I went closer to her bed, took her hand, and she said to me, "I have to go soon."

I replied, "Yes. And it will all be all right. We're all connected, you and me and Susan, and that won't change."

The following evening, Susan and I were downstairs in the living room, reading. With Dee sitting by Rita's bed, we hadn't been up to see her since lunch time. She wasn't awake most of the time, and Dee would text me when she was.

Out of the blue I heard an inner voice telling me, "Go upstairs to Rita." I rose and told Susan I was going upstairs, and she came with me.

Rita was asleep. Or unconscious. It wasn't easy to tell by this point. I received another inner voice, "Play *Wanting Memories* for Rita." I got out my phone and found the song on YouTube.

When it finished, another instruction, "Play *Breaths.*" One of the first songs I ever sang with the newly formed Portland Lesbian Choir. Another YouTube search for Sweet Honey in the Rock. Susan and I were on either side of Rita's bed, lightly touching her. Dee was sitting in a chair in the corner, watching with bated breath.

> Listen more often to things than to beings
> Listen more often to things than to beings
> 'Tis the ancestors' breath
> When the fire's voice is heard
> 'Tis the ancestor's breath
> In the voice of the waters
>
> Those who have died have never, never left
> The dead are not under the earth

> They are in the rustling trees
> They are in the groaning woods
> They are in the crying grass
> They are in the moaning rocks
> The dead are not under the earth
>
> Those who have died have never, never left
> The dead have a pact with the living
> They are in the woman's breast
> They are in the wailing child
> They are with us in our homes
> They are with us in this crowd
> The dead have a pact with the living
>
> Listen more often to things than to beings
> Listen more often to things than to beings
> 'Tis the ancestors' breath
> When the fire's voice is heard
> 'Tis the ancestor's breath
> In the voice of the waters
>
> ~words by Birago Diop
> ~music by Dr. Ysaye M. Barnwell, 1987[70]

Rita took a last rattling breath midsong, at the lyric, "The dead have a pact with the living." And was gone. Dee was looking on throughout Rita's dying, her eyes getting increasingly huge. She and I waited with Susan a respectful time, then I said to Dee, "Let's go downstairs," giving Susan a private goodbye.

Dee and I sat in the living room, and I told her stories of Rita as I remembered her. I was in my own state of grief. Half an hour later, Susan came downstairs, shell-shocked and holding Rita's wedding ring. RIP Rita, August 13, 2019.

I had never witnessed human death before. As I listened to those last rattling breaths, then silence, looking at Rita with goodbye in my heart, there was a distinct point when I recognized, *Rita isn't here any longer*. From one

---

[70] Permission to use lyrics by Birago Diop and music by Dr. Ysaye M. Barnwell provided by Dr. Ysaye M. Barnwell, email June 7, 2023.

heartbeat to the next, I felt that I was in the presence of a mannequin. If I hadn't already had a spiritual awakening, that evening would have done it.

The Aftermath

Susan was barely putting one foot in front of the other in the days following Rita's death. I stood by her, behind her, watching over her. Every which way she needed, I was there, unobtrusively. She needed support, and, at the same time, space to grieve in her introverted way without attention called to her process. A therapist brother was perfect.

I went through various address books and stacks of old Christmas cards, notifying everyone I could find. I sent emails, made phone calls, mailed cards. I went over to Little Shin Shin and told Dennis of Rita's death. I went across the street to Alan, who maintained the neighborhood email list, and asked him to notify the neighbors.

As the days went by, friends or neighbors would call or drop by. Susan held court, telling the same stories over and over, one person at a time, as I brought tea for our visitor. She marveled time and again that she established her therapy practice at the time she got involved with Rita and now, thirty years later, both ended at the same time. Through it all, I was with her. Witnessing. Processing. Witnessing August 31, the last day of her therapy practice. Having closed my own practice in 2012, I understood full well the significance of The Last Client.

I can't say my 64th birthday was much celebrated that September 1. Friends and family tried, but how could we? What a year! One year before, I'd celebrated my birthday singing *Never Ever* in the Forbidden City in Beijing.

I finished the bulletin for Rita's memorial service, with Susan's blessing. The day before the service, I went to the store to buy suitable clothes. The shorts and t-shirts I'd brought for a vacation weren't going to do it.

On September 7, I read:

> I am standing upon the seashore.
> A ship, at my side,
> spreads her white sails to the moving breeze
> and starts for the blue ocean.
> She is an object of beauty and strength.
> I stand and watch her until, at length,

she hangs like a speck
of white cloud just where the sea and sky
come to mingle with each other.

Then, someone at my side says, "There, she is gone."
Gone where?
Gone from my sight. That is all.
She is just as large in mast,
hull and spar as she was when she left my side.
And, she is just as able to bear her load
of living freight to her destined port.
Her diminished size is in me - not in her.

And, just at the moment
when someone says, "There, she is gone,"
there are other eyes watching her coming,
and other voices ready to take up the glad shout,
"Here she comes!"

And that is dying...[71]

---

[71] See fn. 37.

Chapter Twenty-Nine

Back and Forth...and Back...and Forth

September means PGMC to me, back from summer break. This particular September meant a once-in-decades opportunity to sing in the audition chorus to select the new artistic director for PGMC. I signed up early in the summer to participate, with no idea what the summer held in store for me. Now, the date was approaching.

I kept a close eye on Susan. A few days after Rita's memorial service, a month after her death, I could see Susan was letting it sink in that she now lived alone—for better or worse. She began talking about various groups she might join now that she was retired. I did a little research on her behalf and found a community chorus I thought she would enjoy now that her time was going to be entirely her own.

I invited her to visit Portland for PGMC's December concert. Susan hadn't seen the chorus in some years and was enthusiastic. During a phone conversation with Sue, I brought the phone over to where Susan was sitting and they had a brief conversation, Sue encouraging my sister to visit for the concert.

Susan woke up to the fact that I'd been doing her laundry. And all the cooking. And all the shopping. She started shooing me out of the kitchen at lunchtime, assuring me that she could heat up her own leftovers. I could see it was time. My introverted sister wanted to be alone again, ready to start building a new life for herself. And increasingly aware that I wasn't living my own life in Portland.

Back North

With sadness in my heart, I left Kiko with Susan, assured by several friends and relatives that they were looking diligently for a new home for her. I already had Figaro and Susanna. They would not willingly incorporate a third.

On September 11, that fateful anniversary again, I pointed the car north with great excitement to be home again. I flew up I-5, home in ten hours. So excited! The next several days were joyous. Chorus! Bear hugs around, much sympathy for my summer. Auditioning three stellar artistic director candidates.

The third audition was done on Saturday afternoon, and I went home to Cristina saying, "He's the guy. That third one." I couldn't remember his name precisely, Johnny Something. I knew it started with A and had a certain number of Italian-sounding syllables, so I called him Johnny Arugula.

The following Tuesday evening, my phone chirped, and I saw Susan's oldest was calling. I picked up, eager to talk with Kathleen again.

At first, my brain kept saying, "No. No. You aren't hearing this because Kathleen can't be saying what you're hearing."

I sought out Cristina, Kathleen still talking. Coming in mid-conversation, Cristina slowly woke to the same message my brain was denying.

Neighbors had noted newspapers piling up on Susan's porch. Though concerned, they also knew how introverted Susan was and didn't want to intrude during her time of grief. One neighbor had Kathleen's phone number, so called to relay the neighborhood concern.

Kathleen came over and, with a sense of foreboding, saw the house entirely dark though it was only about 8:00 in the evening. A complete night owl, there is no way Susan would be lights-out at that hour. She was apparently home, as her car was in the driveway. Kathleen had a key, so came in and turned lights on throughout the downstairs. Nothing. Heading upstairs, Kathleen was by this time fairly sure what lay in store.

Susan was peacefully lying in bed. Borderline diabetic, with wildly fluctuating blood sugar, she hadn't had time to take the diabetes classes that were on her list of "things to take care of" now that she was retired, and Rita was gone. Kathleen found her on her bed, hand raised apparently trying to feel the pulse in her neck. Piecing it all together, it appeared Susan's blood sugar had dipped low enough that she slipped unconscious and was gone. She died almost exactly one month after Rita and six months after her twin brother, John.

One of the remarks Susan had made time and again as she held court with those offering sympathy for Rita's death: "I'm going to start taking care of my health better now that I have the time and space. My family lives to be in our 80s and 90s, so I'd better take good care of myself, so I'll have a good quality of life." She didn't connect all the dots—Jan died at 62, John at 75. And now, so had his twin, Susan.

Kathleen had last seen Susan on Saturday afternoon, as I was participating in the last audition of PGMC's new artistic director candidates.

Kathleen helped her up to bed to take a nap, and found Susan exactly there some days later, wearing exactly the same clothes.

Back South

I pointed the car south again the morning after getting the news. I was in shock, grieving all the more deeply for the unexpectedness of Susan's death. I arrived back in the Bay Area on September 18, exactly one week after I'd so jubilantly headed home. And exactly 19 years from the day I'd pointed the U-Haul north after graduating from JFKU.

I met Kathleen and sister Sharon at Susan's house, and we commiserated together, grateful Susan was spared the slow and public decline that Rita had experienced. The very shock of Susan's death was part of the blessing—sudden, unexpected, alone—exactly how she would have scripted her own passing.

Kathleen, Sharon, and I spent the next week or so preparing for Susan's memorial. *Déjà vu* all over again. Contacting friends and family. Once again, I went over to Little Shin Shin and informed Dennis that Susan also had died. Once again, he was grief-stricken. I texted Rita's caregivers, Dee, Lish, Vashti, and JoJo. Susan and I had bonded profoundly with them during Rita's decline, and I knew they would want to attend Susan's memorial. One and all were shocked to hear Susan had also died.

I created the bulletin for Susan's service from scratch. There was no folder titled "Susan's Memorial." She had left post-it-note sayings and thumbtacked quotes all over the house, inspiration handy no matter where she was. I chose a few and added hymns I knew she liked.

Finding Bible readings posed no problem. Susan's appointment book spoke to the rhythm of her therapy practice: a weekly inspirational quote written at the beginning of each week, with daily inspirational Bible quotes written next to the client names for that day.

Kathleen, Sharon, and I soldiered on through reams and mountains of paper. Susan, why did you keep the box of documentation of your 1979 divorce? "You never know," would have been her response. And she would wince to realize how much work this thoroughness created for the family left behind. A life well-lived and well-paper-trailed.

As we sorted through the house, we came across photos, keepsakes, and family memorabilia that had come to Susan from our mother. We invited family members to come over and take whatever they wanted. It was a balm to my soul to see various family members gather in Susan's house, choosing keepsakes and mementoes, reminiscing, finding 40-year-old photos, laughing at themselves and each other.

Back North

With Susan's memorial scheduled for October 7, exactly one month after Rita's, I drove back to Portland. I'd had quite enough of that house for one summer and didn't want to stay the two weeks until the memorial. I'd rather drive home and back again!

Kathleen and Sharon pressed me to take *anything* I wanted from the house, wanting to honor me for all I'd done for the family over the past few months. I now have two coffee mugs, one obviously Susan's and the other Rita's, though I'm not sure which is which. One mug says: "It's not the years in your life that count, it's the life in your years." ~Abraham Lincoln. The other mug: "Yesterday is history. Tomorrow is a mystery. Today is a gift[72]." ~Eleanor Roosevelt. Either saying suited them both.

In addition to coffee mugs and a few other odds and ends, Kiko traveled with me. She had lived alone in that house with a dead Susan for some four days, untended, unfed. This cat had a lot of recent trauma to recede into the background. I couldn't leave her behind.

I prayed as I steeled myself to catch her into the cat carrier. On the third traumatic try, I had her. She yowled as loudly as I've ever heard a cat, and I cringed as I thought of the long drive home. Surprisingly, she quieted down immediately we were in the car.[73] I texted Cristina from the road to prepare a place for this new cat companion of ours.

Upon our arrival that night, Cristina had a new cat box in place, with food and water awaiting our new companion. We put her in the TV room, opened her cat carrier, and closed the door behind us so she could be alone to acquaint herself with her new abode.

I slept the next few nights on the futon in that room. I laid down that first night and, for the first time since I'd known her, Kiko jumped up beside me, purring and rolling around as I petted her, rapturous gratitude in every

---

[72] That's all that fits on my coffee mug, but there is another line to that quote: "That's why it's called the present."

[73] As I got to know Kiko, I came to understand that her yelling was from being picked up. She quieted down as soon as I put her in the carrier, no longer picked up. As time went on, she somewhat tolerated being picked up, though her entire body remained tense as she waited to be put down again.

movement. I had never rescued a cat from such dire circumstances before and have never regretted it since.

Susanna had had diabetes for years; by late October, it was clearly time for her to move on. I said to Cristina, "When she stops purring, we'll know it's time." And so, it proved to be—RIP Susanna, 11/1/19. I called our vet to make the appointment. When I arrived, I found the vet had prepared an exam room: lights off, candles lit, a fleece blanket and cozy cushion on the exam table. As the vet injected Susanna to send her on her way, she told me, "Take as long as you need with her."

I have this vision of heaven as this little line of cats waiting to greet me. And because it's heaven, they all get along. And no cat boxes. There were now eight cats in that line, Leon at the head.

So Kiko and Figaro were the cats now in our household, intolerant of each other just as other cats I've lived with in the past have been. Kiko jumped in my lap and up onto my chest at any opportunity, barely waiting for me to settle before wanting her strokes. If she'd had her way, I'd be her lap 24/7, as Rita was in the months prior to needing full-time caregivers.

Back South

I drove back down to the Bay Area in early October for the weekend of Susan's memorial. Susan came full circle having her memorial service at First Baptist Church of Berkeley, on the campus of the seminary where she had received her Master's of Divinity in the mid-1980s. Pam and Bill from Good Shepherd participated in Susan's service, and quite a few Good Shepherd congregants were in attendance.

As I got up to read during the service, I glared at my family, sitting in the first few pews, and said directly to them, "I don't want to read this again for a *long time*." And I read:

> I am standing upon the seashore.
> A ship, at my side,
> spreads her white sails to the moving breeze
> and starts for the blue ocean.
> She is an object of beauty and strength.
> I stand and watch her until, at length,
> she hangs like a speck
> of white cloud just where the sea and sky
> come to mingle with each other.

Then, someone at my side says, "There, she is gone."
Gone where?
Gone from my sight. That is all.
She is just as large in mast,
hull and spar as she was when she left my side.
And, she is just as able to bear her load
of living freight to her destined port.
Her diminished size is in me - not in her.

And, just at the moment
when someone says, "There, she is gone,"
there are other eyes watching her coming,
and other voices ready to take up the glad shout,
"Here she comes!"

And that is dying...[74]

Back North

After the memorial service, the family went to Little Shin Shin for a farewell dinner. We toasted Susan and Rita, reminiscing and sending them on their way with laughter and tearful joy. Dennis was our waiter, which seemed fitting.

Next morning, I went across the street to Alan and Julie's house and hugged them goodbye. I took myself off to Gaylord's on Piedmont Avenue and said farewell to the barista I'd joked with half the summer. I went to the church service at Good Shepherd, saying goodbye to these folks with whom I'd bonded while attending services for half the summer. Pam. Lauren. Bill. The other Bill. Hugging goodbye at coffee hour, the car pointed north once again, and I was back home late that night.

---

[74] See fn. 37.

Chapter Thirty

Change is Still the Only Constant

Back to Chorus. I gradually relaxed into being home, profoundly changed by my summer, deeply thankful for having gone and for being home again. Chorus without Bob was depressing, and the holiday concert was difficult. Mary had her work cut out for her, leading the subgroup, Cascade, as she'd always done and now filling in as interim conductor for the entire Chorus.

Johnny was slated to start work on the spring concert in January, ironically a 40-year retrospective concert commemorating a milestone organizational birthday. I viewed the role of interim conductor as being similar to the rebound relationship after the break-up of a long-term partnership. I didn't envy Mary!

Thanksgiving approached, and I was so grateful for my Portland family of choice with which to share it. Rick and David hosting. A dozen or so laughing and toasting each other.

In early December, as the last family memorial service was finally receding into past tense, my friend Max contacted me to have coffee. The program manager for SAGE Metro Portland, Max was excited to tell me their workplace (Friendly House) had received a grant to hire a staff member with the glorified title "SAGE LGBT Community Inclusion Specialist."

I'd been looking for a job off-and-on for three years, to add to our income but also so I would have healthcare benefits. Once I experienced the summer of 2019, it became clear to me why I hadn't yet found a job! Knowing I'd been looking for work, Max encouraged me to apply for the position.

Back South

Excited though I was at the prospect of a job, first things first. The weekend following PGMC's December concert, I pointed the car south for the fourth time that year (a personal record) and drove to the Bay Area.

For the first time in 2019, my travel south had nothing to do with death and everything to do with celebration of family life. When my mother and Jan both died in 2004, our family stopped having regular, you-can-count-on-it family gatherings. With all the recent death in my family, it was so important to us all to gather in December once again. I stayed with niece Lisa. We would be hosting the family.

Without planning, without prior discussion, our gathering organically fit us as we now were. On a whim, I made spiced tea, reviving a family tradition. Susan had made it for every family gathering, decades earlier. Lisa didn't even have the recipe. I texted Cristina, and she texted me a picture of the recipe, found in a family cookbook I'd inherited from my mother.

None of us at this family gathering had ever made spiced tea. I hadn't liked it, while my niece Sharon recalled being shooed away from it as a teenager. As I added rum (per the recipe), she exclaimed indignantly, "No wonder I never got to drink it! I didn't know it was a Drink drink!"

As people gathered to leave, we spontaneously stood in a circle, toasting each other and our re-found sense of family togetherness. I recognized this as a new family tradition in the making. My cousin Dave, a complete introvert, took the moment with his toast. "Today's my birthday. Some of my co-workers asked me what I was going to be doing to celebrate, and I told them I was going to a family reunion. One said, 'Oh, I'm sorry that's how you have to spend your birthday!' And I said, 'No, you don't understand, you don't know my family.'" And with that, Dave raised his glass to us.

I sat on the couch, watching my family morph into a new family unit, with new alliances, future issues to deal with, rekindled friendships, new generations carrying on. Despite all the loss of 2019, my newfound faith in God wasn't shaken. Rather, I felt the connections with those who went before me all the stronger. While John was living 7,000 miles from me, we had less connection than after his death.

My siblings all now reside in my heart, and I feel a sense of committee connection supporting me through my life. My triumvirate of older siblings, laughing at the idea that the baby of the family is now the oldest. And cheering me on at the same time. I smile every time I pray in front of the altar, Jan's picture smiling back at me.

A New Opportunity

Upon my return, I went online and found the SAGE job on the Friendly House website. Over the years, I've found various aspects of my life reconnecting in unexpected ways. I'd often led workshops at various events held at Friendly House, never dreaming I might one day work there.

This job—helping make senior living facilities warm and welcoming and safe places for LGBT seniors to live—made me think of Nick immediately when I read the job description, and how much he could have benefited from someone advocating for him in his small-town rehab facility.

Mid-January brought exciting news—an interview! In early February, more excitement—a final interview!

A day or so later, a text from my friend Paul: "Max just called me because you listed me as a reference for the SAGE job…"

Paul's text overlapping with a phone call from Max: "I'm calling to see if you would accept the job."

Ya think?!

A New Era for PGMC

Johnny moved to Portland from New York City, his home base. Cristina and I had him over for dinner, helping welcome him to Portland and to PGMC. The Chorus began rehearsals for our 40th anniversary concert. Yes, I missed Bob intensely. And it was GALA choruses that fed my soul, giving my heart to various directors over the years—Ali, Lynda, Ray, Bob. And now Johnny. Not Arugula after all—Atorino.

We began rehearsals in early January, and I knew immediately that Johnny represented the next 26 years of PGMC. Nevertheless, it was an odd feeling, singing a retrospective concert of music I'd learned under Bob, now directed by Johnny. Johnny and Mary worked well together, collaborating to lead PGMC in new directions.

And then…

Didn't See That One Coming…

I started my new job on February 14, 2020, attending a Valentine's Day social at Hollywood Senior Center, meeting many of the seniors who participate in the SAGE program. Being staff for the first time.

And then… another "didn't see that one coming"—a pandemic. Really? From March 17, working from home. The first scare came a few days after attending my first work meeting, a fellow committee member informed us that she had tested positive for Covid-19. None of us got it from her, and Brenda survived. But it sure brought home the risks.

In late June, laid off for the foreseeable future. How could I do the job I was hired to do when senior facilities were necessarily focused on keeping their residents alive through strict quarantine? Despite being laid off, the most profound impact the pandemic had on me personally was in chorus. Cut off from each other.

> **March 29, 2020 blog**
> **Seeing Each Other Home**
>
> In December of 1993, we got the news at a Bridges Vocal Ensemble rehearsal: come soon. We had known that call would come eventually, since June of 1992, when Trent had told us between sets at the GALA choral festival that he had AIDS. No matter how much time we'd had to prepare emotionally, no matter how many friends we had lost in the meantime, Trent was the first of our tight-knit chorus.
>
> That evening after rehearsal, we all went over to Trent's house. All 20-something of us packed into his living room, standing around the chair he never left at this point, singing every song he knew. He mouthed all the words with a half-smile on his face, too weak at that point to vocalize. After an hour or so, we filed past him one by one, shaking his hands, kissing his forehead, saying each in our own way, "Goodbye for now." Trent died the next day.
>
> The current Covid pandemic is triggering to many who survived the AIDS era. Some younger people have asked those of us who were there, "How did you get through it? What tips do you have for us?" I've been asked myself, and have found myself at sea, unable to answer.
>
> Today, it came to me why I've been unable to answer: because nothing that helped me then applies today. If Trent were dying of Covid-19 today, we would not be surrounding his chair, singing along with him, kissing him goodbye, later all grieving together at his memorial service. Singing. Together. At his memorial service. And, we would not have had a year and a half of watching him slowly decline, wasting away toward an inevitable death. AIDS never took us by surprise unless a miraculous person survived. The death rate was nearly unanimous.
>
> I accidentally discovered the power choral singing holds for me in 1986 and have never been without a chorus since. One reason GALA choruses are so powerful today, such a

presence in their communities, dates back to the AIDS era. Sharing the air through choral singing is one of the most powerful ways in which humans can bond with each other. Sharing the air helped us survive the loss of so many, back in the day. Today, sharing the air is most of what causes Covid losses.

I have been a member of the Portland Gay Men's Chorus since 2008. A few years ago, a member died of Alzheimer's. It hit me then that in the years I'd been in the chorus, no one had died of an AIDS-related cause. Time was, the chorus sang at one or two chorus member memorial services a month, all dying of AIDS.

When I joined, the chorus had a tradition: the first rehearsal of each month, those who were celebrating a birthday that month would get up on the stage of our rehearsal space and we would sing, "Happy birthday." A nice warm tradition. And back during the days of AIDS, a way of saying, "We're still here."

Sharing the air is precisely what we *can't* do these days. We can Skype. Zoom. Talk on the phone. But we can't rehearse. On occasion, someone will post a humorous little questionnaire on Facebook: favorite ice cream? ocean or mountains? morning person or night person? favorite day of the week? Monday. Because chorus rehearses Monday nights. Or used to. In my 34 years singing in GALA choruses, I have never had a concert canceled. A GALA chorus festival postponed. Sharing the air, music to my soul, isn't going to be what gets me through this time. So, what will?

I do have a useful takeaway from the AIDS era. We are resilient, life will go on, nothing will be the same, but that doesn't mean there will be nothing. My chorus is going to experiment with remote rehearsals, using available technology, adapting it as we can, doing what we can to stay connected. To see each other through. This, too, shall pass.

The PTSD of the AIDS era is kicking in for many, triggered into reliving the pain of loss. And realizing the old ways of coping aren't there—hugging, singing together, being together, embracing loss together. All the more bereft. Triggered into the past in a way that might be making it hard to embrace what connection there is available today. And really, if Zoom and Skype had been available to us during the heaviest days of AIDS, we would most certainly have taken advantage of this technology as well. We needed it then, we need it now, whatever will work.

So, isolated as we may be in our individual spaces, keeping ourselves physically safe, let us keep ourselves emotionally and spiritually safe as well. Reach out with whatever form of technology you have and connect. Have a virtual party. Cook together, each in your own kitchen. Raise a toast to each other from your various dining room tables. Put on a mask and take a meal in a bag, handing it to a homeless person. Feed the crows in downtown Portland, now bereft of much of their usual source of food. One of my favorite spiritual images is that we are all just seeing each other home. That remains the goal, though the means of doing so has changed so much, so fast.

Not long after our trip to China, PGMC sang a song titled "*Nia*." One of the seven principles of Kwaanza, *Nia* means "purpose in life." Since that concert, I've focused on my *Nia*. With each new revelation of identity throughout my life, I have come closer to the center of who I am as a person, thus approaching my *Nia*.

I love to cook for people, bringing them together over food. I love to sing *for* people in chorus, making them cry and laugh and sing along in unity. I love to sing *with* people in chorus. There is a reason choral singing originated in spiritual contexts. Sharing the air through music thins the boundaries between us, making our interconnection apparent. Building bridges as we sing side by side.

As the pandemic deepened, we sang… together… sort of… via Zoom. We could spot each other across the bridge as we sang. I cooked for people but couldn't share the food at table with them. Nurturing, yes. Building bridges? Not so much. I missed the physical presence of my friends with an ache Zoom couldn't quite assuage.

I had been asking, "How can I build bridges if we can't share the air?" Now, I found myself asking, "How *do* I build bridges now?" I hadn't always been sharing the air with the vast majority of people in the world, so that couldn't be the only way to establish the interconnection that I feel so strongly.

I discovered various unexpected silver linings from Covid. One is that I was forced to learn PowerPoint, not just relying on my ability to connect with people in person. True connection is difficult via Zoom, even if everyone appears on one screen. I discovered I have an unexpected talent for creating Zoom presentations. I presented at virtual conferences, and for national committees I could never have attended in person. I stopped attending conferences some years ago, as Cristina needed more in-person attention and, more recently, as my own mobility has been severely challenged.

PFLAG also discovered silver linings. People who live in small communities some way from Portland are able to attend Zoom meetings, which have been quite successfully supportive. This format is here to stay. We will have a few social gatherings every year—a summer picnic, a holiday party—and our bimonthly support circles will be all Zoom, all the time.

Some describe their spiritual awakening by saying God entered their heart. The bridge-builder in me experiences spirituality differently. My heart opened wide in China and God emerged, becoming the bridge between me and the rest of life, the universe, and everything. During the depths of quarantine, I felt a profound interconnection every time I prayed before my altar. No, I couldn't cook for you—and yet, we're still connected. No, I couldn't share the air with you—and yet, I still do.

What was missing wasn't the connection, but the ability to physically manifest connection. God gifted us with the power to connect with each other through touch, and that was denied us for a couple of years. We were all the more overwhelmed by the intensity of this loss at the beginning of the pandemic. Those of us who survived the AIDS epidemic had the feeling in the back of our minds, "This quarantine could last decades. I may never see some of my closest friends in person ever again." We had no way of knowing vaccines would become available as quickly as they did.

Goodbye, Mr. Blue Eyes

In mid-August of 2020, Figaro suddenly stopped being able to defecate, and was barely urinating. He spent some hours at an emergency vet clinic, undergoing tests that found a swollen lymph node. High probability of cancer. August 20, 2020—RIP Figaro, just one week after we noticed a problem.

Just like Figaro to create a problem with the timing of his passing. Quarantine meant not being with him at the vet, as we had been with Susanna. We asked around and contacted a company that makes house calls to help pets cross that rainbow bridge at home. Figaro died in my arms, and now, we have his collar and a snip of his fur on the altar.

Nearly a year after her journey north, Kiko had the run of the house, gradually turning into a real cat, formerly feral receding into her history. Figaro has joined the line of cats in heaven, shoulder to shoulder with Leon. Susanna is hidden behind them, well-protected.

It was a huge shock, losing part of my quarantine family, and so suddenly. Quite like Figaro. In early August, he was wandering the house, in and out as he pleased, sunning himself all afternoon on the back patio. Into everything he wasn't supposed to be. Never quiet when awake. And from mid-August, residing only in our hearts.

It Ain't Over 'Til it's Over…

And transition ain't ever over!

I applied for Medicare in early August of 2020, about to turn 65. Shortly before my birthday, I received a letter in the mail from Social Security, telling me to call not just a phone number but a specific person, named in the letter. I couldn't imagine what would warrant a letter telling me to call an actual person.

I called Usha, and a real person answered the phone. O.M.G.! Really??? She looked up my name and asked me security questions to verify it was really me. Then, she said the absolute last thing I would ever have expected:

"The gender you checked on your form doesn't match what's in our system."

As a therapist, I advised hundreds of trans people: "Before you ever start telling people you're going to transition, before you ever start taking hormones, right now, start making a list of all the places your name and gender appear. Include phone numbers, email addresses—whatever information will help you make the change once you reach that point. Add to the list as you think of new things. Library card. Your bank. School. Believe me, you will be so grateful to not have to create this list once people are reacting to your transition, especially if you're also going to be dealing with a shifting hormone balance."

No one ever gave me that advice 25 years ago. I never dealt with Social Security 25 years ago. I changed my name in the Social Security system as soon as my name change was legal, but I changed my name long before I started taking hormones and *could* change my gender. There is no gender indicated on my Social Security card. I forgot I'd never made that change to the Social Security system.

Usha: "Do you have paperwork that will verify your gender change?"

Me, nearly falling over laughing, "I might have a file... somewhere... maybe." [75]

Usha, beginning to laugh herself as the ludicrousness of the situation was clear, "Ordinarily, you'd have to take paper documentation to your local Social Security office along with your ID, to prove it's you. Because of Covid, the offices aren't open, so I'm going to waive this requirement and process your application. You'll still have to go in when the offices open up, but this will get you benefits in the meantime."

I was reminded of the woman at the Yreka DMV, jumping through computer systems to help me register Jan's car in my name.

So, trans folks reading this, make sure you've changed your name *and* gender everywhere you need to! And if, like me, you have transitioned long before you're dealing with Medicare or Social Security benefits, double check that you've changed your gender in their system!

Not a Birthday—A Lifeday

Early in 2021, there was such uncertainty about vaccines. Who was eligible? How to find one? At this time, the most widely publicized vaccines in Portland were available at the Oregon Convention Center, with rumors of long waits in line. My knee pained me to walk very far; standing in a line was unthinkable.

Cristina is the techie in our family. She monitored vaccination possibilities for me. March 6, 2021, my first vaccine. April 3, 2021, my second. [76]. I was not bothered at all to drive 60 miles to Salem Costco to

---

[75] Once again, Toby Meltzer proved himself as an ally and an all-around nice guy. When I had my chest surgery, he'd given me a notarized letter stating I'd had sufficient surgery to be considered male. I couldn't find this letter, 25 years on, so contacted his office. He sent me three notarized letters within a week of my request.

[76] October 28, 2021, first booster! Now, I've had three. PGMC requires singers to be up to date. No one can visit rehearsal without showing proof of current vaccination. We do our best!

receive my lifeline. It mattered not at all that I felt like I'd flown to China and back in one day after each shot, completely flattened with fatigue. I will always remember these dates not as a birthday but as a Lifeday.

Cristina's second vaccine shortly followed mine. Later that month, I accompanied Sue as she received her second vaccine. My friend John had been fully vaccinated since February. Mark, Sandy, David, Rick, Max, Rebecca… One by one, we were all given our Lifedays, breathing a sigh of relief as each of us received some degree of fortification in the era of Covid.

My friend Brenda, having to notify us back in February of 2020 that she had tested positive, is now part of a Long Covid study. She still has difficulties. And she comes over for lunch most Fridays. Life goes on.

Turning 63, singing in the Forbidden City. Turning 64, in the aftermath of Rita's death. How could I have predicted the circumstances of turning 65??? My church held a fundraising auction during the summer of 2020, of course virtual. I donated a Zoom dinner, offering to teach up to ten folks how to make dal. I didn't tell them in advance that the date was my 65th birthday. And it was such a wonderful moment when they all sang happy birthday to me in Zoom un-unison! As Sue put it, "What a fabulous quarantine birthday celebration!"

Living Quarantine

At the beginning of Covid quarantine, PGMC scouted about for various ways to keep members engaged and to support each other. Several people volunteered to host Zoom socials. My friend Mark hosted a Saturday morning Coffee Chat. The same people tended to show up every week. During the summer of 2021, this social went live, finally able to just… meet for coffee.

My friend John and I hosted a Friday evening hour-long social we called "Chorus Night In," since we couldn't have Chorus Night Out for some time to come. At the beginning of quarantine, vaccines weren't on the horizon, and we had no way of knowing how many years we might be hosting "CNI," as we came to call it.

When we first thought of hosting CNI, John and I tried to plan each Friday, thinking we would show chorus videos or play YouTube performances. We were quite concerned about how to make sure each hour was planned as a rehearsal would be, with no dead space.

Over time, we often forgot until the day of that we hadn't set up the Zoom call. One of us would text the other, "It's Friday already! Can you set up the Zoom?" We didn't plan anything at all, except to try to be on time so we wouldn't keep anyone waiting on the Zoom doorstep for the host to show up. John and I talked over when would be the last Chorus Night In, and decided—when PGMC resumed rehearsing in person, which happened in September of 2021.

I became used to showing up for morning Zoom meetings in my pajama bottoms and slippers, with a reasonable shirt. I took for granted being able to get up at 8:00, knowing I'd easily be on time for an 8:30 meeting after showering, making coffee, and grabbing a yogurt to eat during the meeting. It was all Zoom, all the time.

And, for many of the regular meetings I attend, it will continue to be all Zoom, all the time. We have discovered the joys of not driving to a meeting, hunting for a parking place, and then driving home past our bedtime. Kiko loved it when I attended Zoom meetings with her on my chest. She appears in the attendance of a number of meeting minutes: "Reid (accompanied by Kiko)."

During the height of quarantine, I had some actual in-person deliveries to make and realized, with a shock, that I was going to be late for the first delivery because I'd forgotten to build in sufficient travel time to my schedule. Human resilience is amazing. We adapt without knowing we've done so until we look back at the beginning.

It remains to be seen how quickly we will adapt to a new normal if Covid quarantine recedes into history, the disease morphing into just another annoying virus. Shopping without a mask—maybe. Hugging—perhaps not without a pause. Sharing the air in song, sharing meals in a crowded restaurant. I have faith that we will continue to adapt, though it will take longer for some of my friends than others as we continue to pivot in response to new Covid news. None of us will ever take our physical togetherness for granted again, no matter where Covid takes us.

"Normal" will mean different things to various of us. Some may never shop without a mask again. Some may always avail themselves of grocery delivery, a new concept to them prior to Covid. Some of us are far more familiar with GrubHub than we would ever have imagined. We are forever changed, regardless of what normal means to each of us in the future.

Thank God - I Survived

A bit at a time, a shelf here, a drawer there, I organized my office during Covid quarantine. At one point, I decided to order my old journals chronologically. I opened one only to see the date October 11, 1986.

It's always easy for me to get distracted when doing some tedious project, like organizing. But, in this case, I might be forgiven. October 1986—right around the time of the formation of the Portland Lesbian Choir. I hadn't read these journals since their writing, so was quite interested to "hear" what I had to say about the choir at its inception.

Excitedly, I sat down and began reading. Good thing I was sitting down, for in no way was I prepared for November 11, 1986.

> I've felt alone since I was born, and the feeling has only grown stronger as time passes. More and more, I am estranged from those of my age as they grow and develop and become more whole people. I withdraw more and more, feel more isolated as each year passes. I don't know how long I can go on like this. I am perpetually miserable.
>
> I don't think I used to be like this. That's one purpose of old journals. Sure, I used to get upset and depressed over various women, but I don't read any thread of suicide in my past writings. It's sure there now, make no mistake. Something is quite wrong with me, and I have managed to convince myself it's the way I am and nothing I can change. Which, of course, makes the suicidal thoughts all the stronger. If I can't change this, that means I will be this miserable all my life. And I simply can't want that for another *50 or 60 years*. I can't do it.

With shocked sympathy for my younger self, I read on, to November 23, 1986:

> Well, kid, you have to hang tough and keep open, because every now and then something actually will fall into place. I went, against my feelings and with nervous trepidation, to the Lesbian Community Project meeting. And afterward came the best thing of all—Sally announced the

formation of a lesbian chorus and gave the address. The next meeting was that evening, and I went with a couple of friends. We went to sing for the evening, and I am now part of the Portland Lesbian Choir. This day, I did something extremely important and good for myself.

In fact, I had joined the group that gave me a reason to live, a purpose in life, for the next nine years until I finally realized *why* I'd felt so increasingly isolated and depressed and miserable. Oh, my God, indeed. I have often looked back to that winter night in 1995, reaching out, saying miserably, "Help me, I can't do this anymore." Re-reading my 1986 self, I see now that 1995 wasn't the first time the hand of God saved me.

Yet another profound difference between the voice of then and the voice of now. How did I describe the formation of the Choir when I wrote Volume I of this memoir, twenty years ago?

> In October of 1986, a fledgling organization, the Lesbian Community Project, produced the first lesbian conference Portland had ever known. Over 400 women attended workshops on a variety of topics. I went, though I had no intention of joining any political group. Politics (and particularly processing) bored me. However, something happened at that conference that changed my life once again.
>
> A few women had been trying for a month or so to form a women's chorus in Portland but had had little success. Only four women had shown up at the first few meetings. Their advertising had been a little too minimalist. One member offered to announce the formation of this group at the Lesbian Community Project conference.
>
> With two friends, I heard the announcement, and all three of us decided to go to the next rehearsal to check it out. We did, and I stayed. For the next eleven years, the soon-to-be-named Portland Lesbian Choir was my spiritual center and the only place I ever felt truly at home in the lesbian community.

Well… yes… a good description of events, but not showing my heart. Ironically, the Choir saved me until 1995, when I was ready to face the knowledge that I needed to transition. Then I had to let the Choir go in order to do so.

I recently came across a meme[77] on Facebook that perfectly captures the depth of change necessary to transition.

> Grief Isn't Just For Death
> Relationships that have ended
> Losing your community
> Missing the certainty you once had
> Questioning your judgment
> Releasing who you once were
> Feeling lost and unanchored
> Losing traditions you loved

Yes. To every one of these, yes. I gave up the Choir. I gave up everything I thought was true about myself in order to pursue the unknown. Paradoxically, the life lesson I gleaned from this was: I don't pursue the unknown, I live it. I have always resonated with this particular bit of Rilke's writing, which came my way in graduate school. I included this once before in this book, and it bears repeating:

> Have patience with everything
> unresolved in your heart
> and try to love the questions themselves.
> Do not search for the answers,
> which could not be given to you now anyway,
> as you would not be able to live them.
> And the point is, to live everything.
> Live the questions now.
> Perhaps then, someday far in the future,
> you will gradually,
> without even knowing it,

---

[77] I tried without success to find out who to attribute this meme to. Please contact me if you know who I can thank for this incredible synthesis.

live your way into the answer.
~Rainier Maria Rilke

Life Inevitably Moves On

In October of 2020, I received notice from the DMV. Time to renew that car registration that took such angst to acquire in the first place. Really? Two years gone? In some ways, it felt like yesterday, and simultaneously Covid has stretched time to decades. The non-events of 2020 Covid quarantine created a huge gap back to 2019, which had already left 2018 in the distant past. 2018 and my trip to China, my spirituality finally front and center—2017 might as well be the nineteenth century. And as I write this, it's December of 2022. Into what black hole did 2021 disappear??? Where did 2022 go?

I have wondered about my siblings and how they would have adjusted to Covid. Like me, Jan and John were extroverts and would have used Zoom as I do, a lifeline to connect with others. Rita would have organized their street such that they would have had matching masks, undoubtedly the first street in Oakland to be fully vaccinated.

Susan would have retired from her practice before she would have considered using Zoom or any other form of telehealth for therapy appointments. A devout Luddite, she barely functioned with email. As an introvert, the biggest effect Covid would have had on her life was an inability to go to church. That deprivation might have forced her into Zoom along with the rest of us.

In early October of 2020, somewhat adjusted to Figaro's death in August, Cristina began looking at Craigslist and various humane societies, searching for a dog. I had come with Rikki when we met, and we had both been driven to rescue Figaro (and tagging along, Susanna) from the Humane Society. Kiko wouldn't socialize with anyone but me. Cristina had wanted a dog for years, and now was the time. Not only for companionship—she also felt a dog could be trained to be of service to her.

Perry is a handful of a German Shepherd. We laugh (sort of) as we watch him into everything, marveling that we thought Figaro a destructive and ruinous force of nature. He's a sweet-natured dog who came to us with absolutely no training. At first, he didn't even know we were trying to train him as we taught him to sit and not pull us everywhere when we tried to take him for walks. He had no idea what a leash was, or why we were trying to fasten one on him. The first time he heard the doorbell ring, he ran into the hall, where the bell is attached to the wall. He didn't connect it with the front door as we'd never had visitors. Perry is a Covid pup, born at the bare beginnings of Covid, his first ten months of life quarantined in a backyard.

As I told Cristina, "Take the long view. We can train behavior. You can't train temperament, and he's a sweetheart, well worth the effort to train." And effort it is, as well as a fabulous distraction from quarantine.

Kiko had the run of the house after Figaro and Susanna both died. She had become accustomed to emerging from her room to sit in my lap as I watched television at night, barely letting me settle on the couch before demanding her place. She was appalled at the sudden appearance of a 75-pound behemoth in the house. She and Perry eventually reached a *détente*. She didn't hiss at him if he didn't sneak into her room and devour her food at one gulp. Which he would do if the door was open and we weren't vigilant. I told Cristina she should be grateful he wanted her food and not her cat box.

Wrapping Up Quarantine

In the spring of 2021, I made chicken soup for a transman friend recuperating from chest surgery. As I was stirring in the chicken, it hit home what a different world we live in. I came home from my chest surgery on December 10, 1997 to find Lisa had set up a Christmas tree for me. She and some of my other friends did various things for me as I recovered. All were old friends of mine, friends from the lesbian community that I was leaving behind. Though supportive of me, there was also some grief at my transition. How could they be wholeheartedly happy for me?

I had two trans friends local to me, and one was Alan, with whom I had little contact by the time of my chest surgery. Great online support, via email, yes, but not much in person. I experienced a degree of isolation in my transition that would be foreign to a Portland resident today. Isolation today would be by choice. So glad for Charlie that I could make him soup, one of many friends (trans and otherwise) supporting him as he recovers.

I typed this section in June of 2021, sitting in bed with my computer in my lap, not at my desk. My leg was supposed to be elevated as much as possible. A word of caution: don't step down onto painted concrete, wet from watering the yard, without deliberation of movement. You will likely find yourself flat out on the ground before you can blink. Perhaps with a broken ankle. In a non-walking cast for a month, then a walking cast for another few weeks.

In retrospect, I have to laugh at the irony of it all. A couple of years ago, I was helping Susan maneuver Rita to a bedside commode. During this broken leg recovery period, I had a commode myself and counted my blessings that I didn't have to get to the bathroom. I became an expert at maneuvering around the house with a walker we had acquired years ago for Cristina's use.

I looked on this time as a retreat into quarantine. During the summer of 2021, I didn't leave the house except for orthopedic appointments. The difference is that it wasn't strict quarantine any longer, and I could have friends visit me. Sue visited me regularly, as did John. Other friends brought us home-cooked meals. Wonderful support!

All my friends have gone through profound change during Covid. Sandy went through a divorce after nearly 30 years with her wife. Several friends moved cross-country, closer to family while leaving a long-time Portland life behind. Sue now lives at the coast; quarantining for a year in her beach house made her realize how much she loved the rhythm of the ocean. Her weekend beach house get-away is now home. Covid has turned all our worlds upside down, none of us even close to the same people we were two years ago.

Back to the Future…

This date was momentous and will go down in PGMC history—October 3, 2021, the first time since March of 2020 that the entire chorus met in person to sing. Masked though we were, with some distance between our chairs, I looked at the open windows and knew the folks in the apartments across the street were back on their balconies, crying as they listened to us returning to a semblance of normal. Many had become season ticketholders after listening to our rehearsals, feeling blessed by happy accident to have moved across the street from our rehearsal space. Masked, yes. Singing, yes. Resilient? The epitome thereof.

Our choralographer Sara was there to teach us movement to a silly song. Later that evening, she posted to Facebook: "I was utterly devastated by how glorious that sound was. And the energy. Like palpable, audible love."

Covid wasn't done throwing us curveballs, however. In mid-October, Johnny sent out a bombshell of an email to the chorus. He had reached the end of his own resilience, giving his all to shepherd us this far through Covid quarantine. Our December concert, his first live with our audience, would also be his last. He was returning to his home base, New York City, needing so badly to rejuvenate and recharge himself.

So unfair, the timing of it all. We had five rehearsals with Johnny in early 2020 and then—quarantine. Our audience only saw him in virtual performances. He had never had a chance to develop his own support system here in Portland and felt keenly the long distance between himself and his family, both biological and of choice. PGMC has existed through ups and downs and AIDS and Covid. We will go on. And once again, the future is completely up in the air and who knows where we will land, or with whom.

Another milestone: the weekend of December 10, 2021, back on stage once again at the Newmark Theater, performing masked for a live audience. Nearly two years to the day since our last live musical venture. The concert started with the chorus invisible behind a scrim, Erik singing a solo. The audience lost it when the curtain came up mid-song, the chorus full-voice singing directly to our audience: "Come in from the rain."

Home again to the stage, singing for our lives, singing for our audience. Making people laugh and cry and shout with joy, giving them hope in the face of wherever their lives turn. A masked chorus. Not at full strength as yet. Providing a beacon of hope toward resiliency. We're back.

Chapter Thirty-One

Ends... New Beginnings... Ends

Yes, we were back. And once again, *déjà vu* all over again, about to embark on a director search. Fortunately, the chorus had just put together the infrastructure for a director search, and the same committee would reconvene. But first...

Ends

Johnny's first live concert with PGMC, December of 2021, was also his last. Our audience saw him in person long enough to wave goodbye. My on-stage experience completely overshadowed for me the momentous occasion of our first live concert in two years. My knee was so painful by that point that I used a walker to get around. I had no choice about using a stool on stage; no way could I stand for three concerts in one weekend.[78] The stool was uncomfortable, but who knew it was also hazardous to my health?

Midway through the first half, performing a rollicking song that had us swaying with our arms overhead, I felt a hand on my shoulder. I might have thought the guy behind me had accidentally touched me while doing choralography had I not heard a whisper in my ear, "Your stool is breaking out from under you."

I froze mid-movement, toning it down to nothing as I hardly dared breathe. The curtain came down mid-song as the piece transitioned to a quiet solo, and a stagehand dashed onstage to whisk my stool away. I stood for the last two songs of the first half. My stool was magically back in place after intermission. The stage manager later told me they put about 100 screws in it.

The next day, I sought out Ann, that miraculous stagehand, and gave her a Starbucks gift card. Turns out, she had noticed my stool giving way.

---

[78] A year later, I was determined to stand for all three of our December concerts. I did so, though it took a lot out of me. Total knee replacement comes with a long recovery process!

She had written a note on her iPad, in the largest possible font, holding it up from the nearby wings to warn me my stool was breaking. I didn't see her note, but the guy behind me fortunately did. What a showstopper that would have been, not to mention what I might have broken had Ann not acted so quickly.

Though we had reasonable audiences for all three shows, it wasn't the celebratory atmosphere we might have expected. Our audience was a bit anxious in the presence of so many people after two years of quarantine. Johnny was leaving. Covid was still very much in the fore, the Omicron variant having recently emerged. Our moods were dampened, chorus and audience alike. Johnny took off back for New York within days of the final holiday concert.

New Beginnings…

Rehearsals for the March 2022 concert, again with Mary leading as interim conductor, started without me. I have put some thought into determining the last time I'd taken a deliberate leave of absence from any chorus. My conclusion was—never. I didn't sing in Bridges when my voice began changing via hormones, but I didn't view that as a leave of absence. I came to rehearsals, and I helped produce a concert I didn't sing. This time, I didn't even attend the concert. It would have been a bit much of an undertaking a week after total knee replacement.

Despite not singing the concert and not even attending the performance, I did participate some weeks later in the auditions for our second new director. I had been disheartened when Johnny resigned. My thought was, *First there's this Covid thing, and then there's the fact that our last new director quit so soon after taking the job—who's even going to apply???*

Despite my fears, we had three stellar candidates audition. Braeden had auditioned in the first go-round director search in 2019. By the end of the second audition process, I went home to Cristina and said, as I had of Johnny, "He's the guy!" I admired Braeden for putting himself out there to audition again when he hadn't been selected the first time.

Our rehearsals with Braeden started in September of 2022, fabulous and high energy from the get-go. Over 90 people came to our first rehearsal and nearly 40 potential new members auditioned, more than I've ever seen in one term![79] Physical therapy and chiropractic were helping me regain mobility after knee replacement, walking without pain for the first time in some years. And—it's always something…

… Ends

September is complicated for me. My birthday leads off the month. Mid-month, several other family birthdays, including my mom's, then the anniversaries of Susan's and Jan's deaths a day apart.

Not long after my birthday, I heard a cat yell and hobbled a run into Kiko's room. She had lost control of her bowels from both ends. My heart sank, as I recognized this trajectory as the beginning of the end.

I spent as much time with Kiko as I could in the last weeks of her life, telling her repeatedly how much I loved her, how honored I was by her trust, how blessed we had been. Cristina and I had moved to a house that couldn't be more perfect for offering this particular cat a home. Her own room, with a side window view of trees and a fence-line squirrel highway. No cars or people in sight. Her own window perch that I called her "reality TV." A big bed covered with fleece blankets.

And me, her guy, saying, "Hey, girl" to her multiple times a day as I sat on the bed. Before I could get comfortable, she would be on me, on my heart. Her spot. Kiko died on September 21, laying on my heart, as the visiting vet injected her with the drug that would release her from pain. As she died, a chapter in my life closed as well, the last remnant of Susan's and Rita's life now gone. Kiko has joined that line of cats awaiting me in heaven.

Okay… time to end now. It's the middle of life, and there's just no good way to say, "The End."

---

[79] That record didn't stand long—in the fall of 2023, over 60 people auditioned, and 48 new members were accepted!

Epilogue

I quote myself from 2000:

> It's hard to know when to end an autobiography. If anyone had told me five years ago where I would be today, I would have thought them crazy. God knows where (or who) I will be five, ten, twenty years from now. Well, that will just have to be the next volume of this work in progress, this growth process that is my life. God, I love it! I wouldn't trade places with anyone.

This time, however, I'm going to publish Volumes One and Two. I don't take for granted my time here. I'm not feeling morbid. I'm a total optimist because I know there will be a future, as there has been a past. Life goes on. I just don't know how long I go on in this iteration of life.

I don't have a feeling of impending doom, or that I'm going to die of Covid. I don't feel I'm going to die any time soon. And yet, I have been driven to finish this autobiography. And now, I'm following an impulse to include other writings, not book length unto themselves. So, you get a bonus! Enjoy!

Finale

Volume III

I hadn't thought to begin writing Volume III until some unforeseeable point a decade or more in the future. I intended to rely on life events to catapult me into writing. A pandemic provided the catalyst for Volume II. And now, here's chapter ½ of Volume III. Life events have already catapulted me into writing. A word of advice from this 68-year-old: don't even try to think you know where life will take you.

Several years ago, I took on the task of answering emails for the Portland PFLAG chapter. On January 9, 2023, I fielded the following email:

> Hi, I'm in the UK., Mum to a 17-year-old transgender son. A friend of his arrived in the UK from the states in July after getting away from a very abusive family situation. He messed up his student visa and has to go back to the US at the end of this month.
>
> We've exhausted all avenues over here to keep him in the UK. He'll have to stay in the US for between 4 and 6 months until we can sort his visa. I'm trying to find an organisation who could help us temporarily house him or offer any advice on what we can do. He's a very vulnerable 18-year-old, and I'm terrified for him going back.
>
> Any help or advice would be really appreciated.
>
> Many thanks

Wendy[80] is that UK mum, a prototypical PFLAG parent, though she'd never heard of the organization until the day before she sent the above

---

[80] I wrote several blog entries about this whole saga. At first, I gave pseudonyms to all involved—Wendy was Kathy, and the youth she was sheltering was known as Tim. As the

message. For reasons I may never know, a New York transwoman and someone in Texas specifically recommended (unbeknownst to each other) that Wendy contact Portland PFLAG.

I replied to Wendy's email, and that afternoon we had an hour-long Zoom call. She told me some time later that she thought my email response was an autoreply; I got back to her within seconds of her sending her original email. For my part, the PFLAG email is one of several accounts that appear on my phone screen. I happened to be looking at my phone and saw that an email had come into the PFLAG account.

During that first Zoom call, Wendy told me, "I sent several hundreds of emails all over the U.S., trying to find help and guidance. No one stepped forward to help. Some organizations said, 'Maybe we can help if you bring him to our doorstep. Maybe.' All Theo could say about it was, 'Anywhere but California.' And then, you responded person to person."

I have seldom felt the hand of God guiding my life so strongly. Every step of the way, I acted out of confidence in the hand that was guiding me. On January 29, 2023, Wendy flew with Theo to Portland, getting him settled with me and Cristina.

Before their arrival, I put out a Facebook post, inviting support for Theo and outlining what might be needed. Several people stepped up and proved invaluable from the start (thank you, Abigail, Bo, Heidi, and Charlotte!).

Wendy stayed a week; by the time she left Portland, Theo was registered with the Oregon Health Plan (our insurance plan for those who are low-income), had an appointment with a trans clinic to begin the process of getting hormones, and had filed his paperwork for a legal name/gender change with the state of Oregon.

A month later: Theo's name and gender change were official. He had a new driver's license. He mailed his paperwork to get a new passport. He had an appointment a few weeks down the road that resulted in a hormone prescription. He'd been singing for several weeks with our local queer youth chorus, and he had been hired by a local grocery store as a cashier.

Wendy told me, "It's such a long process in the UK to get hormones. People end up on a waiting list for some years."

---

months went by, however, the need for pseudonyms went by the wayside, so now, I'm using their real names.

Not only will Theo be on his way with hormones before returning to the UK,[81] he has also accomplished bureaucratic steps that could only be done from within the US—his legal name and gender change, obtaining a driver's license with his new name and gender, his new passport. Returning to the US was the last thing he'd wanted to do, and yet, the silver linings are so apparent in his having to make the journey.

In December of 2022, we received a new cat, out of the blue. Susan's oldest Kathleen brought Harmony into our lives, a rescue kitty who needed a stable loving home. Knowing Kiko had died, Kathleen thought of me. Now here was Harmony, settled in for a month and quite ready to welcome a companion sleeping in her room with her every night. Theo was gifted with a loving cat companion to keep him company as he settles to sleep each night. For her part, Harmony was happily snuggled in with a cat whisperer once again. Mitigating Perry's attempts to gain access to her food bowl, she hisses him away as best she can, following in Kiko's footsteps.

Magical Families
(from August 16, 2023 blog)

It's been seven months since I first wrote about needing to form Team Tim, seeking support for a young man transported from England to Portland to take care of bureaucratic issues around a visa.[82]

How times have changed… Now, it's fine to use his real name, Theo. He no longer fears his biological family has any power over the course of his life (and he's right).

Let's see… Theo landed here with Wendy (his UK mom) on January 29. He started hormones on March 17 (a day he will celebrate every year as I celebrate June 20) His speaking voice began to have baritone overtones to it within a few months. I tease him about that, as I'm a baritone in the Portland Gay Men's Chorus and Theo sang in the first tenor section in the June Pride concert, a Disney extravaganza. I am the baritone section rep, and threatened to be Theo's section rep were he to sing with the chorus

---

[81] It's much easier to renew a hormone prescription in the UK than it is to get the initial prescription.
[82] See https://reidvanderburgh.com/2023/02/26/team-tim/ and https://reidvanderburgh.com/2023/02/26/what-a-great-town-we-live-in/ for the back story.

again. As it is, Cristina is the first tenor section rep, so he would be switching from one member to the other of his current family.

As we were rehearsing the concert, the chorus was told there were opportunities for two-minute storytelling scattered throughout the show. The story category "Life's a Journey" spoke to me, so I submitted the following story and told it during the concert:

> "The path toward happiness in life along the wrong gender trajectory isn't an easy one. You don't know it to look at me, but I'm a transman. In 1974, I fell in love with a woman, and it seemed to explain everything: 'No wonder I always felt different, like I didn't fit in. I must be a lesbian!!!' However, over the next twenty years or so, I still felt uncentered, not fitting in with myself.
>
> Eventually, I realized I'd misunderstood my identity back in 1974. I wasn't a lesbian: I was a transman.
>
> Long before I transitioned, I ventured forth several times on solo cross-country bicycle trips. I was having lunch in a Midwest café, at some point, and got to talking with a local guy. When he found out I was riding my bike cross-country, he joked, "That's what trains and planes are for!" However, Boston was my destination; the journey was my goal.
>
> Do I wish I'd understood myself back in 1974 and transitioned when I was 19? Not really. My journey through life was meant to be convoluted. Do I wish I could have snapped my fingers back in 1995 and hey, presto, I'm a man? No, an authentic life requires a journey, not a snap of the fingers."

The category that spoke to Theo was "Magical Families," and he read this during the concert.

> "Growing up in a conservative city in California, I understood two things relatively young: one: I was a boy, not a girl, two: that I would not be safe in the family I was born into.

Thankfully, I met my boyfriend online. Jack just happened to live in Manchester, England. Two weeks after I turned 18, I ran away from home, boarded a plane from LAX to the UK, and told my biological family not to contact me until they were able to love me not as their daughter, but as their son.

The plan was to unite with my boyfriend, Jack, and begin university in the fall. When I arrived, I instantly felt more loved and supported by Jack and his parents than I ever had at home. Unfortunately, it quickly became apparent that I didn't have the time or the funding to secure a student visa. We tried everything, but, in the end, I would have to go back to the United States until I could get my visa for the next school year.

Knowing that returning to my biological family was not a safe option, Jack's mother, Wendy, sent thousands of emails to charities across the US, looking for somewhere I could stay. Months went by with no response, and I had to leave England in only a few weeks. I was terrified. I had nowhere to go. Finally, someone replied: Reid Vanderburgh from the Portland PFLAG chapter. We threw together a plan. As soon as I arrived in Portland, an overwhelming connection and love sprouted—just like it had in Manchester. These people took me into their home, saved my life, and, as a bonus, I now sing with PGMC.

As I expected, I haven't spoken to my biological family since I left California. But with the loss of one family, I've gained not one, but two *chosen* families who I now can't imagine my life without."

Wendy and Jack made the journey from Manchester to see this concert. They were here for a magical week. Wendy and Jack both fell in love with Portland, and Wendy told me if she was twenty years younger, she'd transplant her family here immediately. As it is, by the end of their visit, we had come up with a new last name for all of us—Vandermingdale, combining all our last names into one. Theo no longer feels he has two families. We are all one family to each other now.

Oh, and by the way, Theo had chest surgery on August 15. His visa process went smoothly, and he was on his way back to England on September 3 with all his early transition goals checked off or in process.

Thank you: Abigail, Bo, Sue, Mark, Carissa, Jordan, Charlotte, Dennis, Mary, Bridging Voices, the Portland Gay Men's Chorus, and Portland PFLAG. It's taken a village.

That's it for Now

September 1 is my birthday. Theo did me the honor of not leaving back to England on my birthday. Our sense of loss in this household was profound. In the seven months Theo was with us, he was able to achieve everything related to early transition—legal name and gender change (affecting everything from his driver's license to his passport), beginning hormones, and having chest surgery.

Just as important are the invisible changes—centering into himself as his hormone balance aligns with his identity. Initially Theo was running away from an unsupportive biological family. Now he's focusing on his new life, new possibilities, moving forward with confidence rather than running away into an uncertain future.

Cristina and I took Theo in as a *mitzvah*, what our church would see as an example of "good works." It wasn't long, however, before we viewed him as a grandson who had been missing from our lives. Now, I am a neograndad, gifted with a new generation of family. I recently came across a meme that perfectly captures our experience.

> A young boy sits on a tree branch, speaking to an injured sparrow in a cage next to him.
>
> The boy says, "I'll take care of you until you can fly again."
>
> The sparrow responds, "But then, I may leave you."
>
> "Yes," says the boy, "that's the point."

Fly free and far, Theo!

Stay tuned at some future time for the continuation of Volume III of this work in progress, my life.

Appendix

Make Mine a Tailwind: Stories from the Road

My mother sold her last car in 1960. I was five years old. I grew up in the heart of San Francisco. To set the landscape—San Francisco is a peninsula of a city, 49 square miles. It will never be larger than 49 square miles, bounded by the Pacific Ocean and San Francisco Bay. The houses in most parts of the city are right up against each other. Building up is the only way to accommodate an increase in population.

With this level of population density in such a geographically small area, two things are truisms: you're never far from public transportation, and most people don't need a car to conduct activities of daily living.

I grew up walking seven blocks to the grocery store with my mom a few times a week, each of us carrying a bag home. Walking to school. Walking to Golden Gate Park to feed the squirrels in the Arboretum. Walking half a block to a bus or streetcar to go anywhere I wanted in my city. My mom walked to work each day at UC Hospital. I grew up independent of cars.

Driver education was a required high school class at that time. This class consisted of sitting in the driver seat of a simulator in a portable trailer in the cement school yard, essentially playing a video game with me as a car driver. This novel class was quite fun. It pre-dated video games, so bore no resemblance to anything else in our lives as high schoolers in the early 1970s.

Driver training was the next-step class, taking turns driving with several classmates and a teacher, in a real car, on real San Francisco streets. At the end of this class, I received my learner's permit, allowing me to practice driving at home with a licensed driver in the passenger seat. The goal was my eventually acquiring a driver's license.

And just how would I practice without a car in the driveway at home? It didn't seem worth the effort to organize practicing driving with someone, then taking the test to get my license. What use was a driver's license to me? Buses and walking were a much more practical way to get around my congested city. I had a bicycle, but rarely rode it anywhere in my city of hills. And living in San Francisco, why would I want to go anywhere else? Even as a child, I knew I lived somewhere "special."

Despite growing up somewhere "special," I moved to small-town Oregon in 1976 to go to college. I lived about a mile from campus. I dusted off that bicycle and rode to school each day. As I had with my mother throughout my childhood, I walked to the grocery store a few times a week. I walked to the library to check out books. I walked to my local movie theater. I never felt constricted by lack of a driver's license or car.

At one point, I had an appointment in a town some seven miles from home. Ordinarily, I would have taken the bus. For reasons I don't remember, the bus wasn't an option that particular day. What to do??? I looked at my bicycle with new eyes. Perhaps this would work.

There was something about the idea of riding to an entirely other town that seemed insurmountable by bicycle. I loaded my backpack with enough water and food to climb Mt. Everest. I left hours early. And was hours early for my appointment. I was there in less than half an hour.

I felt such a sense of accomplishment and freedom! I was now conscious of a constriction I'd never felt while growing up. I no longer lived an easy bus and walk to anywhere I'd like to go. There was a degree of logistics and planning involved, less spontaneity. My bicycle shifted significance in my life from my daily ride to school to my form of transportation, the ticket to my regaining a feeling of independence.

I bought a bicycle repair book and took my bike apart, cleaning derailleurs, chain, brake cables, learning how it all worked and fit together. I bought a subscription to *Bicycling* magazine. I was more intrigued by bicycle touring than racing. I didn't care how fast I got there. I was more interested in reading stories of people like me, using their bicycles for transportation. Bicycle touring was an intriguing expansion on tying the rhythm of daily life to riding a bicycle.

I was hooked when I read about the Bikecentennial, a cross-country trek a group had undertaken in celebration of the 1976 bicentennial of the birth of the United States. My imagination was captured by the idea, and I determined that I would someday do a bicycle tour myself. However, my $50 Sears bike wasn't going to be the vehicle to take me there.

By this time, I'd learned brands—which bicycles are good, which are best, which components are more appropriate for racing, and which for touring. A woman cyclist wrote an article in *Bicycling* that caught my attention: men's and women's bodies[83] are differently proportioned; the geometry of bicycle frames should differ based on who was going to be the rider. Women have longer legs and shorter arms, on average, than a man of the same height, who will have shorter legs and longer arms.

The author was a physical therapist. She had noted that a number of women cyclists had come in complaining of severe back pain. Her conclusion? The geometry of their bicycles was designed for men, with longer arms. To reach the handlebars, the women were having to reach further than was good for their backs. Their bikes fit their leg length, but not their reach. At the time, the only solution was a custom bicycle frame. There weren't yet any commercially produced bicycles taking this physiological difference into account.

Life was pretty cheap in small town Oregon. I saved money my mother sent me for birthdays and the like, and money I earned from a part-time job working the cash register in a small shop. Within a few months, I had enough money saved for a custom bicycle frame. I built my bike up from the frame. I chose my components with care. I even built my own wheels, taking them to my local bike shop for inspection before daring to actually ride on them.

The result was a lightweight touring bike that fit me perfectly, weighing in at 22 pounds. The first ride I did of any length was 30 miles into Portland to visit friends for a weekend. It was a short step from there to believing I could go anywhere on my bike. As a result, I didn't acquire a driver's license until I was 44 years old. My childhood experience—walking and bussing everywhere—carried forward into adult life, with the addition of my bicycle. I took great pride in not contributing to air pollution through driving a car.

During the 1980s, I ventured forth on four bicycle tours of varying lengths and with varying destinations. And with stories to tell as a result…

---

[83] As a transman, I am well aware that the wording here is problematic. My wording reflects what I gleaned at the time, not how I feel now about gender identity and terminology.

The Bear

It was a placid June afternoon. Not much breeze through the brilliantly blue skies. My first trip through eastern Oregon, I was riding a deserted road in the Umatilla National Forest. Across a valley of trees, I could see the interstate traversing the foothills of the Blue Mountains, not out of sight, but fortunately out of earshot. The interstate paralleled my route, drawing all car traffic from my little road, slowly cracking its way back to oblivion, supplanted by I-84.

I took my time, in no particular hurry. The road switch-backed its way up, occasionally flattening for a stretch, then around a bend to switch-back up some more. Though it was over 90 degrees out, I wasn't much bothered by the dry heat. I stopped now and then when I encountered shade trees, straddling my bicycle in the middle of the road, sipping from one of my water bottles. Reveling in the sage and pine of the air and the quiet breezes of nature.

I rounded a bend and froze to a fast stop. A hundred feet or so ahead of me, mid-road, was a sleepy bear, facing sideways to me. I gradually breathed again as it became clear the creature had no awareness whatsoever of my presence. I knew nothing about bears. Black? Brown? All I knew was…a bear. Sitting mid-road sunning itself. Not at all concerned about no traffic.

I stood straddled, pondering, breathing. Sipping water. How long we communed like this, I have no idea. Eventually, my companion slowly lumbered feetward and ambled on across the cracked pavement, disappearing with some rustling into the bushes crowding the edge of the road. All sound died down. Gone.

I waited a few more minutes, listening carefully to the silence. Then, slowly, onward and upward.

The Cemetery

I rode by the cemetery late afternoon. Though a bit earlier than I usually stopped, I pulled in. My favorite place to camp was a country cemetery. No one ever comes there after dark. Wheeling my bicycle off road, picking a spot shielded from the road by bushes, no one was the wiser that I was there. As a woman, I felt more vulnerable camping in a campground. People saw me, and that I was alone, and traveling by bicycle. The only advantage of a campground was the occasional shower.

This particular cemetery was several miles from the nearest small town. As my can of soup heated on my one-burner stove, I wandered around, considering how many stories were buried here. Half the names were "Smith" and the other half "Jones." And I'd bet many of the women had switched one name for the other. One family plot caught my attention—three children, all dying in 1918. Of course. The Spanish flu. I saw what must have been their parents, surviving their children by several decades. What sorrow this family had known.

Other dates of significance caught me, seeing various military symbols on graves. Some dated back to the Civil War or World War I. Several graves with fresh flowers, reminding me to consult my journal, verifying the day of the week. Saturday wasn't the time to camp in a country cemetery. Of all days of the week, Sunday morning was the most likely for a visit to the cemetery to pay respects. I never camped directly on a grave, nevertheless, I didn't want anyone to feel I'd desecrated their relative.

As I ate my soup, I heard a rustle in the bushes beside me and a small calico cat emerged, looking at me curiously. Bicycles are not modes of transport deep in the country. Camping in the cemetery was a novelty to this creature, I could tell from its expression. Finishing my soup, I sealed the bargain by allowing the purring cat to lap the remains of my dinner as I stroked its fur. It probably lived on the farm I'd passed around the last bend.

Curling into my sleeping bag as the last remnant of sunset faded and the fireflies were out in full, I left the door of my tent unzipped and clicked my tongue invitingly, hoping. I would trade a few mosquito bites for cat company. A few minutes later, rewarded by a snuggling ball of purr. I was six weeks removed from my beloved Bear Cub, patiently awaiting my return so she could be my snuggling ball of purr once again. I felt gifted that night, falling asleep with a cat curled into me.

The Original Remark

1987 marked the longest bicycle trip I undertook—over 5,200 miles, gone nearly five months. Twenty-two states and two Canadian provinces, I rode cross-country and halfway back. Dipping my wheels in the Pacific and Atlantic Oceans, a tradition among cross-country bicycle tourists.

I heard the same remarks time and over again all summer. From men, in a jocular tone: "That's a heavy load you got there!" From women, with great concern: "You're not doing this alone, are you?" And from everyone, upon hearing Boston was my destination: "You've got a long way to go!" (I had to laugh when I heard this remark in western Massachusetts, 50 miles shy of my Boston destination.) Along about Iowa, I experimented telling people I was heading to Portland, just to hear them say what a long way it was.

By mid-September, I was nearing the end of my trip, approaching Portland from the north via the Olympic Peninsula of Washington State. It was a momentous day when I came in sight of the Pacific Ocean, feeling the pull of home. Toward the end of the day, I pulled into a campground on a bluff overlooking the ocean. I rode slowly around the loop road, looking for a vacant spot to set up tent.

I was riding a sturdy all-terrain bicycle, with full panniers front and rear. For this trip, I'd made a carry-all bag of waterproof nylon to strap to my rear rack, shielding my sleeping bag, foam pad, and tent from any kind of weather I might encounter. A full handlebar pack, with eight cassette tapes for my Walkman, and the map of the week. 80 pounds' worth of home.

As I rode along, walking pace, an older gentleman emerged from a dirt path close to the cliff's edge. He was carrying a load of firewood. He stopped to let me pass, gazing at my home-on-a-bike, and said admiringly, "That's not a bike! That's a small pick-up!" The only original remark I heard all summer.

How Surrealistic

As a woman biking alone cross-country, as a lesbian venturing through the Midwest by myself, I wanted to connect with my own along the way. I had subscribed to *Lesbian Connection* for years, a monthly publication consisting entirely of letters written about various topics, and letters in response to letters in response. Announcements of coming events. And a "Contact Dyke" list, in service of community connection for lesbians on the road or moving to a new place. I had been a Contact Dyke since I'd first subscribed to *Lesbian Connection*.

In the fall of 1986, I put an announcement in *Lesbian Connection* that I was riding my bicycle cross-country the following summer. My route would be partly determined by responses I got from Contact Dykes offering a place to stay and a bit of connection with some of my own people.

I wasn't entirely surprised my first contact ended up being in eastern Kansas. From there on east, I had fairly regular contacts, but a lonely span of 1,800 miles lay between me and that first contact. The states I would be riding through in the meantime—Idaho, Wyoming, Utah, Colorado—didn't have a stellar reputation as lesbian-friendly places to live, especially since I avoided cities. The lack of representation among the Contact Dykes was hardly surprising.

I met nice folks along the way, had offers of places to stay the night from locals, ate many meals at the family dinner table. Nothing like an 80-pound bicycle to start a conversation! And I felt the lack of lesbian community, looking forward to that first contact in Kansas.

Along about eastern Colorado, nearing Kansas, still four days from my contact, I was battling sidewinds and worrying about roiling black thunderclouds looming overhead. A pickup truck passed me heading west on the sparsely traveled state highway. In my mirror, I saw the truck turn around and head back east, passing me and pulling off on the shoulder. I was irritated: "Please don't make me stop with small talk about how far I've got to go and what a heavy load I've got! I want to get under cover somewhere before the rains hit!"

I was of a mind to ride on past, but as I approached, the driver got out and leaned against the truck, arms folded. Lesbians of that era used to joke that only on the east or west coasts did "gay-dar" work to spot lesbians. In the Midwest, all bets were off. Many women, straight or otherwise, wore their hair short, didn't wear makeup, and wore jeans and flannel shirts all the time. However, even in the Midwest, I recognized this woman was a lesbian. I practically skidded to a stop.

She asked, "Are you Nancy?"

My mouth fell open in astonishment. It had been 1,600 miles since anyone had known my name.

Her name was Ann. She was on her way to a conference in Denver. She'd been unhappy over the timing, as her best friend was all excited to be a Contact Dyke about to host a woman biking from Portland...

I sat in her truck for half an hour, and we chatted while the thunderstorm blew in and over. As I got out again, the air fresh from the heavy rain, Ann waved and called out, "I'll call Marcy when I get to Denver and tell her that I saw you and that you'll be there in a few days!"

God's Bedroom

Trail Ridge Road. 12,183 feet. The highest continuously paved road in the continental United States. The summit of this road is higher by 1,000 feet than the tip-top of Mt. Hood, that glorious mountain just east of Portland. Featured in an article in *Bicycling* magazine in the early 1980s, I knew this road was destined for a future bicycle tour. How could I possibly resist such a challenge! The centerpiece of my 1987 cross-country trek became Trail Ridge Road.

Riding east from Portland felt like one mountain range after another. Right off the bat, the Cascades. On through eastern Oregon, over the Blue Mountains, cutting a corner of Idaho, over the Uinta Mountains in Utah, a rare east-west mountain range. Turning left to head east into Colorado, the Rocky Mountains gradually dominated the skyline. Turns out all previous mountains were practice runs.

The Rockies don't appear as high in western Colorado as they would from western Oregon. Portland has an average elevation of about 60 feet above sea level. From this perspective, the mountains I was approaching would have seemed high indeed, with peaks 14,000+ feet above sea level. 3,000 feet higher than Mt. Hood.

Western Colorado, however, is already more than a mile above sea level. Climbing to leave Portland, and never quite getting the full descent on the other side to the high desert of central Oregon. Climbing some more, and never fully coming down the other side before hitting a plateau before climbing some more. From western Colorado, the Rockies appear shorter than the Cascades are from Portland.

From a bicyclist's perspective, my body was already acclimated to over a mile high. Good thing, since I was about to add another mile to my altitude and back down again in one day's ride.

The Rocky Mountains extend nearly 2,000 miles, from northern British Columbia down through Colorado, fading into the deserts of New Mexico. Grand Lake, Colorado marks the western entrance to Rocky Mountain National Park, home to the highest peaks in the entire mountain range.

Grand Lake is a small touristy town nestled in the western foothills of the Rockies, over 8,000 feet in elevation, with a disproportionate number of restaurants and bed-and-breakfasts. Whether about to embark upward or just returning from the heights, whether biking, backpacking, or car driving, calories would be in high demand.

Shortly after noon, I leaned my bike against the outer wall of a café and went inside for yet another meal. The attraction of this particular café was the "all you can eat" sign out front. For a fixed price, I could go back to the buffet for seconds. And thirds. And fourths. "All you can eat" made no money off me that summer! I couldn't keep up with the calories I was expending.

As I ate and got more food and ate again, I chatted with Rhonda behind the cash register. Upon learning I was heading east on a bicycle, she said, with great concern, "You're not going over Trail Ridge *today* are you?" I said no, next morning, and she said, with even greater relief, "Oh, good, cuz you're gonna be in God's bedroom up there."

Finally, The Day. I fortified myself with the largest breakfast or two I could find, knowing I'd have no way to eat more than granola bars on the way up and over. By all accounts, there was no place to stop on the way up beyond a very occasional porta-potty. No infrastructure on this road beyond the road itself.[84]

When approaching a mountain range, there is a period of foothills that is seductive: "I'm climbing the mountains now." Then, you reach the mountains and realize, "Oh. *Now*, I'm climbing the mountains." The road out of Grand Lake is mountains. Immediately. And for a *long time*. Next stop: Estes Park, over 40 miles ahead to the beginning of the other side of the country, across the Continental Divide.

The trees grew shorter and more scraggly with each twist up of the road. Further apart as the air thinned. Patches of snow in the shade became walls of ice narrowing the road. The peaks of Trail Ridge are aptly named: the "Never Summer Mountains."

The trees straggled, and then were gone. Above the treeline, even near summer solstice, the ice never melts. This is tundra country. No shoulder going either direction, the walls of ice encroaching on the pavement, obliterating the white line indicating road's edge. This road was only open about two months out of each year. May 31 was the earliest it had been open in over twenty years.

And the wind. Always the wind. Nothing to break it any longer. It shifted, never consistently from one direction. I was nearly blown across the road numerous times. On a rare stretch of road that was downhill, I had to

---

[84] There is a visitor's center near the summit. I didn't stop, as I knew it would be too difficult to pry myself back out onto the road again and the day was fast fading.

pedal downhill through a headwind. Some four miles from the top, the headwind was so strong I had to push my bike for half a mile or so uphill.

The sky was thin, and I felt I was living above the atmosphere, as if I could take off for outer space with very little effort because I was already halfway there. The sun looked so close. I couldn't catch my breath and felt quite out of shape. My admiration for those who climb Mt. Everest soared to hero worship. Over twice as high as I was now.

As I approached the top, I looked with great anticipation for a summit sign. Every bicycle tourist learns to recognize "The Top." A crest of a hill, then a gradual flatness, a shifting of gears, and then no need to pedal any longer. And—a sign we live for, a photo op for the bicycle leaning against a sign that says—there was no summit sign.

I felt cheated. Of all the summits I'd achieved, this was the hardest won. I was to learn later, on the other side, that there is no summit sign for Trail Ridge Road to prevent cars from stopping mid-road for the photo op of the highest such sign in the continental U.S.

As I considered the descent, I was a bit desperate. It had taken me 'til midafternoon to get to the top, over 20 miles up from Grand Lake. As I continued east, down the back side of the Rockies, I was leaving the sun on the west side of the mountains. Dark would come fast. I still had nearly 20 miles to Estes Park.

I hitch-hiked down. As I stood with my thumb out, I looked out east, and, in the distance, a bit south and a long way down, I saw the smog of Denver, the mile-high city, a mile below me.

Jane and Roger stopped to pick me up. My gear and bike filled the back of their station wagon. They drove me into Estes Park. As we talked, I was astonished to learn that they'd already passed me going the other way. They were heading over Trail Ridge Road to go home to Grand Lake. They had just moved there a few months before. They'd never driven Trail Ridge Road because it had just opened for summer season. They were touring in their new community. They saw me hitch-hiking and *turned around* to do a good deed. As Roger described it, they were moved by the desperation in my face.

This was an even bigger good deed than they initially realized. Trail Ridge Road closes at 6:00 each evening, which they had not known. The Forest Service patrols the road to rescue those left behind when the gates are locked. Jane and Roger drove me to Estes Park, and then had to drive around the Never Summer Mountains via the interstate, not over the top. Their day was extended by nearly 100 miles beyond what they anticipated.

I spent the next couple of days recuperating in Estes Park, gazing from the porch of my motel at what I'd accomplished. I was so depleted on arrival I couldn't even go to dinner. I ate my last granola bar and collapsed in bed.

The next day, I went no further than the café a couple of doors down, tired out by that small level of activity. I'd fully drained my considerable strength and stamina on that trek into the heights of the earth, fueled only by breakfast and some granola bars, gaining and losing nearly a mile in elevation in one day. God's bedroom indeed.

It's a Journey

While doing laundry in a small Illinois town, I went to a nearby café for lunch while my clothes washed. I ate at every opportunity, trying to replenish the thousands of calories a day I was burning. Sitting at the counter, I got to talking with a man on his lunch break from work. Upon finding out I was biking cross-country, heading to Boston, he laughed and said, intending humor, "That's what trains and planes are for!"

As I rode away from his town, I thought about what he said. On one trip, I rode to California. Ten days on the road. I filled a journal and shot five rolls of film. I had ridden to a music festival and met up with some friends from Portland. By previous arrangement, I rode back to Portland with them. A van up I-5, home in two days. I wrote a few entries in my journal and took zero photos.

An hour or so into my afternoon, I finally articulated my response to the man in the café: Boston was my destination—the journey was my goal.

The Vagaries of Wildlife

Late one Monday afternoon, I pulled into a deserted campground in rural Vermont. I'd just shopped a few miles back for the next day or so—cans of soup, granola bars, a loaf of bread. Some apples. A bag of nuts. According to my map, I was heading into the Green Mountain National Forest and wouldn't encounter another town for thirty miles or so—most of a day's ride in mountain country. This food had to last through tomorrow.

As I rode into the camping area, I saw a large sign warning me: "Keep All Food in Your Car." Racoons. Bears. Various other non-human entities would eat it. Further instruction? Not. In. Your. Tent. Well, what am I supposed to do, with my bicycle and my tent?

As I heated my soup for dinner, I pondered my options. There was no one else around that I could ask, "Can I put my food in your car for the night?" So… Tent my food and end up mauled by a bear who was after my granola bars? Leave my food in my panniers and find them torn to shreds in the morning, useless for the remaining 2,500 miles of my journey? Put all my food on the picnic table, as far from my tent as could be, and hope for the best? Not much else I could do!

Next morning, a few cans of soup and some scattered wrappers. Not even an apple core. I hope that animal was grateful for its feast. Dammit!

Canadian Camaraderie

Among the Contact Dykes I met up with were Jane and Kerry in London, Ontario. I'd never been to that part of Canada before. After crossing the Canadian border into upstate New York, I rode along the north edge of Lake Ontario. Some weeks earlier, I'd ridden along the south edge of Lake Erie, making my way toward Boston. What a difference. No industry on the Canadian side, just a road meandering its way alongside a gorgeous lake. Along the south shore of Lake Erie, I couldn't see the lake for American industry.

As I approached Toronto, I was impressed with the cleanliness in general of my suburban and then urban surroundings. I didn't want Toronto to end, this beautiful city! I found myself too distracted by traffic to fully appreciate my surroundings, so got off my bike and walked it through the entire city.

I had planned my route to avoid cities as much as possible. Navigating unfamiliar territory while surrounded by urban cars is no fun at all. Walking through this vibrant city, with the grandeur of its British-legacy architecture and full of friendly Canadians, was a treat to this city kid.

At one point, stopped at a street vendor for a soda and snack, I got to talking with a man who was excited by my trip. He too was intrigued by bicycle touring but had yet to undertake a venture. I eagerly recruited him to the fabulousness of seeing the world from the seat of a bicycle; it didn't take much convincing.

We'd talked for some twenty minutes when his girlfriend joined us. He went off in search of a bathroom, and his girlfriend said that she'd tried to talk him out of bicycle touring because of the dangers. I felt a small stab of guilt, knowing I'd fully talked him into it.

When I reached London, Jane and Kerry were eager to show me a good time. I'd told them about my bottomless appetite, and they chose a particular pub to see history in the making: the baskets of chicken wings, or fish and chips, contained so much food, they typically ordered one to split between them; even then, they never finished it all. I said I'd probably be able to finish one basket all on my own. By the time I was done with mine, I nibbled bits from their basket as well as they watched in awe.

Pride 1987

I was gone nearly five months in 1987. No such thing as an internet—cell phones, texting, the internet, the stuff of science fiction. The most advanced technology available to me was my Walkman with ear buds and cassette tapes. Going on a bicycle tour at that time meant being *gone* gone. No one had a way to contact me, nor did they expect to hear from me beyond postcards and the occasional letter.

Five months is a long time to miss friends, however. So, in the planning stages of my trip, I chose half a dozen small towns along my route. I wrote to the post office in each town and said I would like them to hold mail for me, to be picked up by a certain date. I let all my friends know when and where each town was along my itinerary.

Those were special stops, picking up packets of mail. My friends wrote me faithfully, letting me know the doings of their lives. My late June stop was particularly heart-warming. I received a letter in the mail from a PLC friend, with a concert flyer and cassette tape enclosed—a joint concert featuring the Portland Gay Men's Chorus with their special guest, the brand-new Portland Lesbian Choir.

As a founding member of the Choir the preceding fall, I was so sad to miss this performance, though I cheered for them from the heartland of America. I rode away from that Iowa post office with the cassette playing the cheering Pride audience, applauding the only city in the country to have a lesbian and a gay chorus that used the L and G words in their name. That cassette was my Pride celebration of 1987.

Dumb Cows

Western Kansas had little distraction on the roadside. Little traffic on the state highways I chose to ride. Not much need for changing gears. After traversing one mountain range after another since leaving Portland, I took some time getting used to the fact that clouds low in the east were not mountains that I was approaching. With the Rockies in my rearview mirror, there were no more mountains until the Appalachians 1,000 miles east of me, and I'd be riding north of them.

No trees. Some corn. More wheat. And cows. One afternoon, I rode by a fairly large herd, grazing near the fence. As I stopped to sip some water, they raised their heads in unison and munched thoughtfully while gazing at me. *Never seen a bike*, was my amused conclusion. Given how many bicyclists I'd seen in this part of the country (read, none), I was pretty sure I was a novelty, breaking up the monotony of their day. We communed contentedly for a while, then I rode off, their gaze following me with the typically mild interest of cows.

A few miles down the road, a town. As always, I stopped for a soda at the local market. Seeing my bicycle propped outside, the woman behind the counter asked, "So, are you going to catch up with the others?" Seeing my obvious confusion, she continued, "You know, Biking Across Kansas."

Upon further inquiry, she filled me in. An every-year event, Biking Across Kansas was a 400-mile trek across the state. Several hundred bicyclists had ridden through town the day before. But first, those same bicyclists had ridden past a certain herd of cows. So much for being a novel experience!

Biking with Others

I encountered other bicyclists on occasion. In a small Illinois town, I met Henry and Patricia in a grocery store. They enjoyed short bicycle tours and had a lifelong goal of doing a tour in every state in the country. So far, they'd been to eighteen states. Our conversation turned into an invitation to stay the night at their home. Over dinner that evening, I told them stories of what I'd seen, and they told me stories about states I had yet to experience.

The idea occurred to all of us at once, so I don't remember who said it aloud first. The next day was Saturday, and they rode with me that day, all of us staying the night in a motel some fifty miles from their home. They returned home on Sunday. I didn't often ride with others, and it was a novel treat. Their bicycles together weighed considerably less than mine. They weren't carrying their home with them!

Patricia was much shorter than I, but Henry was about my height. It fit him to take a turn riding my bike while I reveled in briefly riding a bike that weighed next to nothing in comparison. A mile or two later, we switched back, Henry enthusiastic in his admiration of my fortitude and physical endurance. The following year, they added Oregon to their list of week-long tours. I rode along with them, showing off a bit of my state.

Some hundreds of miles east of Henry and Patricia, I saw a racing cyclist by the side of a Pennsylvania road, briefly resting to sip some water. I pulled alongside him, and we got to talking. Fred had never toured before and was somewhat condescendingly curious. I offered to let him take a spin on my bike. As he wobbled along, nearly falling several times, I held my breath, hoping he wouldn't damage my home-on-wheels. He didn't dare try to turn around. He got off the bike and wheeled it back to where I was holding his 19-pound racer. Condescension entirely gone, Fred was now incredulously respectful that I'd ridden this behemoth all the way from Oregon!

Pretty Much Flat—Yeah, Right

Wyoming is a beautiful state, photo ops in all directions. In western Oregon, we know to look to the west to find our weather. If it's raining at the coast in the morning, we're looking for rain in Portland that afternoon. Rarely does our weather approach from any other direction than the Pacific Ocean. In Wyoming…!

Ruth had never lived anywhere outside Wyoming. A waitress in a café, she served me a huge lunch as we chatted. She said, "Here, we say, 'If you don't like the weather, wait five minutes.' It's always coming from different directions."

As I pedaled away from lunch, I was thankful to have eaten substantially. The wind swirled and shifted all around me, at times trying to blow me across the road. I stopped at one point, holding my bike for dear life as a particularly powerful gust tried to blow us into a neighboring pasture. As I planted myself to earth, I saw a cowboy in the pasture, herding cattle in our direction. We waved to each other, and he tipped his cap to me.

Mid-afternoon, I pulled into the town of Kemmerer. Munching a granola bar outside a store (I was always munching something when off the bike), I got talking with George, cheerfully helpful when consulted about the road ahead of me, trying to determine just how much food shopping I might need to do that day. He told me my route was "pretty much flat" all the way to my next town, Vernal, Utah.

Unless they also have experience biking, car drivers are notoriously unreliable sources of information about hills or distance. Asked how far the next town might be, "Oh, it's just over that hill. A mile or two," may easily mean five miles with several significant climbs that don't register from behind the wheel of a car. I have to say, though, George took the cake. "Pretty much flat"—other than the long descent into and climb out of Flaming Gorge, a mini version of the Grand Canyon. Oh yeah. There's that.

I would never have expected traffic jams in Wyoming. Unfortunate coincidence: I traversed Flaming Gorge on the Saturday of Memorial Day weekend. The reservoir at the bottom of the gorge opened for boating season on Memorial Day. Every boat owner for a hundred miles around was towing their boat on my road, preparing for summer on Flaming Gorge Reservoir. I was more than hot and bothered by the time I climbed the other side, now in Utah, relieved to no longer share half the shoulder with a literal boat of a car.

Journey's End

The first solo bicycle tour I undertook was in 1981, riding from Portland to my home base in San Francisco. There was some timing involved in this trip. I was planning to attend the West Coast Women's Music Festival in Yosemite. However, I had another agenda item prior to the festival—attending my family's annual September birthday party. Five family members, including my mother and I, had September birthdates to celebrate.

I love surprising people. I told my mother that I wouldn't have time to come to the Bay Area prior to heading to Yosemite and couldn't attend the family party that year. With the connivance of my sisters and brother, however, I made arrangements to be the pinnacle surprise in celebrating our mother's birthday.

I had decided to ride down to California along the east side of the Cascade Mountains. I thought this would be a nice introduction to parts of my adopted state that I'd never visited. I crossed over into California near the Nevada border. Continuing south, I crossed back west at Mt. Lassen, the last peak in the Cascade Mountain range. I then angled down toward the Bay Area, through the Napa Valley and down Highway 101.

It was a glorious moment when I crested a hill, and there was San Francisco Bay laid out below me, the Golden Gate Bridge prominent in front of me. I walked my bike over the Bridge, home again. What a long distance I'd come, from the time it seemed insurmountable to ride to the next town over from Forest Grove, seven miles away! What a difference five years made!

I'd toured by bicycle once before but had ridden with someone who had a bad back. Riding at her pace, we averaged about 30 miles a day. I didn't actually know what I'd be capable of all on my own. I estimated a three-week trip. It was a serene uneventful tour, a perfect introduction to solo long-distancing. No rain. No extreme heat. No flat tires or other bicycle mishaps. Convenient places to wheel off-road each night and camp unseen. I ended up a week early for the birthday party. What to do? I still wanted to surprise my mother, so where would I stay for those seven days?

As I rode that last day, I planned and schemed. I would stow my bicycle in the depths of my mother's basement. Certainly, she wouldn't spot it in the week it would rest there. I would bus my way to stay with one of my siblings that week.

I arrived in San Francisco late that afternoon, too late to put my plan into action. My mother was horrified to find out later that I had camped that last night in the bushes of Golden Gate Park, a five-minute walk from her house.

I knew my mother's schedule to a T. After she'd left for work in the morning, I let myself into the house and carefully packed my bike behind various boxes in the basement. I ate some food, feeling a bit like a family burglar.

Around 11:00, I walked around the corner to a laundromat and put my clothes in the wash. At 11:30, I watched my mother walk by the laundromat on her way home from work for lunch. Half an hour later, as my clothes were finishing in the dryer, I watched her walk back toward work, lunch break over. It was all I could do to restrain myself from opening the laundromat door and surprising her then and there.

I hopped on buses and BART (Bay Area Rapid Transit) and spent the next week in an in-law apartment behind my sister Jan's Oakland house. I had lived houseless by choice for fifteen days and reveled in cooking on four burners, with a roof over my head and a big bed to stretch out in at night after a hot shower in a bathroom with running water. The bicycle tours I've done have given me a profound sense of thankfulness that this is the basic standard of living in this culture, and I have never taken it for granted since that first trip.

My mother was overjoyed to see me at the birthday party.

Other Publications by TransGender Publishing

Publications Available from TransGender Publishing
Publishing Transgender Life Stories and Non-fiction
https://transgenderpublishing.ca/

Life, Liberty, and the Pursuit of Happiness (2023)
Dee Arianne Rockwood
I gave an oath that day. I promised to always try to do the right thing, to help each person or persons that crossed and/or touched my life, to give comfort to those in pain, support to those in need, to teach both by words and example, show compassion, never to judge, always look to each person's worth, believing evil is a circumstance and bad decisions, that good is inherent in each of us, to use each of my skills and powers, both God-given and learned, natural and supernatural, for the good of mankind and not my own selfish needs. I swore to carry myself with dignity and confidence but without pride. I was now a Shaolin Tao Buddhist Priest.

I am not so sure that I have lived up to that oath over the next 40 plus years, but I never have forgotten it either. (https://transgenderpublishing.ca/life-liberty-and-the-pursuit-of-happiness/)

Emergence From Stealth (2023)
Ronnie Gordon, PhD
Imagine a choice, live your life being the facade people believe, or transform into the person you know you are. Being "stealth" describes simultaneous existing as both male and female yet not one person ever knows of this dichotomy. This is my journey of starting a mid-life male-to-female transition, perhaps a different retirement strategy than others. Confusion in early childhood, tumultuous adolescence, a stalled career, considerable chaos, and ample resilience, all merge into cautious optimism. It took some time.
(https://transgenderpublishing.ca/emergence-from-stealth/)

The Stranger Within: Living with Multiple Personality Disorder (2023)
Judith Skillings, Psy.D.
While *The Stranger Within* is undeniably a story about coming to terms with being transgender, I found I often identified with the struggles of both "Stacey" and "Jack." I think we all have vulnerable aspects of ourselves that we are afraid to expose to public scrutiny. We have all experienced rejection and pretended to be something we weren't to gain acceptance. I suspect we have all ached, at one time or another, to *be* different in some magical way other than how we are—smarter, taller, richer, wiser, funnier, prettier, healthier. In that sense, this story is everyone's story. They both played the hand they were dealt, changed what could be changed, and accepted the rest. And did it with great flair.
(https://transgenderpublishing.ca/the-stranger-within/)

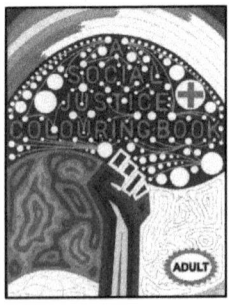

A Social Justice Colouring Book (2022)
Nicola Spurling (and the Flag Shop)
I came up with the idea of *A Social Justice Colouring Book* because my style of artwork lends itself well to this format and because colouring, for me, is a meditative experience that allows my brain to tune out distractions and process information. I will often colour during important conversations, so I can retain information more effectively. Since I would like to see people become more aware of social justice issues, I figured that would be an important topic to focus on. I created 20 pages with each page dedicated to a different major world issue. My intention is not to tell you how to think, but rather to depict the issues in a raw, realistic, and symbolic way. This book contains a brief description of each page, to give you a starting point, and, through the colouring process, you will have time to reflect on how you feel about each issue and form your own stance.
https://transgenderpublishing.ca/a-social-justice-colouring-book/.

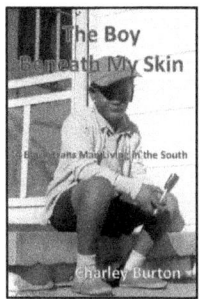

The Boy Beneath My Skin: A Black Trans Man in the South (2022)
Charley Burton
For years, I have wanted others to read my story and hear my voice. I do not think that I am a unique person, although my travels in life have been different. But for many, my path will be one that is recognizable.

This book is about the many journeys that I have taken to become the man that I am today. From a child born in a small rural town, who at the age of eight knew that I was different, to my path of recovery from drugs, alcohol, and food, and moving into my transition from female to male, this is a story of struggle, disappointment, and triumph. It is a story of digging beneath my skin to become whole.
(https://transgenderpublishing.ca/the-boy-beneath-my-skin/)

The Transgender Compendium: Medical, Psychological, Social and Legal Aspects of Gender Diversity (2022)
Diane Saunders
With Contributions from Joanna Clark and Jude Patton
We all know what LGBTQ stands for, but how many of us know that the "T" in LGBTQ stands for "transgender"? What does "transgender" mean? How many people fall under that "umbrella" term, which, over the years, has come to encompass more than just one aspect of gender?

The Transgender Compendium discusses gender as a part of who we are, how we perceive ourselves, and how others perceive us. But gender is not necessarily set in stone. It is inherent in our makeup as human individuals, but not everyone perceives themselves as male or female. Human diversity is truly amazing, and *The Transgender Compendium* takes you on a journey that explores the many aspects of what it means to be transgender.

The Transgender Compendium delves into these subjects and, in doing so, reviews the legal, medical, and social research, the diagnostic criteria in the medical, psychiatric, psychological, and sociological literature, and the legal landscape regarding the civil rights of transgender people. *The Transgender Compendium* also provides information on the LGBTQ community more generally and reviews the professional resources available to help others understand the transgender experience along with the treatment options available. Come along and enjoy the ride.
(https://transgenderpublishing.ca/transgender-compendium/)

Inspired: A Guide to Becoming Your True and Authentic Self (2021)
Stella Paris

Inspired is about being your true and authentic self, of overcoming challenge, embracing change, and becoming all that you can be—not in spite of change but *because* of it. We have all been through a momentous period with Covid and lockdowns, and many of us have struggled with issues around mental health, negotiating our changed world, and questioning life's purpose. Now, as the world slowly comes to a new normal, with old freedoms regained, many in a new form that require an altered way of thinking about the familiar, I believe that transgender people can inspire non-transgender people to embrace change and understand that thinking about things in a new way is OK. It's healthy and can lead to greater satisfaction with life. The lesson to be learned here is the importance of being one's authentic self. (https://transgenderpublishing.ca/inspired/)

My Life Inside the Chrysalis (2021)
The Chrysalis Series Book I
S. Jane Hill

My Life Inside the Chrysalis is an autobiography about what moulded me from birth to transition to the present. It is a sometimes brutal, often philosophical, story of my life and that which moulded me into the true self I am today…the strong woman that I have become.
(https://transgenderpublishing.ca/my-life-inside-the-chrysalis/)

Mr Winky Goes to Melbourne (2022)
The Chrysalis Series Book II
S. Jane Hill

Mr Winky Goes to Melbourne, the second book in the *Chrysalis* series, begins where *My Life Inside the Chrysalis* ends. Detailing what has occurred since, *Mr Winky* uses flashbacks to reflect on the time when the author first met her (then) alter ego and culminates in the lead up to and experiences during and after gender reassignment surgery.
(https://transgenderpublishing.ca/mr-winky-goes-to-melbourne/)

A Trans Feminist's Past (2021)
Forest Handford

Forest Handford was brought up male, but never felt comfortable with that gender. As early as preschool, it was clear that she had interests and habits that were considered feminine. While Forest has supportive parents, they didn't have the knowledge to alert them that she was transgender, a word that wasn't even widely known until long after Forest was an adult.

What little information Forest found about being trans was misleading and harmful. It took cosplaying her favorite Dr. Who character, Clara Oswald, in 2018 for her to find acceptance in feminine clothes. Forest soon discovered that she met the definition of transgender. For a short time, Forest considered herself genderfluid because she didn't believe transition was possible due to misinformation she had been taught to believe. A non-binary friend of Forest's mentioned that their therapist had recommended that they try hormone replacement therapy (HRT). Curious why a therapist would make such a recommendation, Forest did some research that revealed that not only was transition possible for her but that trying a small dose of HRT was a safe way to determine if it could help with her gender dysphoria.

Forest's transition began when trans rights were under attack in her state of residence (Massachusetts). In 2018, Forest knew multiple trans folk who were fired due to their gender identity. Forest had to balance her trans rights advocacy against her safety as a frequent business traveller to Egypt, where being LGBT comes with a 10-year prison sentence.

Forest's memoir covers details of her life and the historical context in which it has been lived. Many of the stories in this book reveal the challenges of being feminine. While those challenges were painful, and some aspects of transitioning during her midlife were difficult, she values the views she has had on both sides of male privilege. She uses this rare perspective as an analogy for her understanding of white privilege.

While many trans stories exist, Forest's perspectives as an Eagle Scout, as somebody who lived in Egypt, and someone who transitioned while in a management position, bring new dimensions to the space, further illustrating that there is no single trans narrative. (https://transgenderpublishing.ca/a-trans-feminists-past/)

Triple Trans: One Woman's Journey to Freedom (2021)
Rose Barkhimer

For me, *Triple Trans* means:
Transgender, the knowledge that one has been born with the incorrect physical body,
Transverse myelitis, a neurological affliction that was a catalyst in my decision to change gender and,
Transition, the process of change.

It is my hope that *Triple Trans* finds its way to at least one individual who is wrestling with the conundrum that is gender dysphoria and that my story helps them to understand their own journey. I also hope that my story will explain to the general public the experiences of one transgender individual

and demonstrate that, despite our differences, we are all human beings struggling with life's journey.
(https://transgenderpublishing.ca/triple-trans-one-womans-journey-to-freedom/).

Journey of a Lifetime (2021)
Karen M. Vaughn
For all of her life, Karen has struggled with gender dysphoria and her true identity. Frightened, confused, and tired of living a lie, she embarks on a journey—one that will change her life, her marriage, and the world she thought she knew. This is her story of coming to terms with who she really is, her struggles to find her way, and the life-altering changes that came along with her journey.
(https://transgenderpublishing.ca/journey-of-a-lifetime/)

Before My Warranty Runs Out: Human, Transgender and Environmental Rights Advocate (2021)
Joanna (Sister Mary Elizabeth) Clark and
Margot Wilson
Joanna (Sister Mary Elizabeth) Clark is an elder trans woman and advocate. During the 1980s and 1990s she was an LGBTQ+ activist and speaker. She was the first person to serve as a man in the US Navy and as a woman in the US Army. Later, as Sister Mary Elizabeth, she was the driving force behind the AIDS Education and Global Information System (AEGIS) database. These days, her focus is primarily on environmental activism. *Before My Warranty Runs Out* is a personal narrative that recounts Joanna's life experiences.
(https://transgenderpublishing.ca/before-my-warranty-runs-out/)

TRANScestors: Navigating LGBTQ+ Aging, Illness and End of Life Decisions (2020)
Volume I: Generations of Hope
Edited by Jude Patton and Margot Wilson
This volume (and the ones that follow) have been in the works for some time. What finally emerges after many months of assiduous advertising, recruiting, editing, and organizing is a volume of intimate, nuanced, and heartfelt stories that reflect the wide diversity in the ways in which trans, non-binary, and Two-Spirit people have come to recognize, signify, embody, and celebrate their difference as their authentic selves. Moreover, with an increasing emphasis on the experiences of trans youth, elders constitute a routinely overlooked, disregarded, and/or silenced segment of the community. In response, this volume documents the myriad ways in which trans elders are coming to terms with the real-life challenges of aging, illness, and end of life decision-making.

TRANScestors is planned as a series of edited volumes that address the issues of LGBTQ+ aging, illness, and end of life decision-making and will be published by

TransGender Publishing. Additional volumes include: Volume II: Generations of Change, Volume III: Generations of Pride, and Volume III: Generations of Challenge. (https://transgenderpublishing.ca/life-trips/)

TRANScestors: Navigating LGBTQ+ Aging, Illness and End of Life Decisions (2020)
Volume II: Generations of Change
Edited by Jude Patton and Margot Wilson

Generations of Change is the second volume in the TRANScestors series. These stories are, by turn, heartfelt, revealing, inspiring, sad, joyful, humorous, irreverent, and incredibly varied. And yet, strong, common themes of courage, persistence, honesty, resilience, and authenticity emerge clearly through the detailed recounting of the individual lives lived. Each author details those specific circumstances that have led them to the places and situations in which they find themselves today. On the whole, these are places of comfort, confidence, revelation, and affirmation. The wide range of attitudes, expressions, and worldviews held by the LGBTQ+ elders presented here challenge us all to carefully consider and adjust our perspectives on our own aging processes and, ultimately, on finding our own places in the world.
(https://transgenderpublishing.ca/live-trips-vol-ii-generations-of-change/)

We are God's Children Too (2020)
Rona Matlow

At the heart of Jewish experience is narrative. Around the dinner table, we tell stories of our families, recalling the quality of a grandmother's cooking, the kindness (or stinginess) of a particular uncle, the ways in which traditions have developed and shifted in our families. In synagogues and Jewish schools, we read the Torah, which is filled with stories of our religious patriarchs and matriarchs. And then there are the stories of Diaspora—the history of Jewish communities existing in exile for over two millennia. There are family stories and history books dedicated to our many wanderings. All of these stories help Jewish people connect to their heritage and lineage. What of the queer Jew? Even as more and more Jewish communities emphasize inclusivity and find a place for queer congregants, Jewish stories do not. The Bible offers no queer lessons, leaving queer Jews split in two; a Jewish heritage and a queer present. Enter Rabbah Rona Matlow, with hir queer *midrashim*. Midrashim are stories which approach Biblical texts from new perspectives, often exploring areas of confusion or possible contradiction within the Bible. Unlike Torah, they are not presented as factual, but as possibilities. Fictions which might yet be possible alternate histories. *Midrashim* bridge gaps. Rona's queer *midrashim* bridge the gap between the contemporary queer Jew and the (seemingly cisgender and straight) Bible, offering a way for us to see ourselves in our Jewish tradition.
(https://transgenderpublishing.ca/we-are-gods-children-too/)

Transgender Heart: Life Stories from the Inside Out (2020)
Bodhi Thompson Gardner
Transgender Heart is a collection of short stories that trace the heart-journey of a small farm kid, youth, and adult, from rural Saskatchewan, across the binary landscapes of life. A deeply grateful soul emerges, while exploring all the hidden nuances of the people, places, and things that held them together. Hidden comforts are revealed from the inside out, an inner harvesting of an authentic self. Their true self searching for somewhere to belong, finds love, acceptance, and authentic connection in the most intriguing and unusual spaces. Black hockey skates not only enrich their game but authenticate their heart. Spaces of unconditional love come from four-legged wild beasts, two-legged mentors, matriarchs, warriors, and elders. An RCMP officer who saw their struggle and offered a hand instead of handcuffs, gifts of nature, and family support abound: however, the biggest surprise of all is their most cherished treasure, the one thing that kept them alive for over 50 years. Transgender Heart highlights the courage and tenacity of the human spirit to rise up!
(https://transgenderpublishing.ca/transgender-heart/)

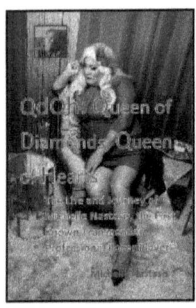

QdQh: Queen of Diamonds, Queen of Hearts, The Life and Journey of Michelle Nastasis, the First Known Transgender Professional Poker Player (2020)
Michelle Nastasis
QdQh: Queen of Diamonds, Queen of Hearts is the life story of Michelle Nastasis, the First Known Transgender Professional Poker Player.™ Michelle is courageous whether going head-to-head with the best poker players in the world, speaking out on television for LGBTQ+ rights, or marching in parades to celebrate being transgender. She is calm, cool, collected, and absolutely fearless. Possessed of fierce intelligence, Michelle is a beacon for younger transgender people. She shoots straight from the hip. She's blunt, loud, sarcastic, and occasionally irreverent. So, sit back and enjoy the ride. (https://transgenderpublishing.ca/misunderstood/)

Dancing the Dialectic: True Tales of a Transgender Trailblazer, Second Edition (2020)
Rupert Raj
Rupert Raj is a trailblazing, Eurasian-Canadian, trans activist, and former psychotherapist, who transitioned from female to male in 1971 as a transsexual teenager. Dancing the dialectic between gender dysphoria and gender euphoria, cynical despair and realistic hope, righteous rage and loving kindness, this Gender Worker tells us all about his lifelong fight for the rights of transgender, intersex, and two-spirit people—and his later-life role as a Rainbow Warrior working to free Mother Earth's enslaved animals.
(https://transgenderpublishing.ca/dancing-the-dialectic-true-tales-of-a-transgender-trailblazer-second-edition/)

Glimmerings: Trans Elders Tell Their Stories (2019)
Margot Wilson and Aaron Devor (editors)
Tell us your story. A story about growing up before the age of global communication, at a time when the Internet and worldwide connectivity were still visions of the future; when inflexible, dichotomous categories of male and female, men and women, existed; when heterosexuality was the only sanctioned form of romantic attraction or sexual conduct; and when any expression of interest outside of these strict prescriptions was severely censured.
   Tell us your story about living in a time when those whose preferences, perspectives, and behaviours contravened the prevailing paradigms and prohibitions, when you had to negotiate dark, prejudicial places where fear, shame, guilt, despair, isolation, and a little bit of hope. Contributing authors include: Stephanie Castle, Joanna Clark, Ms. Bob Davis, Dallas Denny, Jamison Green, Ariadne Kane, Corey Keith, Lili, Ty Nolan, Jude Patton, Virginia Prince, Rupert Raj, Gayle Roberts, Susanna Valenti, and Dawn Angela Wensley.
(https://transgenderpublishing.ca/glimmerings-recognition-authenticity-and-gender-variance/)

My Untrue Past: The Coming of Age of a Trans Man (2019)
Alex Bakker
Born the youngest daughter in a small-town family in the Netherlands, Alex Bakker underwent gender reaffirming transition when he was twenty-eight years old. A new beginning, in the right body, he literally put everything that reminded him of his old life into boxes, never to be opened again. More than fifteen years later, he has finally gathered the courage to face his past. In *My Untrue Past*, Alex goes in search of the painful truth. What does it mean to be betrayed by your body, to be immensely jealous of boys, and to decide that everything needs to be different?
(https://transgenderpublishing.ca/my-untrue-past-available-now/)

Girl in the Dream: Stephanie (Sydney) Castle Heal, a Transgender Life (2018)
Margot E. Wilson
Girl in the Dream is the life story of Stephanie (Sydney) Castle Heal, an advocate, activist and elder in the Canadian transgender community. The outcome of an almost four-year collaboration of storytelling, recording, analysis, and writing, *Girl in the Dream* is a first-person narrative that depicts in intimate detail Stephanie's transgender journey. An enthusiastic and accomplished *raconteuse*, Stephanie tells her story with the verve, passion, and expressiveness of a veteran storyteller. (https://transgenderpublishing.ca/girl-in-the-dream/)

Feelings: A Transsexual's Explanation of a Baffling Condition, Second Edition (2018)
Stephanie Castle
Edited and Introduction by Margot E. Wilson

Feelings is written in a style that reveals Stephanie Castle as a woman of great confidence, conviction, and humour. It reflects her attitudes toward life in general and transgender issues in particular, and definitively emulates the intricacies of her personality and character. *Feelings* provides a very personal view into one transgender woman's journey, a metamorphosis that is as vital, authentic, and significant today as it was when she wrote it. A complementary volume to *Girl in the Dream*, *Feelings* provides a comprehensive and in-depth view into the nature of the transgender experience based on the intimate, challenging, and often poignant experiences and perspectives of one singularly remarkable woman. (https://transgenderpublishing.ca/feelings/)

Coming in 2023/2024 from TransGender Publishing
Publishing Transgender Life Stories and Non-fiction
https://transgenderpublishing.ca/

PUBLICATION EXPECTED IN 2023
Black Trans Men Can Cook Presents
Transmen Can Cook
Charley Burton and Margot Wilson (editors)
THROUGH FOOD AND FELLOWSHIP, WE SEEK OURSELVES
For centuries Black Trans Men have seen how good food and fellowship are as a source of strength to get us through both the trials and celebrations of life.

Black Trans Men have watched mothers, grandmothers or aunties create the magic in the kitchen. Some of us have been able to master the craft of cooking and baking while others are wanting to learn. Our love of food and fellowship is generational.

We have formed a group of Brothers who need fellowship and safe spaces to enjoy food with each other and create brotherhood.

Black Men Can Cook is more than about food. It's about living our lives surrounded by each other.
(https://transgenderpublishing.ca/black-transmen-can-cook/)

PUBLICATION EXPECTED IN 2023
Celebration! Recipes and Life Lessons from Leona's Kitchen
Charley Burton (editor)

I wanted to share my mother's world of food through her recipes. But when I started to plan this with my wonderful publisher, Margot Wilson, I realized that this was more than about food. What Leona Burton did was create a language of stories and tales woven around the food she prepared. Through her love of creating beautiful sights and smells, she celebrated her accomplishments and the people in her life. People enjoyed her culinary creations, and every dish had a story behind it. And how she could tell a story!

She would happily tell you how she was sent to culinary school. But then, with her quick smile, she would also tell you that she was the best student!

This cookbook is not new as my mother made a little cookbook years ago and shared many of her wonderful recipes. This cookbook includes those same delicious recipes but also the wonderful stories that go with them, stories which, at a young age, I often felt forced to listen to. As I got older, however, I began to appreciate those stories, heard from her bedside, an important part of her worldview, and I yearned for more. (https://transgenderpublishing.ca/leonas-kitchen/)

PUBLICATION EXPECTED IN 2023
The Love Beneath: A Journey to Love and Womanhood
Diamond Stylz-Collier

They say hindsight is always 20/20. But even as an adult looking back on the many facets of love in my life, it's still a little blurry. When I got older, I realized how important love was to my survival and sanity, in my coming-of-age story. I started openly telling these stories on YouTube in 2008. These were vulnerable and honest stories about intimate relationships and how my burgeoning transness impacted the world around me. These entanglements were sometimes full of joy while some were poignant and hard to relive. So many people across identities related to the underlying themes of these videos, so I decided to write a book that combined those experiences, my reflections, and my audience reactions. This book is a reflection of moments of love throughout some of the darkest and happiest times in my youth.
(https://transgenderpublishing.ca/the-love-beneath/)

PUBLICATION EXPECTED IN 2023
Gender de Novo
Lawren Burroughs
Edited by Margot Wilson

Many would consider our family conventional, maybe even a bit boring by all accounts but one. We are a two-parent household fortunate to thrive on a single income with a stay-at-home mom, rearing our four children together in one of the "best large cities" in the United States.

As the father, the stoic head of household, and eventually sole breadwinner, I devised my life journey meticulously from an early age to compensate for the deficiencies I assigned myself. I found a way to blend in, and I mastered the art of observation. I was most likely to speak only when spoken to, and I didn't dare draw too much attention to myself lest I be exposed—for what, even I was too afraid to explore. I felt inadequate in every way possible and am convinced I must have been the one Clance and Imes had in mind when they breathed life into the term "imposter phenomenon."

The level to which I would go to hide from myself knew no limits. I was different. I didn't fit in where society expected me, and I derived too much happiness from things meant for others. My life was an existential crisis. I played the role of manhood like a seasoned Method actor, teetering on the ledge of sanity in the stratosphere of my delusions. And with nothing left to give and nowhere left to hide, I finally stepped out, onto thin air, and I learned to fly.
(https://transgenderpublishing.ca/gender-de-novo/)

PUBLICATION EXPECTED IN 2024
My Journey from Dyke to Dude and Other Sordid Tales
Zander Keig

My Journey From Dyke to Dude chronicles the life of Zander Keig, a man who was presumed dead in the womb, assigned female at birth, paralyzed following vaccination at age six, joined a Mexican gang in middle school, was admitted to a mental hospital as a teen, dropped out of high school, enlisted in the military, became an undercover narcotics agent, graduated college and obtained three graduate degrees, became a social worker serving homeless veterans at the Department of Veterans Affairs and transgender servicemembers for the US Navy, and was awarded the National Social Worker of the Year by the National Association of Social Workers. Zander's story goes beyond telling people that it gets better and humorously explains how one person changed their life in almost every way possible and thrived amidst the chaos. (https://transgenderpublishing.ca/from-dyke-to-dude/)

PUBLICATION EXPECTED IN 2023
The Thunder Roars, The Lightning Illuminates
Jonathon Thunderword and Margot Wilson
(https://transgenderpublishing.ca/the-thunder-roars/)

PUBLICATION EXPECTED IN 2024
TRANScestors: Navigating LGBTQ+ Aging, Illness and End of Life Decisions
Edited by Jude Patton and Margot Wilson
Volume Three: Generations of Pride
Volume Four: Generations of Challenge
Studies indicate that LGBT+ people are still discriminated against in most health care settings and in long term care facilities despite advances made in the past few years in gaining more rights. Evaluating physical and mental health care needs, facilitating access to health care providers, and advocating for clients' right as well as end of life decisions and planning for personal legacy options are important aspects of navigating LGBTQ+ aging. Having served as a health navigator for clients with chronic illness and offering end of life doula services to LGBTQ+ community members, Jude Patton collaborates with and advocates for his clients to successfully manage their health care needs. Jude is a proud, open, and out, elder trans man, who has worked with under-served populations for most of his career, including LGBTQ+ folks, geriatric clients, developmentally disabled adults, homeless/chronically mentally ill and drug addicted clients.
TRANScestors is planned as a series of edited volumes that address the issues of LGBTQ+ aging, illness, and end of life decision-making and will be published by TransGender Publishing. Additional volumes include: Volume II: Generations of Change, Volume III: Generations of Pride and Volume IV: Generations of Challenge. (https://transgenderpublishing.ca/life-trips/)

PUBLICATION EXPECTED IN 2023
Taking Care of Angela
Angela Wensley and Margot Wilson
My name is Angela, and I am a transsexual woman. I have always believed myself to be female, even though I spent the first forty-two years of my life being socialized as a male. To be transsexual is no longer a new phenomenon, although many misconceptions still surround it. One thing has remained unchanged is the great pain and personal upheaval that necessarily accompanies the transition from one gender to another. Looking back now, many years after having had gender reassignment surgery, it seems impossible for me to have accomplished what I have. Changing from man to woman involved no less than a total restructuring of every single relationship in my life, with my spouse, family, friends, workplace, and my everyday interactions in society. For me, being transsexual is a beautiful gift, an honour, an evolutionary jump, as it were, to a higher state of being, one in which I am closer to God and to all humanity.

My personal journey can be likened to casting off in a boat without oars into a swiftly flowing river. Standing on the banks of that river, intrigued but not knowing where it would lead me, I had dipped my toes into the water, even waded out to where it was deeper, where I could feel the tug of the current. How I longed to be swept away by the river: however, my fears kept me from the test, and I always retreated to the security of the shore. Ultimately, spying a rowboat on the riverbank, I climbed in, pushed off into the stream, and waited as the small craft inevitably became caught up in the stronger current of mid-stream. Without oars, I could not return to where I had started and had little ability to control my course, though my direction downstream was certain. I was little prepared for the swiftness of the current, or the treacherous rapids and canyons that lay downstream out of sight. How easy it would have been to flounder in a back-eddy or to wreck on the many rocks that projected from the dark waters. Fortunately, with what little control I had over my course, I avoided destruction and travelled the long and lonely distance. Finally, one day, the current slowed, and I found myself past the mouth of the river, in the ocean that is woman. (https://transgenderpublishing.ca/taking-care-of-angela/)

PUBLICATION EXPECTED IN 2024
Both Sides of the Great Divide
Nikita Carter
Nikita Carter tells her story about awakening. At 60 years of age, a series of shattering experiences led to her being broken open to the awareness that she was a trans woman, and she had to make the changes in her life to reflect that truth. Her life has comprised extraordinary experiences and people throughout, which includes being a musician, composer, educator, Artistic Director, producer, and trans woman. (https://transgenderpublishing.ca/both-sides-of-the-great-divide/)

PUBLICATION EXPECTED IN 2024
Inside My Husband's Closet
On Friday July 24th, 2020, my husband asked me, "Can we talk?" This was a question that only I had ever asked.
He proceeded to tell me he wanted to dress as a woman, hair, makeup, clothes, shoes, everything. He wanted to do this part time and referred to it as "cross dressing." Eventually, he adopted the gender identity of "trans."
Ten days after this conversation, I began to journal, my goal being to capture my feelings in real time.

Inside My Husband's Closet is the story of the first year after my husband went into the closet, hiding who he was from everyone but me. He requested that I join him there and not discuss his decision with others.

Having been an ally to others in the LGBTQ+ community for many years, I thought I would understand what lay ahead. I did not.
(https://transgenderpublishing.ca/inside-my-husbands-closet/)

PUBLICATION EXPECTED IN 2024
Between…
Stan Deetz

Stan was a girl growing up in a male body in a small, conservative, religious, farm community in Indiana in the 1950s without an understanding nor language of trans.

Stan a child undecided, caught in a life of cows, responding to ever changing sets of circumstance with intersections of family trauma, gender, and class, thrown into a world already defined, often lost and bewildered.

Living life stealth, running hard to be normal, to catch up, to be noticed. Then getting noticed, being included, respected. Making believe that respect and inclusion were the same as finding a home, being whole.

Older, alone, and being more out, still a home and community painfully elusive through the struggles of self and others figuring out how to relate.

Some are born of the mountains and some of the sea, and some left to navigate the fog between. (https://transgenderpublishing.ca/between/)

PUBLICATION EXPECTED IN 2024
Gender Odyssey: Journey of an Intrepid Androgyne
Ariadne (J. Ari) Kane and Margot Wilson
Ariadne (J. Ari) Kane is a gerontology specialist with Theseus Consulting & Coaching Service. (S)he has developed several workshops focusing on issues of gender, sexuality, and health in the latter decades of the lifespan. Many are designed for the LGBT Community. (S)he has been a leading authority on gender diversity in postmodern America and has given presentations at many universities and institutes in the United States and Canada. (S)he is one of the creators of the Gender Attitude Reassessment Program, a workshop on gender

for sexologists and healthcare professionals. (S)he co-authored *Crossing Sexual Boundaries* with Professor Vern Bullough. *Gender Odyssey: Journey of an Intrepid Androgyne* is the distillation of 40+ hours of recorded conversation that provide a decadal representation of an intrepid traveller who has forged an idiosyncratic path through gender exploration, variance, and expression. (https://transgenderpublishing.ca/gender-odyssey-journey-of-an-intrepid-androgyne/)

PUBLICATION EXPECTED IN 2025
From Shame to Freedom: A Gender Variant Woman's Journey of Discovery
M. Gayle Roberts
Born in England during WW II, Gayle Roberts immigrated to Canada in 1951 and is an UVic alumnus with an MSc in Physics. She transitioned in 1996 as her high school's Science Department Head and science teacher. Gayle coauthored the guidebook Supporting Transgender and Transsexual Students in K-12 Schools and is author of *From Shame to Freedom: A Gender-Variant Woman's Journey of Discovery*. Gayle feels strongly that trans individuals should document their life experiences. She utilizes specific literary writing techniques (creative nonfiction) to create factually accurate narratives. *From Shame to Freedom* is one of those narratives. (https://transgenderpublishing.ca/from-shame-to-freedom/)

PUBLICATION EXPECTED IN 2025
Young Kid, Old Goat: Transgender Journey to Understanding the Man Within
Jude Patton and Margot Wilson
Jude Patton is an elder transman and LGBTQ activist, advocate, and educator since before his own transition in 1970. He founded Renaissance Gender Identity Services in the early 1970s and began publishing *Renaissance Newsletter* in the mid-1970s. Jude started one of the first informal support groups for FTM men and incorporated these into The John Augustus Foundation. Joined by Joanna Clark, these became known as J2CP Information Services, taking over Paul Walker's work with Erickson Educational Services. In *Young Kid, Old Goat*, Jude's personal life story and ongoing work is highlighted.
(https://transgenderpublishing.ca/young-kid-old-goat/)

PUBLICATION EXPECTED IN 2025
Unconditional Love: Stories of LGBTQ+ People and Our Emotional Bonds with Companion Animals
Edited by Jude Patton and Margot Wilson
Our experiences with marginalization often affect our feelings of self-worth. While many people in our lives are unable (or unwilling) to provide the emotional support we need before, during and post-coming out, or transition, our companion animals never fail to see us as we truly are and never fail to express their unconditional love for us. No wonder we love them and derive multiple benefits from our relationships with them. They are woven into the fabric of our lives. *Unconditional Love* is planned as an edited reader that tells the stories of how the unconditional love of (and for) our companion animals has supported, encouraged, confirmed, validated, endorsed, and sanctioned our authentic selves. Our reading audience includes those in the LGBTQ+ community who have found sanctuary and validation in the love shared with our animal companions as well as those in the broader community who revel in the company of our non-human loved ones.
(https://transgenderpublishing.ca/unconditional-love/)

Publications from other divisions of Perceptions Press
Perceptions Press www.perceptionspress.ca
Stephanie Castle Publications www.stephaniecastle.ca
Castle Carrington Publishing www.castlecarringtonpublishing.ca
All Genders Press www.allgenderspress.ca

www.ingramcontent.com/pod-product-compliance
Lightning Source LLC
Chambersburg PA
CBHW041311240426
43661CB00065B/2894